WILLIE NELSON

WILLIE NELSON

Red Headed Stranger

Jim Brown

QUARRY MUSIC BOOKS

for Dick Damron, a kindred spirit

The publisher acknowledges the support of the Government of Canada, Book Publishing Industry Development Program, Department of Canadian Heritage.

ISBN 1-55082-255-1

Editorial development and design
by Quarry Press Inc., Kingston, Ontario, Canada.

Typeset and imaging by The Right Type.

Printed and bound by
Vicks Lithograph and Printing Corporation, Utica, New York.

Distributors:

General Distribution Services
325 Humber College Blvd
Etobicoke, Ontario M9W 7C3, Canada.

Music Sales Corporation
257 Park Ave S, New York, NY, 10010 USA.

Music Sales Limited
8/9 Frith St, London W1D 3JB England.

Music Sales Pty. Limited
120 Rothschild St, Roseberry, Sydney, NSW 2018, Australia.

Published by Quarry Press Inc.
PO Box 1061, Kingston, Ontario K7L 4Y5 Canada
www.quarrypress.com

CONTENTS

one

World Wide Willie 9
Country Willie 19
Have Guitar Will Travel 29
Tootsie's Orchid Lounge 39

two

Ridgetop 51
Country Woodstock 61
Outlaws 72
Austin City Limits 118

three

Stardust 127
Willywood 135
Half Nelson 143
Farm Aid 152
Nothing I Can Do About It Now. 161

four

The I.R.S. Tapes 171
On the Road Again 176
Twisted Discography 184
President Willie 196
The Party's Over 205

References 209
Acknowledgments & Credits 218

HONEYSUCKL
ROSE

1

WORLD WIDE WILLIE

It's Monday, August 14, 2000 and Willie Nelson is scheduled to play to what may very well be the biggest audience of his six-decade career. Willie has played some big ones before — Fourth of July Picnics, Farm Aid, Woodstock '99 — but tonight on A&E Network's Special *Live By Request: Starring Willie Nelson*, broadcast on television with internet simulcast, he will play two sets over 90 minutes to a global audience. I wander between the Power Mac in the computer room and the big screen tv set in the living room, checking out both feeds for the audience of friends gathering at my home for some 'barbecue and Willie'. We celebrate with appropriate inhalations and libations. Like, here's to you Willie!

In preparation for the show, Willie has been rehearsing at the Sony Studio in New York for a day and a half, and just before the show, he goes online for an hour-long 'Yahoo Chat', doing what he loves to do most, next to making music and playing golf, visiting with his fans. When at last Willie appears simultaneously on the tv and computer screens, he's honkin'! He's got a smokin' blues band with him featuring Kenny Wayne Shepherd and Derek O'Brien on guitar, Doctor John (Mac Rebeneck) and Riley Osborne on piano and Hammond B-3, and vocalist Francine Reed from Lyle Lovett's Big Band, with a rhythm section of Jon Blondell on bass and Reese Wyman on drums. The music comes from his new MILK COW BLUES album release on Island Records, which features not only the band members on stage tonight, but also B.B. King, Susan Tedeschi, Jonny Lang, and Keb Mo. Willie has played Kokomo Arnold's song *Milk Cow Blues* since he first picked up the guitar, and when the band breaks into *Night Life*, a song he wrote while driving to a gig as a guitar player in the late 1950s, Willie's back where he left off with the blues almost 40 years ago.

When the evening sun goes down
You'll find me hangin' round
The night life ain't a good life
But it's my life . . .

— *Night Life* (Willie Nelson, Walt Breeland, Paul Buskirk)

Flanked by blistering solos from Shepherd and O'Brien, Willie is tearing off some soulful lead riffs himself on his faithful 'Trigger', the Martin N-20 gut-string guitar he's played through a Baldwin tube amp for more years than Roy Rogers and his horse Trigger played the silver screen theaters during the heydays of the singing cowboy movies. The way Willie is a calm presence in the midst of tight arrangements where blues and country are woven into a many colored quilt of sound, he reminds me of Bob Wills, King of Western Swing, his first music idol and eventual good friend. The way he feeds solos to his players, basking in the sheer virtuosity of up-and-comer Kenny Wayne Shepherd and the soulful veteran Doctor John who is night-tripping this night indeed. Willie is as trim and as light on his feet up there as I remember the late, great Stephane Grappelli to be when he toured with a foursome of young guitarists 50 years his junior. Willie's got that secret smile on his face as he nimbly steps in toward the microphone with his trademark phrasing, his ahead-of-the-beat or behind-the-beat style, playfully kick-boxing his way through the lyrics and melodies like the black belt vocalist that he has always been. He seems to be bringing the raw essence of *Austin City Limits*, the innovative live music show he helped launch 25 years ago, right into our living rooms through the prime-time viewing window.

Listen to the blues they are playin'
Listen to what the blues are sayin'
Mine is just another scene
From the world of broken dreams
The night life ain't the good life
But it's my life . . .

Willie Nelson recently celebrated his 67th birthday, but he's not exactly riding off into the sunset tonight. This year, he'll perform some 200 shows in Europe and the United States. He's been at it for half a century but he's still in great shape. "I feel great, everything's working," he told *Country Weekly* in the weeks leading up to this show. "I still do yoga, running and breathing exercises. And I've done 'Tae Kwon Do' for a long time. Now, my whole family's doing it. Annie and the boys are black belt candidates. So I have to keep up — out of self-defence. I'm mellower and more moderate now. I've learned to savor things." Willie hasn't changed his appearance much over the 30 years since he began sporting a red bandanna, a single gold earring, t-shirt, jeans, and sneakers. The once-red beard has whitened, but he's still the Red Headed Stranger, an enigmatic yet charismatic country music chameleon who continues to surprise us with each new reincarnation of himself, including this pure blues set on A&E.

At the intermission, A&E show host Mark McEwen tells us Willie will be right back to take our online and telephone requests. Now Willie's got his Family Band with him. Sister Bobbie Nelson on piano, Jody Payne on guitar, Mickey Raphael on harmonica, Bee Spears on bass, Billy English on percussion, and Paul English on the drumkit. Handling the requests is no problem for this crew. Bobbie's been playing with her brother since they were preteens back in Abbott, Texas, during the late 1930s and early '40s. Paul English has been with him since 1966. Bee Spears showed up when he was 18 — three decades ago. Their group sound is the essence of down-home, a little ragged compared to the svelte blues band we've just heard, but right in all of the right places.

Willie takes calls from several countries on several continents. He dedicates *Angel Flying Too Close To The Ground* to Becky Sparks who had tickets for the live audience show but passed away mere hours before Willie went on stage. Willie himself often appears to be such an angel come to ground here among us, more so tonight than sometimes, a beatific survivor, although during his 'outlaw' years some folks on Music Row had thoughts he might be one of the fallen angels. After coming of age in Texas and wandering as far away as the Pacific Northwest, Willie spent the 1960s in Nashville writing songs and recording for Music Row labels. His songwriting triumphs were many during these years — Faron Young's hit *Hello Walls*, Billy Walkers' hit *Funny How Time Slips Away*, Ray Price's signature song *Night Life*, Claude Gray's hit *Family Bible*, and Patsy Cline's *Crazy*, all frequently requested by his live show and internet fans. *Crazy* was recently named the all-time most played record on jukeboxes in America.

When Willie first arrived in Nashville in 1960, he was a free spirit with a suitcase full of songs. These songs were some of the best he has ever written, sparse, blatantly autobiographical poems inspired by intense experiences, rather than the usual crafted-on-Music Row fare. Willie's angst seems etched into the fabric of country music as if he'd burnt the lyrics to his songs onto the horizon with a lit cigarette. He didn't use very many words, but the way he uses them can stop you in your tracks.

Willie's whole life has been writing songs. He has written hundreds of them. He has never been out of songs. "I can write a song about anything," he once told Bill DeYoung in an article published in *Goldmine*. "Now, whether it's worth a damn or not is debatable. But to any professional songwriter, you should be able to say, 'All right, write me a song about running around naked,' and he should be able to do it. I just think if you're a songwriter, if that's what you do, it's kind of like if you're a farmer. You have a natural talent for plowing a field. I'm a songwriter. It's supposed to be easy for me, and it is." A songwriter's songwriter, Willie Nelson is scheduled to enter the Songwriter's Hall of Fame along with Eric Clapton, Dolly Parton, and Paul Williams in 2001.

Not only has Willie been a professional songwriter all his life, he has acted this role in many feature films, including *Songwriter* and recently *Wag The Dog*. Spin doctor Conrad Brean (Robert de Niro) teams up with Hollywood producer Stanley Motss (Dustin Hoffman) to divert public attention away from the President's philandering during the final countdown to the election. Working together, they decide to stage a fake war that appears real on television, and enlist the aid of an advertising executive known as the 'Fad Man'(Denis Leary) and a songwriter, Johnny Dean (Willie Nelson). Sprung from a mental insitution, Willie arrives at Hoffman's mansion, sits in on the brainstorming sessions, and begins to write the conspirators an anthem for their production. The grandiose *We Are The World*-type anthem Johnny Dean records in a Nashville studio is not the song that does the trick, though. The song that helps change history is a bluesy jam, which Willie and a studio janitor, an old bluesman played by 'Pop' Staples, come up with long after all the big name stars have gone home. It's about an old shoe, a good old shoe. Hoffman and de Niro then press up one record as a 78 rpm single and stick it in a television network's archives to be discovered at an opportune moment in their scam. Willie Nelson has saved the day with a record that he never made, that was never released, and that no one will ever know he wrote, except for a handful of people in the recording studio at three in the morning. Many such songs he wrote at his Ridgetop farm in Tennessee as he waited for his big break as a Nashville recording artist.

When Willie arrived in Nashville, he was simply 'Country Willie', as he declared in song.

You called me Country Willie
The night you went away
With the one who promised you a life of joy
You thought my life was too simple
To spend it living with a country boy

— *Country Willie* (Willie Nelson)

But life soon became more complicated as he struggled to become a recording star. While Willie caught on quickly as a songwriter in Nashville, he was not successful as a recording artist, thwarted at every turn in the road by the Nashville system. "For years nobody would record him because they thought he sung funny," Joe Allison, head of Liberty Records, would later comment in the authorized video biography Willie Nelson: My Life. "We finally decided that the best approach would just be to play rhythm behind him and stay the hell out of his way." This approach yielded Willie's first LP in 1962, and then i wrote. While the album would one day be regarded as a 'classic honky tonk weeper' with a basic guitar, piano, bass, and drums band sound, this Liberty release did not sell well at the time. With Willie's versions of Crazy, Funny How Time Slips Away, and Hello Walls already country hits for other artists, he found himself competing with his own best songs sung by the best in the business. His songs turned into gold records when other people sang them, but after Willingly, a Top 10 duet with Shirley Collie, and Touch Me, a solo effort that peaked at number 7 on the Billboard C&W chart in the spring of 1962, his own records just couldn't crack the Top 10.

When he moved on to RCA, Willie's records were lushly produced at the label's Nashville Sound Studios, but sweetening up Willie's records with strings and choirs did not click. Seven years and a dozen albums down the line, Willie still did not have another Top 10. The relationship with RCA ended. Nashville had a mold that they used for stamping out records by the hundreds and thousands, but Country Willie never fit that mold. He was already inducted into the Nashville Songwriter's Hall of Fame before he took production of his records into his own hands and recorded RED HEADED STRANGER at a jingle studio in Garland, Texas, a concept album that made Willie a superstar and gave us his first number one hit on the radio, *Blue Eyes Crying In The Rain*. Years before while he was working as a disc jockey, Willie had played the Arthur "Guitar Boogie" Smith recording of the *Red Headed Stranger*, originally written by Carl Stutz and Edith Lindeman, each day at noon on his special children's show. A tale about a mysterious rider drifting from town to town on a black stallion, leading his dead lover's horse, the song was a cowboy morality play which Willie adapted for his album, changing the lead character into a preacher seeking redemption after murdering his cheating wife, working into the narrative other country and gospel standards — Fred Roses's *Blue Eyes Crying in the Rain*, Eddy Arnold's *I Couldn't Believe*, Hank Cochran's *Can I Sleep In Your Arms*, and the gospel classic *Just As I Am*. The result was a sort of 'New Testament' of country values and beliefs. "The usual music industry term 'concept' album is inadequate," Chet Flippo wrote in *Texas Monthly*. "RED HEADED STRANGER is more a revival of an oral tradition, of a storyteller who preserves and passes on beliefs and teachings of a tribe or group . . . . Closing the tale is a pastoral guitar instrumental, *Bandera*, which suggests a vision of a second Eden. Listeners with a sense of whimsy may want to file this record, this Willie Nelson Version, next to the King James or the Revised Standard Version." Many listeners did take this album as gospel, and the Red Headed Stranger persona is the Willie Nelson his fans world-wide came to admire, emulate, love, even worship.

After leaving Nashville, fame, nevertheless, came gradually to Willie during the 1970s with the release of a series of critically acclaimed albums on Atlantic, Columbia, and RCA — SHOTGUN WILLIE, PHASES AND STAGES, RED HEADED STRANGER, and, when he teamed up with Waylon Jennings for a series of hit duets, WANTED: THE OUTLAWS. When Willie left Tennessee and returned to Texas, eventually settling in Austin, he became the most visible member of the 'progressive county' music scene there, performing regularly at the Armadillo World Headquarters night club, staging Woodstock-like Fourth of July country music picnics, and appearing on PBS television as a charter performer on *Austin City Limits*. Willie established his own recording studio at the Pedernales Golf and Country Club — the 'Cut and Putt'— in Spicewood, where he could indulge his two passions, making music and playing golf.

At the center of the Austin 'scene', Willie soon became identified with the so-called Austin sound, which Tom T. Hall first encountered when he fled from the politics of the Opry and found refuge with Willie in his Austin home. As Hall recalls in his autobiography *The Storyteller's Nashville*, "I wound up with a set of earphones and a cold beer and sat there with the music humming in my ears. It didn't really sound all that different to me. In fact, by Nashville standards of sure absolute control of every sound coming out of the studio, it sounded a little ragged and unrehearsed. It sounded as if it had been recorded in the same living room in which I was hearing it. It sounded basic, pure, simple — and, most of all, sincere. It took me back to the days when Hank Williams recorded in mono. It took me back to the times when you got what you got — not the overdubbed, mixed, equalized, mastered, stereoed, speeded up, slowed down, slick, polished, echoed, *plastic* music that I had heard for years. It was fresh, honest, and inspired . . . . Willie sat there on the floor and watched me as I listened to the music. He was wearing a pair of sneakers, a bandanna tied around his long red hair, a pair of walking shorts, and a red shaggy beard. He was playing with his children on the floor of the den and sipping on a beer. I knew that Willie had had his hard times. I knew that he had been rejected by the establishment when he had tried the beaten path to success that had worked for so many, even me. He seemed to have found a new picture of what life was supposed to be for a country singer and writer. He seemed at peace with himself. Having lost his bid for success via the Nashville route, he had taken his music back to Texas where it was appreciated."

And appreciated it certainly was, not only by country music fans, but also by the growing number of 'country rock' fans. In the 1970s, cosmic cowboys from across the southwest and up and down the west coast started heating up the FM airwaves with a hybrid of country and rock that set people's radios on fire. The Byrds with their SWEETHEART OF THE RODEO album, Gram Parsons and the Flying Burrito Brothers, Emmylou Harris, Linda Ronstadt, Poco, Doug Sahm & the Texas Tornadoes, Dick Damron, Billy Cowsill & Blue Northern, Jerry Jeff Walker, Commander Cody & the Lost Planet Airmen, New Riders of the Purple Sage, the Eagles. When I met many of these country rockers as they came to town, they would tell me their hero was Willie Nelson. On his home turf, Willie was more than merely a hero. "Willie was like a god in Texas," Waylon Jennings remarks. "People there believe that when they die they're goin' to Willie's house." The music world seemed rife with 'Willyisms'. "Where there's a Willie, there's a way" and "Matthew, Mark, Luke and Willie." Bumper sticker slogans, to be sure, but the gospel according to Willie made sense to many people.

Willie Nelson's YESTERDAY'S WINE, PHASES AND STAGES, and RED HEADED STRANGER were concept albums that encouraged country artists to go beyond simply throwing ten singles on to a 12-inch LP. Willie's albums were held together with a philosophy of positive thinking and a belief in reincarnation, the Buddhist laws of karma, and the Christian golden rule. At a time when country music was a tangle of drinkin' and I-done-someone-wrong songs, Willie became known as a 'Zen Cowboy'. His singles *So You Think You're A Cowboy* and *My Heroes Have Always Been Cowboys* reminded country fans that 'outlaw music' was not a glorification of lawbreaking — it was about the positive values of independence and self-reliance. As Billy Joe Shaver said in his song *We Are The Cowboys*, progressive country was not about "kids with fast guns," it was about cowboys who "love this old world and don't want to lose it."

The Texans are gathered up in Colorado
The kid with the fast gun ain't with 'em today
The cowboys are riding tall in the saddle
They shoot from the heart with the songs that they play

— *We Are The Cowboys* (Billy Joe Shaver)

Shaver would also write *Willie The Wandering Gypsy And Me*, a tribute to his hero, Willie Nelson.

Willie he tells me that doers and thinkers
Say movin's the closest thing to bein' free . . .
Willie you're wild as a Texas blue-norther
Ready rolled from the same makin's as me
And I reckon we'll ramble 'til Hell freezes over
Willie the wandering gypsy and me . . .

— *Willie The Wandering Gypsy And Me* (Billy Joe Shaver)

When in 1988 Willie Nelson and Bud Shrake put his life story and personal philosophy into print in *Willie: An Autobiography*, we learned that not only did Willie believe in reincarnation, he'd mastered the art. Willie's superpowers were no myth. He could charm snakes, hypnotizing them with shadows cast by a twig in the flickering flames of a campfire. The Grateful Dead believed him capable of controlling the weather. Kinky Friedman was inspired by Willie to write his book *Road Kill*, a murder mystery in which this 'cosmic' Willie is pursued by his ex-wives and other renegades. This Willie imparts his world view to Kinky while driving golf balls into the Pacific Ocean and smoking his favorite green herb. As Waylon Jennings told Ray Benson, "Willie was laid-back before people knew what laid-back was."

Willie became something of a counter-culture guru. Repeated reading of *Willie: An Autobiography* can indeed be as enlightening spiritually as reading Kahil Gibran's *The Prophet*, Shunryu Suzuki's *Zen Mind, Beginner's Mind*, Alan Watt's *The Way of Zen*, or P.D. Ouspenski's *New Model of the Universe* and *In Search of the Miraculous*. Contemporary readers find similar inspiration in the sayings of Deepak Chopra. Learning to listen to your inner voice, understanding the laws of karma, grasping the significance of reincarnation, and cultivating the healing powers of the old Kahunas on Mauii — these are Willie's spiritual preoccupations in his autobiography.

At the height of the outlaw days, Willie broke the mold again, repainting his own portrait, with a little help from Memphis producer Booker T. Jones, on his STARDUST album, rehearsed in Brian Ahern and Emmylou Harris' living room in California and recorded in 1978 through the wonder of the Enactron Truck mobile unit. STARDUST would remain on the country charts for a full decade, an unprecedented achievement. By the 1980s, Willie Nelson had transcended all of his various incarnations — Country Willie, Shotgun Willie, Outlaw Willie, Cosmic Willie — and became an American icon, his image an endorsement of all things country whenever it was seen.

Willie's way appealed to die-hard country fans and to others who had never before bought a country record. Willie continued to grow on people. His collaborations with Leon Russell, Emmylou Harris, Dolly Parton, Merle Haggard, Ray Charles, Julio Iglesias, and many, many others, along with his popular covers of standards, both old and recent, kept him in the Top 10 on radio, no matter if it was a country or pop or MOR format station. Willie was in the movies with Robert Redford, Jane Fonda, Gary Busey, and Kris Kristofferson, who had become a box office star playing opposite Barbra Streisand in *A Star Is Born*. Willie was on the U.S.A. for Africa record *We Are The World*, along with his rock and pop superstar colleagues. Then he began his Farm Aid benefits, which evolved from his legendary Fourth of July picnics into his highest profile and most valuable political act. When he was investigated by the I.R.S. (Internal Revenue Service) for income tax improprieties, Willie released a mail order album, THE I.R.S. TAPES, to pay his debt to the government agency and raised more than a million dollars. Everybody on the street wanted to know how Willie was making out with the I.R.S. "Well," Willie commented in *Mix* magazine, "you can tell them I am now in charge of the I.R.S." When Willie showed up at the I.R.S. to sign the papers and settle accounts, the tax men all wanted to get his autograph on more than just the legal forms. Everybody on the planet, even Internal Revenue Service agents, wanted to have their pictures taken with Willie Nelson.

Today his fans include people of all faiths and persuasions and every walk of life. Whether he's entertaining the President of the United States on the White House lawn or a massed throng at a Farm Aid benefit concert, whether he's crooning Hoagy Carmichael's *Georgia On My Mind* or a soulful version of his own *Night Life*, Willie Nelson can shift back and forth between moody and upbeat in the twinkling of an eye. He's *On The Road Again*, where "The life I love is playin' music with my friends . . ." then he's "Crazy for tryin', Crazy for cryin', Crazy for lovin' . . . you." Each request for these Willie Nelson standards brings showers of acknowledgment from the A&E studio audience in New York City. In his golden years, Willie Nelson still delights in entertaining his audience right there in their living rooms with every ounce of heart and soul he's got.

In the 1990s when Top 40 radio no longer charted his studio productions, Willie would again resort to the grassroots, livingroom approach Tom T. Hall witnessed back in the '70s at Willie's home on the albums MOONLIGHT BECOMES YOU and SPIRIT. Willie Nelson was never merely an entertainer; he has always been a musical medicine man whose performances healed his audiences. As his daughter Lana recently said of Willie's show in Atlanta on a night when the Space Shuttle *Atlantis* was launched into orbit, "the real blast off occurred at 8:00 when the Willie Nelson and Family concert lit up the Kravis Center. Two hours later, fans still found themselves in orbit, absorbed in the famous Willie Nelson jet stream. A stream that will take the audience through a humble, touching look at life, and they'll come through the other side knowing we're all the same, basically no different than the man on the stage; except maybe, for the pigtails."

Life has buffeted this country veteran, but he has kept on keeping on through the decades, bringing a wider sense of jazz, blues, and soul to a genre that had been homogenized in the 1960s by the Nashville Sound. His country has always been blues; his blues, always country. Willie Nelson has reinvented himself several times over, and each time he's surprised us with new music. Willie Nelson is a human being who breathes the world deeply into his lungs before he lets it out again, conscious of his mortal limits and the need to exert his 'will' upon the recycled dust which is his body in this life. People close to Willie sometimes call him 'Will'.

"Music is a religious experience for me," Willie confides in his authorized video biography, *Willie Nelson: My Life*. "It is for a lot of people. It crosses all the boundaries. It's a mainliner." In a world that has rushed from being a largely agrarian-based economy through industrialization to the info age in one short century, country music and the people who play it, dance to it, and love to listen to it are not the people who once looked to country to sooth their poverty-stricken despair. Willie Nelson has evolved along with the music to become the man he is today. The story of country music, in many, many ways, is his story. He has heard and seen it all and sung a good deal of it his way. The country way of life is something he can truly call "my life."

COUNTRY WILLIE

Willie Nelson never was a William or a Bill. He was always Willie, named by his cousin Mildred, who fetched Doctor Simms from his nearby residence when Willie's mother went into labor. Willie's birth was a family affair, also witnessed by his grandmother, "Mamma" Nelson, who must have seen his red hair about the same time she heard him bawl his first rebel yell as he left the blissful realm of the womb and entered the cruel, cold world. While Willie's shock of rust-red hair set him apart from many other kids his age, his voice would distinguish him in time from most other country singers.

Willie sang at an early age, penning songs when he was only seven years old, eventually developing a unique vocal style. No one ever billed Willie Nelson as the next Hank Williams or Lefty Frizzell — or compared him to anyone at all. Willie was one of a kind, right from the get-go, and, while some country singers (with far less to offer in the way of talent) headed for Nashville before they were dry behind the ears, Willie dragged his heels for years until his first wife, Martha, and other early fans, including Mae Axton, finally cajoled him into making the songwriting capital of the world his home. Even then, he didn't stick it out for all that long. While people in Nashville took to his songs, that meandering voice of his, well . . .

Willie Hugh Nelson first drew breath in Abbott, Texas, on April 30, 1933, the second child born to Ira and Myrle Nelson. Arriving in this world smack dab in the midst of the Great Depression and drought years, baby Willie would soon be left in the care of his grandparents, William Alfred Nelson and Nancy Elizabeth Smothers Nelson, when Ira and Myrle's marriage broke down and they moved on. Ira Nelson and Myrle Greenhaw Nelson were married in 1929 in Pindall, Arkansas, and, along with Ira's parents, they had left the cotton farming country on the slopes of the Ozark Mountains in Searcy County, Arkansas with the hope of better times further west. Surely, they must have thought, that hope lay just over the horizon. Twenty-year-old Myrle left Abbott first. She was a waitress and a dancer who had only briefly alighted in Ira's life during musical get-togethers in Arkansas, a colorful butterfly with gypsy ways, and by the time Willie was six months old, she flew away. The small-town life was not for her. Abbott was small then, a mere 350-to-360 people listed as the total population. It's still small today. "Nothing really changes," Willie says in the authorized video biography *Willie Nelson: My Life*, "when a baby is born, a man leaves town." Life in Abbott could be counted on to be as dull and uneventful as in any of the farming communities that dotted the east-Texas cotton belt in the 'dirty thirties'. The nearest movie house was a few miles away down Highway 35 in Waco. For real action, you had to travel 40 miles up to Fort Worth, where a wide-open music scene in roadhouses and clubs could be found.

Ira would leave, too, before Willie turned two-years-old, to seek work as an auto mechanic wherever he could find it, eventually settling into a groove as the chief-mechanic in a Fort Worth Ford dealership and part-time musician playing weekends in and around Fort Worth. Ira's second marriage, to Lorraine Moon, would be a good one. They had two children, Willie's stepbrothers Doyle and Charles, and 40 years later Ira would still be part of his son's extended family, managing his pool hall in Austin and selling t-shirts at Willie's Fourth of July picnics.

For Willie and his sister, Bobbie Lee Nelson, who was born on January 1, 1931, growing up with Ira's folks, Mamma and Daddy Nelson, didn't turn out to be the worst lot that could have befallen them. While Willie and Bobbie endured a sense of loss because their birth parents were seldom around, they were luckier than some because Daddy and Mamma Nelson did a whole lot more than merely take care of their grandchildren out of some family sense of obligation. Their family life in Abbott, where there were always older aunts and cousins to help in their upbringing, would be filled with love and music, despite the hard times the drought and depression heaped on people in those times. A blacksmith by trade, Daddy Nelson and his wife were both self-taught musicians, graduates of learn-by-mail courses, who had taught music back in Arkansas to groups of school children who would come together at county school houses for two weeks of summer music lessons and the singing of old-time gospel music. Bobbie Lee's first 'instrument' was a cardboard piano, which she would take out under the apple tree in the back yard in Abbott and play for hours before she got a real piano. Willie's first instrument was a tin mandolin, a Christmas gift in 1936.

"They were music teachers. They took a correspondence course from a Chicago music institute," Willie explains in the authorized video biography. "They would study their lessons every night by kerosene lamp and I would watch them. It was some pretty complicated 'shape note' type lessons that they were learning. So I started picking it up and my granddaddy taught me a couple of chords on the guitar."

"We had a real large dining table," Bobbie recalls, "and they would sit there with all this music stretched out. And they would study late into the evening. Gospel music was where we really were. But, of course, we had learned some other music, too." Bobbie would take to the piano and do better at persisting with her music lessons than Willie, who possessed less patience. In *Willie: An Autobiography*, which he co-wrote with longtime friend and collaborator Bud Shrake, Willie credits his grandparents for pushing him and Bobbie into music, but he also notes that the instruction they received had some special aspects, which went beyond the usual training exercises. "Bobbie and I developed perfect pitch. All this means is our grandparents trained us to reproduce the memory of how many vibrations were passing through the tunnels between our ears. Music is vibrations. A housefly, for example, hums in the F key in the middle octave of your piano. Hit that key and see for yourself. The sense of pitch changes with the number of vibrations. A B-flat is 400 cycles of vibrating molecules. G is something else."

This hands-on approach to understanding the basis of how music is formed and how we hear it was a rare gift not usually passed on by piano and voice teachers in those days, an insight that would inform Willie Nelson's unique approach to writing and playing music in years to come. For Willie, though, developing people skills played at least as important a part in his approach to things as music theory. For example, he tells of times he stood up to bullies in schoolyard fights because he wasn't prepared to live in anyone's shadow. To him, at that early age, establishing who you were, even if it took getting in the first punch and challenging any comers, meant that you could hold your head high and not have to eat crow, even when you had been given the nickname 'Booger Red'. Willie was so dubbed when he gouged his nose with his finger causing a nosebleed before his first public performance, reciting a poem he had written at age four.

A tough, little, freckle-faced boy, 'Booger Red' had a passion for martial arts, which he became attracted to early on through his comic book heroes, and he studied jujitsu and judo through correspondence courses. Later in life, Willie would get more out of kung fu and 'tae kwan do' lessons where he learned to deal with his aggression as well as how to harness the 'chi' life-force. Willie was an active kid who excelled at several team sports (basketball, football, baseball) and participated in such track and field events as pole vaulting and running. He would later take to running five miles a day to keep his body and mind in shape.

While Willie came to respect the disciplined parenting he received from his grandparents, he also held his mother's heritage in his heart. Myrle's family, the Greenhaws, were notorious moonshiners back in the Arkansas and Tennessee hills, known in Searcy County folklore as operators of bandit hideouts, bootleggers who had their run-ins with the 'revenuers' on occasion. He learned this heritage through romanticized stories told him by his birth mother, Myrle, during her visits to Abbott, and, later through his visits to her home in the Pacific Northwest. The Greenhaws were hillbillies whose mixed European and Indian blood led them to operate outside the law where prejudice could be dealt with swiftly and directly. Willie may have missed his birth mother a whole lonely lot during his formative years, but he more than made up for that aching sorrow by loving her fiercely and forgiving her every trespass. As a boy he would daydream of being a modern day outlaw, and, in the South in those days, there were plenty of role models to choose from. In his autobiography, his description of his mother Myrle holds no love back. "My mother was a very strong woman. She had long hair and an Indian profile like Bobbie's and mine."

The Irish-English Nelsons had first settled in the Ozarks where storytelling, singing, and dancing were a strong old-world tradition that flourished in the frontier days and continued as the families moved west. Willie has said that if, before he was born, he might have had a choice of what life he were to be reincarnated into, he would have picked the one he was living, because the life of the troubadour is the one he feels has always been cut out for him. And in 1978 Willie told Pete Axthelm in *Newsweek*, "I have no negative memories of growing up. It was being grown-up that started to be a problem." So, although some journalists and commentators have made a big deal out of his being abandoned by both his parents before he was two years old, Willie has made the most of what he was handed, and seldom (if ever) blamed anybody for any of it.

In fact, the stories his close relatives tell of Daddy Nelson singing him *Polly Wolly Doodle All The Day* and *Show Me The Way To Go Home* when he was still a toddler, sitting him on his knee or cradling him in his arms, focus on just how fortunate his life turned out to be. Willie's grandfather disciplined him once or twice with a leather strap, but he took the time to tell young boy why he was being disciplined. His granddaddy also bought him his first guitar, a Stella model, from the Sears catalog, and taught him his first 'three chords and the truth' lesson, showing him D, A and G, which are the same chords most kids get shown because they are easy to grip. With them you can play most country songs. Country music never was complicated and some of the best, like Hank Williams, never knew how to write or read music, they just played and sang. C chord and F chord come later. These simple chords and this procedure, mentioned by Willie in his autobiography and elsewhere in interviews, were the same chords and procedure that I used during my junior college years in Nelson British Columbia when I picked up pocket money teaching guitar lessons to kids as young as six and seven years old. Several of these students went on to work with teenage bands, and one, Cameron Molloy, to a career as a country recording artist who had national hits in Canada. Cam was a fast learner. He only came by a couple of times. Next thing you knew, he had a band of his own.

Willie Nelson was a fast learner, too, and after his granddaddy Nelson passed away, Willie became a provider of sorts for the family, playing in a polka band on weekends. He preferred doing that over picking cotton in the fields for local farmers. And it paid better, too, four times as much money per night as he'd been making as a farm laborer. When Alanna Nash asked him in an interview later published in her book *Behind Closed Doors* "When did you realize you had made it?" Willie had no hesitation. "I think," he told Nash, "probably the first time was when I went out — I'd been makin' two dollars a day choppin' cotton, and I went out one night and made eight dollars playin' music. I think I was about eleven years old. From that day on, I had it made. That was the turning point. That was it. No more choppin' cotton for me."

Willie did well at school and later told Alanna Nash that during his school days he raised hogs for the Future Farmers of America. "I used to raise one pig at a time, to show." He also offered her this brief, self-portrait. "Well, when I was a kid, 'long hair' meant a long-haired musician. Of course, I wasn't then. I played country music, but I had fairly long hair, and long side-burns. And my hair was always in my eyes for as long as I can remember, except for a couple of times when I got a burr haircut. I usually went from one extreme to another."

With Daddy Nelson gone at the age of 56 in 1939, victim of the side-effect of a sulpha-drug taken during a bout of pneumonia, Mamma Nelson soon found herself financially challenged to make ends meet. She would supplement her work as a field laborer by taking a job in a school cafeteria. Before this, she had routinely taken the children along when she worked for various farmers in the area. Eventually, she had to move herself and the two children out of the family home into a more modest dwelling in a poorer section of town. Bobbie remembers the work in the fields fondly. Willie was never excited about the back-breaking field work, and often only picked enough cotton so that he could use his little sack as a pillow.

The loss of Daddy Nelson and the move to a smaller home, which was more of a shack than the sort of house they were used to, was offset by the arrival of the family's first radio. Willie has often recalled that because the radio was a novelty, "we used to sit around and watch the radio, because it was new in the house. There was somethin' there that had some entertainment comin' out of it." Of course, one of the first radio shows Bobbie, Willie, and Mamma Nelson 'watched' was the *Grand Ole Opry*, but it was not the only music they listened to. Reception in Abbott was good late at night, and Willie would hear broadcasts from as far away as Chicago and New Orleans. Dance bands playing from the Aragon Ballroom in the windy city and jazz groups playing in the Mardis Gras city. "I was up a lot late at night," Willie later told *Goldmine* magazine writer Bill DeYoung, "and I'd turn the dial and listen to anything I could, really. A lot of boogie and blues, back in the days of Freddie Slack and Ella Mae Morse, and Ray MacKinley. And Glenn Miller and those guys."

Willie was hooked on country when he heard Ernest Tubb's *Walkin' The Floor Over You* on the radio, but he would emulate other singers. In 1995, he told Bill DeYoung, "Ernest Tubb was the Texas country music hero, and Frank Sinatra was the bobbysoxer hero back in those days. But I could see similarities. I think it [my singing style] is probably a combination of Frank Sinatra, Ernest Tubb, Floyd Tillman, and Bob Wills, and probably other people that I don't even know. I think, early on, I did do a lot of phrasing. Maybe I couldn't do it exactly the way Ernest Tubb and Frank Sinatra did it, so I would do it the way that made it easy for me. It may sound strange, or even more far off than they think I should be, but as long as I get back in time and the beat is there. I've run a lot of drummers crazy trying to follow me, because I do lay behind or jump ahead a lot." Willie has often named Ernest Tubb and Bob Wills as his earliest heroes, but his wide-open ears also identified Floyd Tillman and Frank Sinatra as kindred spirits. Their phrasing is what he was attracted to. Willie Nelson and Frank Sinatra would later be compared as two of the best. Willie puts it down to breathing. He could hear, right from Frank's early records, that someone had trained him to breathe. "My grandmother gave me voice lessons," Willie told Bill DeYoung, "and that was what she always taught me. Voice control was breathing from way down deep, and how that would strengthen your lungs and your vocal chords. So I started out doing that real early. And I'd heard Frank Sinatra sing, so I knew he had strong lungs. I really don't know if he practised voice control as I did, but he must have had that sort of instruction somewhere along the way." From this radio smorgasbord, Willie's personal vocal style was evolving.

As were his songwriting skills. Willie had begun to write poems at the age of four. Once he learned the guitar, he put his poems to music, and, after his grandfather passed away, he began writing what he has called "cheating songs." At age 11, Willie would fashion his own songbook, with the title "Songs by Willie Nelson, Waco Texas" on the front cover, and the western motif of cowboy hats and a lariat worked into the words "Howdy Pardner" on the back. He placed it on a table side by side with Jimmie Rodgers and Roy Acuff songbooks, practicing the art of positive thinking years before he came to adopt this discipline as a conscious focus to his life. Already ahead of his time, Willie would continue down his individual path, and nothing, not even Ira's advice to quit trying to make a living at playing music and get a steady job, would deter him from his pursuit of what, at times, must have seemed a very illusive goal. In the Johnny Raycjeck Polka Band, playing acoustic guitar along with 15 horn-players at their Bohemian dance hall gigs, Willie was in no danger of confusing the drummer and was paid good money for his efforts. Mamma Nelson opposed it at first. She'd told him she didn't want him 'going on the road', and while the tour circuit from Abbott to nearby West and Ross involved no more than eight-mile trips, they were road trips to her way of thinking. The getting paid part is the only reason she let him keep doing it. They needed the money.

Daddy and Mamma Nelson were Methodists. Mamma played the piano in the church in Abbott. Willie would routinely sleep through the sermons and wake in time to join in for the singing. He was baptized or 'sprinkled' when very young and later developed a compulsion to come forward and be sprinkled again when the preacher called for converts at the finish of his preaching. If he'd been born Catholic, he'd have been a chronic confessor. Of course, for young boys born to fundamentalist families in the 1930s, there were plenty of sins to confess after each rule was broken.

At age 13, Willie got his first country gig playing and singing in a band that Bobbie's young husband, Bud Fletcher, put together. Bud couldn't play himself at first, but he faked it with a broom handle bass, which he whacked to the beat, and fronted the band. For some jobs, Ira sat in on guitar and fiddle. Bud Fletcher was the enterprising entrepreneur who put together the first Nelson Family Band, a formula Willie would come back to 24 years later. Bud paid Willie eight dollars a show, big bucks for a 13-year-old and much needed money for Mamma Nelson in those days. That same year, he and Bud Fletcher put their efforts together to book Bob Wills for a show and dance at the Oak Lodge on nearby Lake Whitney.

"I think I learned a lot from him," Willie recalls in the authorized video biography *Willie Nelson: My Life*, "because he never took a break on the stage. He would go up at eight o'clock and play from eight 'til twelve. And go from one song to another. He would play two and three songs in a row, he'd play the same song twice. He did a lot of things that were sort of unorthodox. But they worked, and they kept the people dancing, kept everybody happy." In his autobiography, Willie notes that "Western swing was just about the only kind of country music you could hear in the state of Texas before Hank Williams came along. Western swing was jazz, anyway you wanted to look at it. It was jazz riffs inside a country lyric with a 4/4 beat behind it."

Cigar-smoking, fiddle playing band leader Bob Wills had his own way of doing things. His formula of tight arrangements, four-part harmonies that were figured out collectively by Wills and band members like Eldon Shamblin, Tiny Moore, and Johnny Gimble, combined with crackerjack vocalists like Tommy Duncan and plenty of stepping out by soloists, was a winning program for getting people's toes tapping and filling dance floors. Bob Wills & His Texas Playboys with their radio program exposure were the prototype Western Swing outfit, and were much imitated in the 1940s. Needless to say, sharing the bandstand with his hero, a 13-year old Willie Nelson was mightily impressed and quick to jot down in his memory some of the hot licks and arrangement tricks that night. Willie befriended Bob Wills and other members of the band, including fiddle player Johnny Gimble, who gave Willie his first Django Reinhardt record. Willie was already familiar with the Belgian guitarist, impressed by Reinhardt's virtuosity and fascinated with Django's innovative style. "I loved his tone," Willie told Bill DeYoung, "I can't do what he did, but I do admire it enough that it's obvious that I try to do what he does. I reach for something, and I don't hit what he hit, but I'll hit something else, accidently. That's where most hot licks come from, I think."

Willie was also aware that the gypsy guitarist, famous for his shows with violinist Stephane Grappelli at the Hot Club in Paris, was connected to what Wills, guitarist Shamblin, and Gimble were doing in Texas. "My dad played fiddle," he told DeYoung, "and he played rhythm guitar. The style that he played, he learned mostly from Western Swing. From Bob Wills and those guys. Now, the fiddle players in there, guys like Johnny Gimble and Cecil Briar, were great students of Stephane Grappelli. Django himself was a hero to all these Western Swing players, who were nothing more than jazz players themselves. Bob's influences were jazz. So I had Django's influences before I had the real thing." Willie also emphasizes Bob Wills' compelling charisma, writing, "He had an aura so strong it just stunned people . . . . Elvis was the same way. You had to see him live to understand his magnetic pull."

Playing in roadhouses and booze cans was against Bobbie's and Willie's raising. It was harder on Bobbie because society looked down on women who entertained in those days. As Willie has said on occasion, musicians and actors were generally regarded as being "shiftless" by the less talented, who, nevertheless eagerly showed up at movie houses and dance halls where these "shiftless" types eased everyone's stressful lives for a paltry price of admission. And playing full-time in a country band was not in the cards for someone attending high school, especially someone like Booger Red Nelson, who won letters playing for the Abbott Fighting Panthers in several team sports. During those years, he and Bobbie found employment where they could, working as janitors and switch board operators. When Bud Fletcher talked the operators of KHBR Hillsboro into putting their band on a regular radio show, Willie became a local hero. He also got his first taste of hanging out, playing checkers, smoking cigarettes, and generally just killing time with a young war vet by the name of Pat Kennedy, the band's first groupie and unofficial roadie. Just when Willie had come to appreciate Pat's company, the vet "fell off a truck and killed himself."

Willie's best friend during these years was Zeke Varnon, also a war vet and four years Willie's senior. They shared the usual explorations that teenage boys do, first dates, first cars, first hangovers, and some activities some young men never experience at all, running wild and crazy, at times. Most of the time, they barely got by. Their lives often seemed to be a juggling act. One of the stories Zeke would perpetuate would be the one about the pawnshop. "He'd hock his guitar every Monday," Zeke remembers with a chuckle in the authorized video biography. "And we'd get it out every Friday, and that went on for years." The story goes that the pawnbroker could play it better than Willie could.

By the time he graduated high school, Willie had outgrown his "Booger Red" nickname and his days as an athlete. He was hooked on music, but he wanted a car, too, and buying a car meant getting serious employment. However, a short-lived (one day) experience working with Zeke Varnon trimming trees in Tyler, Texas, brought home the same truth he already knew from his experience cutting cotton. Willie was not cut out for laboring. This time, it was showing off, grandstanding for his fellow workers in Tyler, that got Willie in trouble and, he claims, convinced him to enlist in the armed services. "I got him a job trimmin' trees," Zeke recalls. "We were takin' some big limbs off a (power) line, you know, away from the wires, and they had to be roped out with what we call a 'bull rope'."

"So," says Willie, reciting his lines to this oft-told tale with a smile, "I grabbed the rope and went up the tree. And I got up there and wrapped the rope around the limb, and I decided that I would climb down the rope — instead of climbin' down the tree — real brilliant."

"Willie got his hand caught up in the rope," says Zeke.

"I got hung up," Willie says. "I couldn't go up, and I couldn't go down." When a friend cut that rope, Willie fell through the high power lines. "Zoom, he fell right to the ground," Zeke says right on his cue. Willie, delivering the punch line, concludes, "And I got up and never stopped. I left that job and went off down the highway."

Zeke and Willie got into more than a few scrapes together, like the time they got their suitcases packed and set out to hop a freight for California. Running alongside the train as it gathered speed, they got their 'luggage' on board one of the boxcars, alright, but Zeke and Willie, well . . . they never did get themselves on board.

But his stint in the U.S. Air Force, where he got into a brawl or two and washed out at radar school, convinced Willie he could also do without a career in the armed forces. When an X-ray examination revealed a lower back problem, an injury sustained while hefting bales of hay, Willie glimpsed a way out of his four-year commitment. He had made it through basic training with no problems from his back, he says, "because I was mainly getting up at 4 a.m. and doing a lot of running." Later, lifting heavy boxes triggered a collapse and hospitalization. Released from his enlistment after only nine months — he wouldn't agree to a surgical operation and the Air Force couldn't insure him — he high-tailed it back to Abbott. Money available to ex-servicemen provided Willie with the opportunity to attend Baylor University in Waco, although he didn't last long there either, later telling interviewers that he had "majored in dominoes."

HAVE GUITAR WILL TRAVEL

When you become a legend, stories told about you, regardless of whether they are based on fact or they are pure fantasy, become bigger than the life you've actually lived — or even imagined you might have lived. Willie's life has proven to be no different than many other country stars in this respect. A case in point is Willie's marriage to Martha Jewel Matthews. Most often what gets told is the story about how Martha once sewed Willie up in a bed sheet and beat on him with a broom. Not so, Martha told Bud Shrake, when Bud was putting together Willie's autobiography. "The truth is," she claims, "I tied him up with the kids' jump ropes and beat the hell out of him." Willie himself has not been retiring in describing his 'lively' relationship with Martha. "One morning," he recalls, "she threw a fork at me across the table, and it stuck in my belly where it wobbled and made a strange humming noise. Another time she threw a shot glass at me. It sailed across the bar, bounced off a wall, and came back to open the face of a friend." With reference to Martha's Cherokee heritage, Willie has quipped, "Every night we staged Custer's last stand." Despite their ongoing battles, Willie's memories of Martha glow with a special fondness. She was, he has recalled, "just flat out the prettiest girl I had ever seen in my life."

Willie was 19 at the time he met Martha. She was barely 16. He was a red-headed, guitar-pickin', honky tonkin', country singer. Martha was a waitress who hung with a crowd of teenage girlfriends who loved to party almost as much as they loved to dance. Willie first set eyes on her from his position on the bandstand and first asked her out when she was working as a carhop at a local burger joint. He has said he was "dazzled" by her beauty. After a false start or two, like the time he and Zeke showed up drunk at that drive-in, trying to pick Martha up in Zeke's car, she joined him in a car he'd borrowed from brother-in-law, Bud Fletcher. Willie was in *love*. He had the *Lovesick Blues* over Martha. It turned out that she felt the same way, too, and, in February 1952, they got hitched by a Justice of the Peace in nearby Cleburne.

They moved in with Mamma Nelson for the first while, but fell into poor times simply because they were so young. Both jealous of every move the other made, they were hitting the bottle and fighting so often that their marriage was in serious trouble. Willie recognized that he needed to get his "Cherokee beauty out of Hill County if we were going to have any chance of this powerful love not tearing us apart," he explained in his autobiography. To his way of thinking, there had to be somewhere in America "where we could accentuate the positive and eliminate the negative, as the Johnny Mercer song says."

Martha and Willie lit out for Eugene, Oregon, where Mother Myrle was living, with but 24 dollars between them, driving one of those 'drive-away' cars that someone wanted delivered to the west coast, just like the ones that Jack Kerouac was always driving in his semi-biographical novel *On The Road*. Little did Willie know then that he would later write an even more famous "On The Road" — in his case, a song — but like the ever restless Kerouac in his formative years, Willie and Martha zigged back to Texas for a while during her first pregnancy, moving in with grandmother Nelson, then zagged back to the Portland, Oregon-Vancouver, Washington, area (where Myrle had moved) for a spell, then settled in with Ira and Lorraine from time to time. Consequently, Willie and Martha's three children were born in three different cities. Lana came first, born in a hospital in Hillsboro, the nearest facility to Abbott. Susie came second, born in Vancouver, Washington. Billy came third, born in 1958 in Fort Worth. Somehow Willie and Martha kept their marriage going and raised their children together for more than a decade, a feat Ira and Myrle had not managed to accomplish.

Willie found work in San Antonio as a lead guitar player with Johnny Bush's band by night and as a deejay, newscaster, commercial announcer, salesman, and jack of all trades by day at KBOP in Pleasanton. But when Martha came to term with Lana, they once again headed for Mamma Nelson's place and the hospital in Hillsboro, then relocated in Fort Worth where Willie secured a job at KCNC. He replaced popular KCNC radio personality Charlie Williams. Willie had his on-air personality down by this time, signing on like a pro with a patter he had distilled from several popular deejays of the day. "This is your cotton-pickin', snuff dippin', tobacco chewin', stump jumpin', gravy soppin', pot dodgin', dumplin' eatin', frog giggin' hillbilly from Hill country, Willie Nelson. Stay tuned . . . ."

Life in the Dallas-Fort Worth area, especially for musicians, was rough, often complicated by turf wars staged by rival gangs and gamblers. In this world, Willie met Paul English. Paul had been running a call girl service out of a "drive-in motel," had been questioned during several murder investigations, had become a fixture on local police "10-most-wanted men posters," and had served some hard time before that night in the mid-1950s when he filled in for his brother, Oliver English, Willie's regular drummer. "It's the first time he'd ever played in his life," Willie recalls. "He'd played trumpet in the Salvation Army. We told him when to hit, and we got the beat started for him. Obviously, he had some hidden talent, and he picked it right up." At some point along the way, Willie and Paul and band would play a club on the notorious Jacksboro Highway strip, a hardscrabble assortment of honky tonks and roadhouses where, on some Saturday nights, violence broke out as regularly as traffic lights changed from green to yellow to red. "They hired us to cover up the noise of this big dice game," Willie has recalled. "We played there nine months," Paul confided to the *New York Times*, "and saw two killings and at least one good fight every night." Paul joined Willie full-time in 1966, and since that time, he's managed the band's security and taken care of the money, which in those days was collected in cash before the band went on and needed to be protected by someone who knew how to handle firearms, especially when Willie began hauling upwards of $20,000 per night in the 1970s. "Willie Nelson is my best friend by far," Paul English told Bud Shrake. For several years, when they were still using station wagons on their tours, Paul and Willie were roommates. "Willie and I make a good pair," Paul points out, "because he's the eternal optimist, and I'm the kind of guy who figures out all the angles."

During the lean years, when the band didn't always get paid, Paul sometimes sold one of his rental properties to help make ends meet. Willie would tell his pal that he'd "make all of this up to you, someday." True to form, Willie has kept his word in both dollars and song. *Me and Paul* is one of his most heartfelt compositions. Paul English is a 20 percent partner in Willie's publishing company, which means Willie shares one fifth of every songwriting royalty that he receives with Paul. "Willie feels safe with me behind him," Paul told Bud Shrake. "I carry two guns."

It's been rough and rocky travelin'
But I finally got both feet on the ground
After takin' several readings
I'm surprised to find my mind still fairly sound
I guess Nashville was the roughest
But I know I said the same about them all
We received our education

In the cities of the nation
Me and Paul

— *Me and Paul* (Willie Nelson)

The first song Willie recorded was *When I've Sung My Last Hillbilly Song*, which started out as a demo, cut in 1955 at one of the radio stations where he was working. The demo was sent to Charles Fitch at Sarg Records, and at some point got pressed onto a 45 rpm record b/w *The Storm Has Just Begun*, a song that Willie is said to have written at age 12. Michael Hall, a musician and journalist who interviewed Willie for *Grammy Magazine* in 1995, brought along one of these obscure 45s to his meeting with the singer. "I discovered Charlie Fitch a couple of years ago," Hall told Willie, "and have been out to Luling to see him a couple of times just talking with him. He's a really good old guy. And it's a great story, how you recorded two songs at the station where you worked in 1955 and sent a tape to him. He passed then, but pressed these 45s up years later. Have you heard it?" Willie responded, "I maybe heard it then . . . I forgot the name of it." Once Hall gave the title, Willie began to sing, "When I've sung my last hillbilly song . . . ." That same year, Bill DeYoung wrote an article on Willie in *Goldmine* that includes an extensive discography, listing no less than three 1955 releases on the Sarg label. These records probably didn't receive much air play, perhaps none at all. Bootleg is just another seven-letter-word when it comes to the rough demo sessions that have been released by Willie Nelson's former associates, including some companies that are known as major labels.

Most sources cite Willie's first 'official' recording as his 1957 single *No Place For Me* with Leon Payne's *The Lumberjack* on the B-side. That record was put together in a Portland garage while Willie Nelson was a deejay at KVAN in Vancouver, Washington. The first 500 copies of the reverb-soaked effort were pressed by Starday in Nashville, although Starday head Pappy Daily did not pick up the publishing rights for the songs, an option often included in the Starday manufacturing contracts at that time. The label on the record read 'Willie Nelson Records'.

Portland, Oregon is set on the south bank of the Columbia River some 100 miles upriver from the Pacific Ocean, with Vancouver, Washington situated on the north bank. The Columbia serves as the state line dividing Oregon and Washington. The lyrics to Willie's debut single on Willie Nelson Records testify to the song being inspired by his time spent there.

Your love is as cold as the north wind that blows
And the river that runs down to the sea

— *No Place For Me* (Willie Nelson)

Willie had a good situation at KVAN with a four-hour show from 10 a.m. 'til 2 p.m. playing country records, the second most popular show in that time slot, surpassed only by Arthur Godfrey's syndicated radio show. His on-air personality was "Wee Willie Nelson," and he was on a roll hawking his record and selling several thousand mail-order copies of it and an 8 x 10 photo for a buck a copy. He was working with a couple of local bands, playing fellow deejay Pat Mason's Wagon Wheel Park in Camas, Washington on weekends, making it possible to provide for his family, but he felt restless. Elvis had broken onto the radio in a big way with Heartbreak Hotel and Don't Be Cruel recording out of Memphis and Nashville. It seemed like things were happening down in Tennessee.

When Mae Axton, who'd written *Heartbreak Hotel* for Elvis, showed up at KVAN during a promotional swing through the Pacific Northwest, which she was making on behalf of Colonel Tom Parker to plug an upcoming Hank Snow tour, Willie pitched his songs to her. Mae was impressed. As she recalled in the authorized video biography *Willie Nelson: My Life*, "He said to me, 'I play all of your songs that come to the station.' I thought, 'Hey, this kid's alright!' He said, 'I'm a big fan of yours. I've been tryin' to write, but I don't know if I'm good enough.'" When Mae heard Willie's demo tape of *Family Bible*, she knew he had something. "My chin," she recalled, "went on the proverbial floor. I couldn't believe what I was listenin' to from this little scrawny kid, this deejay. I said, 'Son, you quit this job. You go to Texas or Tennessee where people can hear your songs." The lyrics to *Family Bible* convey the sense of "family" Willie has carried with him throughout his life.

I can see us sitting 'round the table
When from the family Bible Dad would read
And I can hear my mother softly singing
Rock of Ages, Rock of Ages, cleft for me

— *Family Bible* (Willie Nelson)

Willie and Martha packed everything they had into Willie's new Cadillac and headed south, but a stopover in Springfield, Missouri, where Billy Walker was working the *Ozark Jubilee*, convinced Willie that Nashville doors would be closed to him. So, Martha and Willie hung around Springfield for a few weeks. By this time, Willie and Martha's marriage had become a pattern of 'mutual intolerance', Billy recalls in the authorized video biography. "She was workin' at night, he was babysittin' . . . and then he would go off on a tangent and she would just sometimes beat the tar out of him." Billy Walker would become the first Nashville artist to record a Willie Nelson song when he cut *Mr. Record Man* in 1960, but the song harkens back to Willie's days in the 1950s when when he seemed to be forever on the road.

I was drivin' down the highway with my radio turned on
And the man that I heard singing seemed so blue and all alone

— *Mr. Record Man* (Willie Nelson)

With Martha working some of the time, and Willie not able to find many playing jobs at all, their existence became sketchy and nomadic. "Well, I did a lot of movin' in the middle of the night," Willie recalls in the authorized video biography. "Whenever the rent would come due, we'd head on out the window to find another apartment in the next big town." Of course, this could not go on indefinitely. With a wife and two children dependent on him, and a third on the way, Willie decided to follow Ira's advice and give up playing music for a living. He and Martha stayed with Ira and Lorraine at their home in Fort Worth until he generated some funds. Willie tried his hand at selling bibles and encyclopedias. Then he sold Kirby vacuum cleaners. But the night life was still calling the young couple, and whenever they could find a baby-sitter, they hit the clubs.

On Sundays, though, they attended a Baptist church, and Willie got baptized. Fully immersed, this time, not merely 'sprinkled' as he'd been in the Methodist church in Abbott. He got immersed in teaching 'Sunday School', too, but fell into conflict with the local minister. "We was gettin' some jobs here and there on the side, you know, playin' wherever we could," Ira later explained in an interview with Sean Mitchell, "and that included a bunch of honky tonks. At this same time, both me and Willie was teachin' Sunday School. Well, one Sunday the preacher come up to Willie and he said, 'You can't be teachin' Sunday school and singin' in them honky tonks, too.' So, Willie quit teachin' Sunday school, and I did, too." In his typical pragmatic way, Willie has said that he and the preacher both made the "money decision" — Willie opted for the paying gigs at the night clubs, the preacher accepted the contribution made by the complaining parishioner to the church coffers.

Willie refused to believe that the Methodists and Baptists "had a lock on God." In search of spiritual alternatives, he began researching the situation in the Fort Worth Public Library, which led to his discovery of the Aquarian Bible, and to his coming to believe in reincarnation. Reincarnation, he discovered, was embraced by several religions. Christian visionary and healer, Edgar Cayce, believed it to be true, too. The result of Willie's religious studies has been a personal spiritual quest that has continued throughout his life. When Willie was younger, his mother had sent him a letter in which she laid out a map for positive behavior and visualization. When Willie had first received that letter, he hadn't really known how to act on her suggestions. With the studying he was doing, he came up with his own approach to positive visualization, jotting down some guidelines in a list at the back of his Aquarian Bible. When he compared the two lists of recommendations, his mother's and his own, it turned out that his was not all that different from the suggestions Myrle had made. With the 'self-work' that he began there in Fort Worth, Willie started a transformation which eventually saw him move from writing cheating songs, laced with loneliness, to lyrics that contained powerful healing messages. He might have a few more reincarnations before he perfected himself, but he now had a path to follow. By the time he was rubbing shoulders with the songwriting community in Nashville, he would be known as a positive thinker who seldom lost his cool, except, of course, when he was fighting with Martha.

After Martha gave birth to their third child, Billy, in Fort Worth on May 21, 1958, the family headed for Houston. Willie had heard there were some people there who might want to buy some of his songs, the only equity he had. Giving up playing music and getting a day-job had not worked out all that well. On the way into Houston on the Interstate, Willie stopped off at the Esquire Ballroom where Larry Butler was rehearsing his band and offered his songs to Larry. Willie pitched *Mr. Record Man* and some others to the bandleader. Butler could not believe Willie would be willing to sell these outright for only $10. He told Willie to hang on to his songs, lent him $50, and hired him to play guitar in his band. Willie and Martha located an apartment in Pasadena, just outside the city, and he began commuting six nights a week to the Esquire club. To supplement his income, he began working as a deejay Sunday mornings at a Pasadena radio station.

On a roll, Willie hooked up with Pappy Daily, who had just started his own "D" Records in Houston after selling his interest in Starday Records. Willie's first record for Daily was the 1959 release, *The Storm Has Just Begun* b/w *Man With The Blues*. The artists credited were Willie Nelson & The Reil Sisters. When he was fired, re-hired, and fired again from the radio job for being late, Willie kept after people to buy some of his songs. One of the people he hooked up with in Houston was Paul Buskirk, a musician and music teacher. With some help from Paul, Willie now started teaching some lessons, too. He has credited Buskirk as being a mentor. "We played music together when I was first in Houston, when I first started," he told *Grammy Magazine*. "Paul had a music studio. He taught me how to read music. We have played a lot of gigs together."

Willie's time at the Paul Buskirk School of Guitar was fraught with the fact that he felt the students knew he was faking it most of the time with the lessons, whipping out some fancy pickin' on *Wildwood Flower* or some other number to dazzle their eyes, even though his heart wasn't really in teaching. The thing is, Willie wasn't always bringing home enough to make ends meet. Even though he had a record out with Pappy Daily on "D" Records, he wasn't exactly setting the world on fire. So, once again he found himself trying sell some of his songs, this time to Paul Buskirk. As Paul remembered it for the authorized video biography, "Willie said, 'I've got a song I think you'll like.' And I said, 'Willie, I ain't got much money, how much do you want . . . before we start?' He said, 'I'll take . . . 50 bucks.' He started singing *Family Bible*, and I knew, I said, 'Willie, I'll buy it.'"

Willie had needed the money, but when Paul Buskirk pitched the song to singer Claude Gray, the Tall Texan, and Pappy Daily put Claude's recording of it out on "D" Records, it was difficult to live with the consequences. "I watched it go up the charts to number one, Claude Gray's record of it," he remembers in *Willie Nelson: My Life*. "My name was nowhere around, but I still had a lot of pride. I felt if I could write one good song, I could write another. I had a lot to say back then. So, I wrote a lot of songs. I was playing at a place called the Esquire Ballroom, which is on the Interstate Highway, across Houston, and it's a long drive, about an hour over and an hour back, and I wrote one goin' over and another comin' back. I wrote *Crazy* and *Night Life*."

Many people like me
Dreamin' of old used-to-bes
The night life ain't a good life
But it's my life

— *Night Life* (Willie Nelson, Walt Breeland, Paul Buskirk)

Buskirk also bought *Night Life*, this time for $150, and backed Willie's rendition of it, putting it out on the RX label, then the Bellaire label. "That master was done at Bill Quinn's studio for $180 with friends and Willie singin' and playin' the guitar," Buskirk later recalled. The writers listed were Paul Buskirk and his buddy Walt Breeland. To appease Pappy Daily, who still had Willie signed to his label but had passed on recording *Night Life* because he thought it was a blues song, not country, the artist is listed as Paul Buskirk & His Little Men, starring Hugh Nelson. Daily put out Willie's second "D" Records release, *What A Way To Live b/w Misery Mansion*, but the titles told the story straight up. This time, Willie parked Martha and the children with relatives in Texas and headed straight for Music Row. He would find success there selling his songs but not the day he blew into town. Times would be tough and the marriage he and Martha had clung to would begin to unravel at the seams.

Each night I make the rounds
To every spot in town
A lonely man with lonely time to kill
What a way to live

The jukebox playin' loud
A face among the crowd
So much like hers it makes my heart stand still
What a way to live

— *What A Way To Live* (Willie Nelson)

Driven by poverty and wading knee deep in the blues, Willie was motivated to write in those days. Hunger is a powerful motivator, he has often acknowledged. He wrote so many songs, he gave up trying to demo them all, and began to file them in a stack that grew thicker every day. Some, he wisely set aside for a rainy day, perhaps for that dreaded moment every songwriter fears when the well runs dry. His time in Houston and Nashville would be his most prolific as a songwriter. And, once he got acquainted with the crowd at Tootsie's Orchid Lounge, Willie Nelson would be among friends and fellow songwriters, a member of a songwriting community that was the lifeblood of the country music industry.

TOOTSIE'S ORCHID LOUNGE

Willie has often been quoted as saying he went to Nashville "because that's where the store was." If you had songs to sell, this was where you could sell them. By 1960, most of the building blocks had been cemented together and the "store" was open for business. In the four decades since Marconi's radios and Edison's records first hit factory assembly lines, country music had evolved from a string-based hillbilly style, changed to 'country & western' when Western Swing and silver screen cowboy ingredients were added, and changed again in the early 1960s with the smoother Nashville Sound to 'country music', which was the Music Row solution to competing with rock & roll.

The three most important contributing factors which had led to Nashville becoming the hub of the country music industry were the city's central position on the buckle of the bible belt, the establishment of the southern regional offices of ASCAP (Association of Songwriters, Composers, and Publishers) in Nashville in 1924, and the creation of the WSM *Barndance* radio show the following year. The performing rights organization drew a population of music publishers. The *Barndance* became the *Grand Ole Opry*, quickly becoming the premiere barndance-style show in North America. Spin off tours from the Opry brought booking agents to town. In the 1940s, BMI established an office in Nashville to compete with ASCAP for the country music publishing business. By 1960, Nashville record labels and recording studios had made country music a thriving industry.

Nashville was in its heyday. The set had been built, most of the major players had arrived, and the outrageous and outlandish scenarios Music City has become known for were going down 24-hours a day, 52 weeks a year. Patsy Cline was ascending. Johnny Horton, Johnny & Jack, and Kitty Wells were hot. Jim Reeves was the heir apparent to Hank Williams and Jimmie Rodgers. The pantheon of country & western stars boasted marquee names like Roy Acuff, Eddy Arnold, Faron Young, Webb Pierce, Red Foley, George Jones, Hank Snow, Hank Thompson, Carl Smith, Ray Price, and Marty

Robbins. Chet Atkins was still pickin' and grinnin'. He'd worked with everybody from Archie Campbell and Bill Carlisle to Red Foley, from Elvis to the Everlys, and Mother Maybelle & the Carter Sisters to Hank Snow. Chet was still hittin' on the radio himself with cuts like *Windy & Warm*, and his instrumental albums like TEENSVILLE were in every guitar picker's record collection along with Django Reinhardt, Merle Travis, Duane Eddy, and Ventures' records. Owen Bradley and his brother Harold had their Quonset Hut studio going full tilt. Ernest Tubbs' late night radio show, broadcast from his record shop, kept things hopping on Saturday nights after the *Grand Ole Opry* went off the air.

Nashville was a Barnum & Bailey-style three-ring circus with plenty of sideshow action. Sleazy managers, sleazier agents, and every imaginable mover and groover in the country music business could be found up and down Music Row, bellied up to the trough, looking over the newcomers for their next meal ticket. 'So, y'all want'a make a record, kid?' became an oft-repeated phrase.

People fresh off the train from Hicksville paid small fortunes for sessions, where they were told, "Hank recorded right here where you're standin'" . . . or . . . "Marty or Lefty or George Jones will be in here tomorrow standin' just where you're standin'." They were told, "Don't worry 'bout that little darlin', we'll fix it in the mix . . . ." When their money was gone and all they had was a box of records to take back home, the product was no better than a song demo they could have made for $29 a track at their local radio station, but the made-in-Nashville brand became a stamp of approval. So-called 'girl singers' who couldn't sing their way out of a paper bag, but had a Daddy Warbucks backer or a good ole boy husband with a chain of hotels, made records so bad that you had to pay people to play them, and even then they might peel the paint off your living room ceiling when you did. But there were people who had real talent and a dogged persistence to boot. A few of them became stars.

When Willie first hit town, he looked up Billy Walker. Billy was surprised to see him, as he recalls in Willie's authorized video biography. "What in the world are you doin' here?" he asked. "Well," said Willie, "there ain't anybody in Texas buyin' any songs, so, I just thought I would come over here and see what I could get going." Billy had a little house where he lived with his wife and kids, and Willie stayed there with them while he checked out the action. Right away he fell in with a crowd of songwriters that hung around Tootsie's bar. In those days, the Opry was staged in the Ryman Auditorium, but the converted church was not equipped with the same number of comfortable backstage dressing rooms, rehearsal rooms, wide corridors, and spacious washrooms that the Opryland Theater provides today. Tootsie's Orchid Lounge, located just outside the back stage doors of the Ryman, was the unofficial green room, a seedy lower Broadway venue run by a colorful character who had a soft spot in her heart for songwriters and brown-eyed, handsome, guitar pickin' men, like Hank Cochran, Harlan Howard, Roger Miller, and Mel Tillis. Four years later, Dolly Parton would arrive and fit right in, a 16-year old hopeful from Sevierville with a whole lot more spunk than you might expect from someone a mere five-foot-zip tall, and a song in her pocket she called *Everything Is Beautiful (In It's Own Way)*, which she would record as a duet with Willie Nelson 20 years later.

Before Dolly showed up, the 'in crowd' at Tootsie's was an inner circle of sweaty armpits, male bonding, and macho songwrestling, but the songs those boys turned out set the country music world on fire. Harlan Howard had already penned *Heartaches By The Number* for Ray Price. As Harlan recalls in Willie's video biography, "I didn't realize what a dump Tootsie's was. At the time, I thought I was in hog heaven! I mean, it was my buddies there, and a fantastic jukebox. It's memories. The memories of Mel Tillis, and Hank, and Willie, and all of these different people — memory glosses over and paints a beautiful scene and I think, wow, is this where we hung out?"

Tootsie's Orchid Lounge is portrayed by these songwriters as if it were the rock of Gibraltar, a timeless institution, which had appeared out of the fog drifting off the Cumberland River and creeping up lower Broadway, taking a place beside the Ryman, Ernest Tubb's Record Store, Roy Acuff's Country Music Exhibition, Linebaugh's Restaurant, and Sho-Bud Guitars, sometime during the legendary past. In fact, Tootsie Bess had only recently quit barnstorming with her ex-husband Big Jeff Bess as a country comedienne and ticket-taker to open her nightspot mere months before some of them arrived on the scene. With her feisty, take-charge attitude, and a vicious Diamond-headed hat-pin, she regularly prodded and ejected drunks. At closing time, she produced a shrill police whistle, blew on it, and bawled, "All right, drink up and get the hell out!" Then proceeded to apply the hat-pin to the slow drinkers. But she did have a soft-spot in her heart for songwriters, and the latest, state-of-the-art jukebox, which she regularly primed with the best of the new records, plugging it with her own coins to select the latest recording of the star who had just entered the premises. It was her way of saying, 'Patsy Cline has entered the building'. Some Music Row wags later claimed that if your record had made it onto Tootsie's juke, you already had a hit. Over the years, the walls of Tootsie's became blanketed with autographed glossy 8 x 10 photos of the stars who had sat at the bar, partied in the scarred wooden booths, swapped their songs, and kicked, tilted, and swore at the pinball machine.

The first time Willie walked into Tootsie's, he had a suitcase full of songs and he was writing new ones every day. He was as hungry as ever, and when Martha and the kids showed up unannounced a few weeks later, there were more mouths to feed. When they got settled in Dunn's Trailer Park, where Roger Miller and other songwriters had lived before them, Willie and Martha would come home to a sign that said, "Trailers For Sale or Rent," the very words Miller used to begin his hit song *King Of The Road*. So, there was ambience everywhere, and right away, Martha had herself a job at The Hitching Post, right across from the Opry, which sometimes hurt Willie's pride, but took some of the pressure off paying the bills.

"It was right at the back door of the Ryman," Willie explains, "and all of the acts would come over to Tootsie's for a beer or a coke or whatever between the times that they were supposed to perform." This strategic location proved propitious on more than a few occasions for songwriters eager to pitch their songs directly to the stars themselves rather than leave their fate up to the nine-to-five song-pluggers employed by the publishing companies on Music Row. Mel Tillis knew them all. "Webb Pierce," he recalls, "Patsy Cline, Jim Reeves . . . would come through there, and everybody was pullin' for country music and for each other."

At the time, Hank Cochran had a publishing deal with Pamper Music, Hal Smith and Ray Price's publishing company, where he also worked as a company song-plugger. Right away, he wanted to know who Willie was signed with. "Willie got the guitar," Hank recalls in *Willie Nelson: My Life*, "and started pickin' and singin' some of the tunes he had written, and I said, 'Damn, who's got those songs?' Cause I was workin' for Pamper Music at the time. He said, 'Nobody. Nobody wants 'em.' And I said, 'Get out!' Gawd, I couldn't believe that."

As Willie remembers, "They were gettin' ready to give Hank a $50 a week raise, and Hank said, 'Why don't you give Willie the $50? And don't give me a raise.'" This turn of events would result in Willie and Martha being able to move out of the trailer park into a brick house on an acreage in Goodlettsville, nearer to the Pamper Music offices.

Ray Price was one of the first to lend Willie a helping hand. "We tried to figure out," Ray remembers in the video biography, "a means of keeping Willie alive. Subsistence, really, because we didn't have a lot of money. It may not have been a livin', but enough to keep him from starvin'." Before things got better, Willie would land a job playing bass in Ray's band, faking it at first because playing bass was not a skill he had acquired at the time he applied for the position. Willie had been in good company when he replaced Donny Young, a.k.a. Johnny Paycheck, as Ray Price's bass player. Buddy Emmons, Darrell McCall, and Roger Miller helped him fit in, carrying Willie night after night as he made his way through his bass parts until he got the hang of it. Kinky Friedman would later quip that it took Ray Price six months to notice that Willie couldn't play bass.

The Pamper Music songwriters had a clubhouse of sorts, a less glamorous venue than Tootsie's, but one where they were not distracted from focussing on their craft. "It was a little garage," Hank Cochran recalls, "and we would write and make the tapes and stuff like that." As Harlan Howard remembers,"It was tight in there . . . two or three chairs, a mixing board, and so forth. That's where Hank, and I, and Willie hung out." Willie also recalls just how small it was. "There was no windows. Just one door. I guess, after sittin' in there for so many days, I started talkin' to the walls . . . ."

Hello walls, how'd things go for you today?
Don't you miss her since she up and walked away?
And I'll bet you dread to spend
Another lonely night with me
But, lonely walls, I'll keep you company

— *Hello Walls* (Willie Nelson)

"Hank Cochran was almost a writer on *Hello Walls*," Willie told Ralph Emery. "Hank and me were tryin' to write in a little one-room house out back of Pamper Music. It didn't have a phone. I'd just told him I wanted to write a song called *Hello Walls* when someone came out and told Hank he had a phone call up at the office. I told him I'd start the song while he was taking the call. He was only gone about ten minutes, and when he came back I'd already finished it. It's your basic ten-minute song."

The story of how Faron Young came to record Willie's *Hello Walls* has been given a lively rendition by Willie's wife Martha. The way she tells the story, if she hadn't pressed Faron, who was a regular drinker at The Hitching Post, he would never have recorded this hit song. Martha kept putting the bug in Faron's ear, telling him about this song her husband had written, *Hello Walls*, and keeping after him, saying that her husband was over at Tootsie's . . . but Faron kept sayin' he wasn't interested.

In *Willie*, the sketch Martha paints shows her disdain for all of these men. "Faron Young kept comin' in there," Martha told Bud Shrake, and all the girls just fell all over him. Faron thought this was the greatest thing in the world, because he had this big ego, being a star and all. I would never mention Willie to anybody. I figured Willie would get out on his own and make it . . . . But one night Faron had been sittin' in The Hitching Post for hours and hours." Martha pitched Willie's song to Faron. He feigned his indifference, picked up and walked out. A few minutes later, someone came into The Hitching Post and told Martha that Faron was over at Tootsie's listening to these great songs "this guy from Texas was singing." When Faron himself returned, he said to Martha, "Hey, I got a new song called *Hello Walls*." Of course," Martha relates, "the dumb ass still didn't connect me with Willie." Deejay Ralph Emery added to the legend when he recorded an answer song, *Hello Fool*, which did not amuse Faron at the time it came out, but was a Top 10 hit that same year.

Faron Young tells the story differently, recalling the first time he heard Willie singing *Hello Walls* are he walked into Tootsie's. "Willie had a crew-cut," Faron recalled. "He was the All American Boy. He said, 'I've sung this for everybody.' I said, 'Sing it for me.'"

Hello window, well, I see that you're still here
Aren't you lonely since our darling disappeared?
Well, look here, is that a teardrop
In the corner of your pane?
Now, don't try to tell me it's rain

"He played me two songs. I said, 'I'll take 'em both. I'm gonna record 'em." Before he went into the studio, however, Faron felt the barb of rebuke from his peers. "A few of these guys were sittin' around, and I sang it, and they was goin' 'Hello commode. Hello bathtub. Hello sink. Where *did* you get that terrible piece of material.' I sang it to Sue, she said, 'That's a hit, honey, you cut that thing.' And me and Willie laughed all the way to the bank." In the spring of 1961, Faron Young's Capitol Records release of *Hello Walls* spent nine weeks at number one on the country charts, crossed over into the Top 10 on the pop charts, and eventually sold a million records.

Willie recalls trying to sell the song outright to Faron because Willie had not yet become believer in the royalty collection system. But Faron knew how important it would be for Willie to keep that songwriting royalty. By giving up a 50 percent publishing share, he had someone on his side, a publisher who stood to make an equal amount, which is the whole point of publishing your songs. Some writers have seen this merely as a tax, but just ask that writer if they are prepared to travel across the country collecting their royalties from every jukebox operator and radio station personally, then they get the picture. Performing rights organizations and music publishers police the industry, and without their presence songwriters would be dependent on singing for their supper like the troubadours of old.

"He tried to sell me *Hello Walls* for $500," Faron recalls in *Willie Nelson: My Life*. "I said, 'No, no, don't you sell this song. I'm gonna loan you the money. I loaned him the money, and about six weeks later he got another check for about $20,000." This was, no doubt, more money than Willie Nelson had made in his entire 28 years on the planet. When Willie got that first big check, he went over to the bar where Faron was drinking and kissed him. "He come into Tootsie's," Faron recalls in *Willie Nelson: My Life*. "I felt this arm come over my neck, he wedged my mouth open, and he french-kissed me. It was the best kiss I ever had! And we've been close, ever since." Willie remembers that "I was going to pay him that 500 bucks that I owed him, but he said, 'No, you raise me a cow. And whenever that calf gets old enough to butcher, well, you give her to me." For several years, whenever Willie and Faron would run into each other, the subject of this steer would come up. Faron would ask Willie how big the steer was by now. "It got to be about 7,000 pounds," Willie says with a smile in his video biography. One day, Faron received a message telling him not to leave his office before 3:00 p.m. Sure enough, right on time a truck pulled up. In it was a 3,000 pound registered Simmental bull that Willie's son, Billy, had purchased at an auction. Estimated value, approximately $37,000.

For a while, Willie and Hank became as thick as thieves. Cochran would have many successes during this era, penning songs like *Funny Way Of Laughing* for Burl Ives, *She's Got You* for Patsy Cline, and *Make The World Go Away*, a number 2 country hit for Ray Price in 1963, before becoming a number one crossover smash for Eddy Arnold in 1965 that spent 10 weeks at the top of the country charts. But Hank learned that hanging out with Willie could be downright dangerous at times. He was the unfortunate bystander that night in Tootsie's when Martha threw the shot glass at Willie but hit Hank instead. Willie drove Hank to the hospital where the medics patched him up. Another time, when Willie came into the Wagon Wheel, which Martha was managing at the time, she tossed most of the liquor bottles at him before they could get her calmed down. Things were so stormy between them that everybody, even their children, looked forward to the day they would call it quits. While Willie was carousing out on the road, Martha was cutting her own colorful path through the Nashville night life driving a '59 Cadillac, a black beast of a monster car with the biggest fish-tail fins ever put on a motor vehicle, which they had bought from Ray Price.

In the summer of 1961, Billy Walker's recording of *Funny How Time Slips Away* hit the number 23 spot on the country chart.

Well, hello there, my it's been a long, long, time
How'm I doin'? I guess that I'm doin' fine.
It's been so long now
But it seems now like it was only yesterday
Gee, ain't it funny how time slips away?

— *Funny How Time Slips Away* (Willie Nelson)

"Everybody in the world has recorded the song," Walker reminisces, "and it's been a hit four or five times by different artists." In 1963, pop singer Jimmy Elledge hit number 22 on the pop charts with his version; and in 1964, Soul singer Joe Hinton hit number 13 with his version, released as *Funny*.

Willie's next break came when Decca released Patsy Cline's recording of *Crazy*, a lucky break indeed because every writer in Nashville was pitching her their best material. When performed by Patsy Cline, *Crazy* would become one of the most famous country songs of all time.

I'm crazy — crazy for feelin' so lonely
And I'm crazy — crazy for feelin' so blue
I knew that you'd love me as long as you wanted
And then someday you'd leave me for somebody new . . .

Worry — why do I let myself worry?
Wonderin' — what in the world did I do?
I'm crazy for thinkin' that my love could hold you
Crazy for tryin', crazy for cryin'
And I'm crazy for lovin' you

— *Crazy* (Willie Nelson)

Hank Cochran pitched *Crazy* to Patsy's husband, Charlie Dick, and Hank and Charley pitched it to Patsy and her record producer, Owen Bradley. Willie remembers sitting in Hank's car outside Patsy's house while Charlie and Hank went in to play her the demo of the song. When Patsy liked it, he overcame his shyness and went in and met her.

As Harlan Howard recalls, "Hank and I had written *I Fall To Pieces*. Patsy had to go and record again for her next single. There was quite a fight (a friendly fight) goin' on between all of us writers. We were submitting our best songs, and Willie won." *I Fall To Pieces* had been such a big record, on the Top 40 for 39 weeks in 1961, that Patsy didn't exactly rush back into Owen Bradley's Quonset Hut studio to follow it up. When she did record *Crazy*, it didn't go down all that easily in the studio. "They did a whole three-hour session but it just didn't come off," Charlie Dick recalls. "It just wasn't working. It sounded good, but something didn't fit." They kept the band tracks and Patsy took them home. Patsy had learned Willie's song from the demo of it with Willie singing, and she was trying to duplicate his phrasing. "We had some brandy," Charlie continues, "and then somebody says, 'Why don't you just forget Willie Nelson and sing it the way you would normally sing any other song.' She went back to the studio and one or two takes, she was off and running." *Crazy* was in the country Top 40 for five months, peaking at number 2 in early 1962, and crossing over into the pop Top 10 before sliding slowly back down the charts

"Patsy Cline's recording of *Crazy*," Willie relates in the authorized video biography, "was my favorite all-time song of mine that anyone ever did. There's some close seconds. Ray Price's *Night Life* and Roy Orbison's *Pretty Paper*. Faron Young singin' *Hello Walls*. But Patsy Cline singin' *Crazy* was just a lot of magic."

When Shirley Collie, a yodeling west coast singer, came to town to cut a record, she was introduced to Willie and Martha by Hank Cochran. For a while, Willie and Martha socialized with Shirley and her husband Bif. Martha had her suspicions about the kind of friendship that developed between Willie and Shirley, but Bif remained in the dark until one night Shirley left Bif a note saying she's was going out to buy a dress and appear on a tv show with Willie. She never came back. While she was touring across Canada with Willie and Ray Price, Bif got a bill for several thousand dollars of car rental fees. Then he got divorce papers.

In the spring of 1962, *Willingly*, featuring Shirley Collie and Willie Nelson, became Willie's first chart success, a Top 10 hit on the *Billboard* country chart. Liberty followed this up with *Touch Me*, Willie's first solo hit, a number 7 hit on the chart later that year. Willie Nelson was in his most prolific period. He had something different going on. Something unique, which the other songwriters recognized. Willie could take the cheating song and turn it into something far more fragile. Far more intimate. "A lot of guys in this town," Billy Walker notes in the authorized video biography, "they manufacture songs. He writes songs . . . from the heart, y'know, it's a God-given talent. It enables him to say something different than anybody else says. He says it in such a different way that it catches the spirit of a human bein' and causes them to live with the same kinds of feelin's that he had when he wrote the song." Harlan Howard agrees. "He won't write just anything. It's got to be a pretty unusual idea for him to even get into it. He's not vanilla at all, you know. Most of his ideas, I'd never heard 'em before."

Former Liberty Records president, Joe Allison, remembers these years as a golden era in country music as "it changed from the great stylists like the Ernest Tubbs and the Roy Acuffs to the more melodious artistically talented people like the Patsy Clines, and the Marty Robbins, and the Don Gibsons." While these 'melodious' artists recorded Willie's songs, he was never considered to be such a singer. "He was a very successful songwriter," Billy Walker recalls, "and other people would record his songs. That had already been proven by the time he came in to make records. But his singing style just didn't really catch on." Joe Allison recognized Willie's singing genius, though, and upon Hank Cochran's recommendation, Joe signed Willie to a recording contract with Liberty Records. "Hank brought me a tape of Willie Nelson. I had heard of him as a writer. But this was the first I'd zeroed in on him as a singer. And I said, 'My gosh, why hasn't somebody recorded this guy? He's been around here a couple of years.' Hank said, 'Well, they like him. But they won't record him. They think he sings funny.'" Funny how as time slipped away Willie would become admired as a master vocal stylist.

2

RIDGETOP

Singing toe to toe, eyeball to eyeball into a single microphone with someone is always an intimate moment of truth; you can fake some things in life but you just can't fake intonation. You must hit your notes or the harmonies sound awful. Sharing this intimacy provided more temptation than either Willie Nelson or Shirley Collie could resist, and singing together now that they were lovers became a special rush, especially for Willie because he'd usually chosen his one night stands from the fourth row of his audiences. With Shirley, he felt the stirring of love, as he had so many years before when he first met Martha. Traveling together on the road with Ray Price & the Cherokee Cowboys on a Canadian tour, where for a while Shirley remained hidden when they thought she might be spotted by one of Bif Collie's pals, solidified the relationship as something more permanent than merely a series of one-night stands. And when Ray let them off the bus in Goodlettsville, Willie told Martha that he was leaving her to be with Shirley. Although she knew in her heart that the marriage had run its course, Martha blamed Shirley at the time. Bif blamed her, too, and, during a time when Shirley returned to the west coast to collect her belongings, tried unsuccessfully to have her committed to a treatment center.

Martha took their three children and the Cadillac and headed for Texas, where she parked the children with their grandparents and drove up to Nevada to find work and get a divorce. When she caught wind of Willie being in Texas, she picked up Lana, Susie, and Billy and brought them out to Las Vegas. She soon married a man named Chuck Andrews, who proved to be more than a match for Martha, according to Susie. She alleges that he abused her mother when he felt she was out of line. He was mean to Billy, too. Billy would be the first of the three children to live permanently with Willie and Shirley when they found their property in Tennessee. Lana and Susie also liked being there with their dad, when they visited in the summer, and they liked Shirley, too.

At first, Willie and Shirley lived on Shirley's savings. When Willie had first begun receiving substantial checks for his songwriting royalties, he had squandered his money about as quickly as his marriage was disintegrating. All of a sudden," he recalls, "I had a lot of money but it wasn't worth anything because of what I was going through. So I started throwing it away with both hands. When *Hello Walls* was a hit, I was making $30 a night playing bass with Ray Price, and I was flying to all the jobs, renting penthouses and suites, buying everybody dinner — while Ray was riding the bus with the rest of the guys. It didn't take long to go through the first royalty check."

When Willie quit Ray Price & the Cherokee Cowboys, he worked briefly in California, opening a west coast office for Pamper Music, but didn't enjoy being chained to a desk. He then formed his own small group, a trio, with Shirley singing and playing bass, and Jimmy Day on pedal steel. Jimmy and Willie had written *I Didn't Sleep A Wink* in 1961. Yodeling was Shirley's specialty, and their audiences loved the way she did it. At times, she would add comedy routines to their show, too, using Willie as her straight man. When Shirley's divorce became final, she and Willie married, and they settled onto a rural property on Greer Road in the small town of Ridgetop, some 30 miles from Nashville.

After this brief period of performing together with Willie, Shirley found herself gradually shuffled to the other side of Willie's stereo life. She became the homebody at the Ridgetop ranch, the person Willie came home to when he came off the road. Not that Willie forced her to. In fact, Shirley took to Willie's kids — Lana, Susie, and Billy — whenever they came to stay, eventually looking after them on a permanent basis. She took to the farming life, too, raising a brood of laying hens. Shirley was upset, at first, when Willie went into his moods writing songs, but she tried her hand at that, too; and Willie would later record *Little Things*, a song they wrote together.

In late 1963, with his recording deal with Liberty turning sour, Willie decided to come off the road. The way things were going, he was making money from songwriting royalties and losing money being an artist. So, he settled in with Shirley and his children at the Ridgetop farm and became a hog rancher for a while, but raising hundreds of hogs proved to be a lot more challenging than raising one pig for the Future Farmers of America. As Shirley put it in a statement made to Bud Shrake, "He enjoyed being a gentleman farmer for a couple of years at Ridgetop, even though he didn't have much aptitude for it. But when he started going on the road for weeks and months at a time, our family life began slipping away."

"I lost a fortune in pigs," Willie told Alanna Nash in an interview published in *Behind Closed Doors*. "I had the fattest pigs in town. I paid 25 cents a pound for 'em, and fattened 'em up for six months. When I sold 'em, I got 17 cents a pound for 'em. Lost my ass and all its fixtures. It was just that I got into the hog business at a bad time. I found out from the old-timers that you can't just get in it one year and expect to make a killin' and get out. You've got to stay with it and raise hogs every year." Willie's recording career wasn't making a killing, either. With *Touch Me* being his best showing on the charts and album sales not taking off, Liberty declined to release Willie's third album. They parted ways.

Willie had made no compromises to Nashville norms, steadfastly maintaining his unique vocal style. "As a stylist, I think Willie was 'way ahead of his time," Johnny Cash observes in the authorized video biography. "That's why it took the world a little while to recognize his unique tone of delivery." The boredom of singing the same songs, night after night, was also a factor in the development of Willie Nelson's unique style. "There was just certain songs you would have to do if you played nightclubs or beer joints in Texas," Willie explains in the video biography. "*San Antonio Rose* was one, and *Fraulein* was one. You just knew what songs you had to learn. I got tired of singin' the same songs every night. So, I started playin' around with the phrasing." Fred Foster, who headed up Monument Records in those days, remembers, "I thought he was the most different, refreshing, real talent that I'd heard. And I wanted to sign him, and, ultimately, did."

Willie had handed Roy Orbison the seasonal gem *Pretty Paper*, a Top 20 pop hit for the Big 'O' on the Monument label during December 1963. Willie recorded some sides for Monument Records, too, and signed a contract with Fred Foster, the same week Foster signed R&B artist Lloyd Price, but a misunderstanding led to it being torn up. As Foster later explained to Ralph Emery, "I told Willie I was going to take out a full-page ad in *Billboard* to welcome them both to the label. The guy who was putting the ads together was a huge Willie Nelson fan, and he wanted to use purple to indicate royalty, but the color kept running." Plans were made to run Willie's ad the following week, but Foster was not able to track Willie down. He called "all over Texas," but before he got hold of Willie, Willie got hold of *Billboard* and saw Lloyd Price there but not himself. "Willie thought I wasn't sincere about the deal," Foster told Emery, "went out and got drunk and decided to sign with RCA. By the time I finally found him and explained what had happened, it was a done deal. RCA would have sued him, so I agreed to cut him loose."

Ironically, Fred Foster had been interested in Willie *because* he sounded different, not despite the fact that he didn't fit the Nashville formula. "I was looking for someone who could be identified the minute the needle hit the grooves," Foster later told Susie Nelson, author of *Heartworn Memories*. He had signed Roy Orbision for just this reason, and, when he heard a demo of

Willie Nelson at Pamper Music, he became interested in signing him, although he was still with Liberty at that time.

Willie himself knew that what he was doing had gone over with audiences before he came to Tennessee. "I was 20 years old comin' out of Texas," he recalls. "I thought I knew everything . . . but I did know what to play, and what kind of music I wanted to play, and I had just come from where people liked it. So, it wasn't as if I didn't know what I was talking about. I did know that people liked what I did. At least the people in Texas."

The lyrics to his songs during these prolific mid-'60s years often contain ironic overtones, which, although they fit the hurtin' situation of the women they are addressed to, also seem to refer indirectly to all of those people who "thought he sang funny." The images he used were unusual to an extreme and helped effect sudden reversals similar to phrases like "time is out of joint" that poet and playwright Will Shakespeare had used so cunningly so many years ago.

The sun is filled with ice and gives no warmth at all
The sky was never blue
The stars are raindrops searching for a place to fall
And I never cared for you

I know you won't believe these things I tell you
No, you won't believe
Your heart has been forewarned all men will lie to you
Your mind cannot conceive

Now all depends on what I say to you
And in your doubting me
So I've prepared these statements far from the truth
Pay heed and disbelieve

— *I Never Cared For You* (Willie Nelson)

Willie's staccato delivery of these lyrics at ballad tempo — "the sun is filled with ice . . . and gives no warmth at all . . . the sky was never blue . . . the stars are raindrops . . . searching for a place to fall . . . and I never cared for you" — makes a forceful impact as he then gallops onward as if he's caught the pace of the classic *Ghost Riders In The Sky* or Del Shannon's 1961 gold record *Runaway* (which utilizes a similar chord pattern). But country radio programmers thought otherwise at the time. "We did a song of his, *I Never*

Cared For You," Fred Foster recalls, "and we did it with just his guitar, basically, and bass and drums, and just one more guitar. Sort of like the way that he finally did hit. And we shipped it out, and I remember that everybody except the stations in Texas thought that we were 'way off the mark'." However, a young airforce officer was taken by Willie's odd phrasing. "When I was stationed over in Germany," Kris Kristofferson recalls, "there was a disc jockey over there who loved Willie Nelson. He had a program that all the soldiers listened to in the afternoon, and he would talk about Willie every day, and play a lot of the songs that, I guess, weren't big hits, because Willie wasn't a commercial singer. He phrased like a jazz singer, and that was a long way from Ernest Tubb."

In 1963, Bob Wills had written the liner notes for Willie Nelson's second Liberty LP, HERE'S WILLIE NELSON, but the King of Western Swing's health was failing, and a bout of heart attacks and strokes would soon render him unable to play his fiddle. Willie hurt for his longtime idol and friend, remembering the way unscrupulous associates and accountants had treated Wills, bilking him out of the publishing rights to hit songs like *San Antonio Rose* and leaving him to face bankruptcy on his own, but there was little he could do at the time to help out. Willie's records weren't selling much, except in Texas, where Bob Wills' endorsement meant a whole lot.

On November 24, 1964, Willie signed up with the *Grand Ole Opry*, making his first appearance on Saturday, November 28 as a regular cast member and receiving $35 that night. The Opry managers could economize on the wages because country artists reaped their benefits playing on the road where they were known as stars of the Opry. In fact, Opry managers had a hand in some of the bookings, too. So, they pretty well called the shots. As Chet Atkins remembers, "Jim Denny always sort of tried to run me off, because I didn't work the road. He was in charge of booking the artists (for tours)." Susie Nelson also points out that playing the required number of Opry shows also cut into the most lucrative money night of the week. While country fans seldom heard a whisper of these internal political squabbles and economic liabilities, the artists were well aware of the ways they were boxed in by the system.

Soon after, Willie signed with RCA, where he got the best production on his records that the label had to offer. Chet Atkins even tried pairing him up with Elvis's producer, Felton Jarvis, for a session or two, but the song *Once In A Row* which charted at number 19 in 1966 was the best the artist and label were able to do together. *The Party's Over*, *Black Jack County Chain*, *Little Things*, and *Johnny One Time* stalled in the 20s and 30s before *Bring Me*

Sunshine edged into the Top 20 again in the early weeks of 1969. As single after single failed to hit into the Top 10, Willie became disillusioned with the Nashville system. Consistently, however, he blamed the system rather than any of the people. "To me," he recalls in *Willie Nelson: My Life*, "Chet Atkins is a guy in Nashville who did more good for more pickers, for more artists, than any other living human being. He was well respected and still is in that city. But while he was running RCA, he was the guy."

Chet himself, however, was more willing to fess up. As Chet told Bud Shrake, "when we signed Willie on RCA, I said, 'Well he sounds great in Texas. What we've got to do is spread him out of Texas.' So, that was going to be our thing — promote the hell out of Willie and sell his records all over the country. But we didn't do that. I was just about the worst at promotion and sales. I didn't care anything about that part of the business. What time I wasn't working in the studio, I was off somewhere playing my guitar. I would fall asleep playing my guitar. I just didn't have the time — or take the time — to promote and sell records, mine or anyone else's. It hurt Willie a lot to have a guy with my attitude about sales as the one who was supposed to push his product. I guess the timing wasn't right." Waylon Jennings, whom Chet signed to RCA in 1965, says, "the thing was, they had such control over everything, and I'm not sayin' that was all wrong, 'cause a lot of people needed that. But people like me and Willie, we had our own ideas. Good or bad, wrong, right, whatever they were, we had our ideas."

Willie did record a live album for RCA. The lineup that night was Johnny Bush (drums), Wade Ray (bass), and Jimmy Day (pedal steel). The album was titled COUNTRY MUSIC CONCERT, later reissued as WILLIE NELSON LIVE. But the label was not able to promote it successfully to record buyers outside of Texas. Looking back on those years, Chet Atkins sometimes resorts to humor in order to dull the brunt of their collective failure to make it happen for Willie. "Somebody said that Willie didn't start selling records till ugly came in," Chet says with a smile, "and he let his hair grow, and started to get funky, and wear old clothes. But everybody tried to make hits with him, including myself." "It was a noble attempt," Harlan Howard insists. "Chet Atkins at RCA spent a fortune on Willie to try . . . to try to figure out . . . I mean, Willie sang different. He sang a little bit after the beat, likes a little bit of jazz — a little Texas, you know — he's unique."

During his years at Ridgetop, Willie put on a few pounds, took to wearing bib overalls, smoking a corncob pipe, and sometimes letting his beard grow out. He also fixed up a studio situation in the basement of the house where with Hank Cochran and others he continued to write and demo songs, sometimes working long into the night and fueling their creative energies with whiskey and whatever other consciousness enhancing substances they had at hand, which had not been the usual procedure in the officially scheduled writing sessions at Pamper Music. In 1968, Willie and Shirley wrote *Pages* with Willie's daughter Lana and *She's Not For You* together. Despite his lack of success as a recording artist, the Ridgetop years were a success for Willie in many other ways. He'd come to town writing about loneliness and despair, but during the years at Ridgetop a more hopeful tone crept into his lyrics.

Though I travel to strange, foreign places
There's a memory keeps calling to me
Of hollows and flowers and many happy hours
In Ridgetop in Tennessee

By this time the roses are blooming
The grass in the valleys is green
The wind plays the anthem of Heaven
Through the leaves of the white oak tree

— *Ridgetop* (Willie Nelson)

By this time, the 400-acre Ridgetop farm had become home to hundreds of hogs, 200 head of Black Angus cattle, hundreds of chickens, half a dozen horses, dogs, cats, and an assortment of humans who managed to sow and harvest crops and keep up the fences in the grazing pastures. A local old-timer by the name of Hughes, who had started out as a hired hand, coordinated much of the operation. Willie's father Ira and step-mom Lorraine, their children and families, Willie's sister Bobbie Lee, her three children and second husband all moved onto the land. For a while, Willie's mother Myrle and her husband lived just down the road. Martha, happily remarried to a third husband, followed suit, living nearby. When Willie's longtime Fort Worth pal Paul English joined the band, he would also move his family to Ridgetop. The lettering on the mailbox now read "Willie Nelson & Many Others." With the clan gathered and the bees happily buzzing in the pastures, Willie hit the road more regularly. He had a home base to anchor him, and he had become determined to establish himself as an entertainer.

Willie's prospects as a touring artist took an upturn when he hooked up with Texas promoter Crash Stewart, who initially came to Tennessee to book a Ray Price tour. When Price took another offer, a more lucrative one put together by Abe Hamza, Willie and Crash put together a package tour for the dates in Louisiana and Texas. "I told him okay, but told Willie he was not equal to Ray Price at this stage in his career," Stewart recalled for the 1980 *Willie Nelson Family Album* book compiled by Willie's daughter Lana Nelson. "Willie said, 'I know that but we will hire another big star to replace Price and call it the Willie Nelson show starring the other names who are better known than I am." With people like Marty Robbins, Stonewall Jackson, Jeannie Sealy, Hank Cochran, and Johnny Bush signed up, Willie was to be the headliner. At the last minute, Charlie Pride was added to the package show, and Willie found himself being an onstage diplomat. Civil Rights demonstrators had begun to challenge the segregation in the South, but country music fans were simply not used to hearing an African American singing their music. To their way of thinking, black singers sang the blues, not country. Willie knew that once people heard Charlie sing, their prejudice would fall away; Charlie was already a hit on the radio, Chet had seen to that. So, the trick was to get them to sit still and give him a chance. The incident most mentioned is the time Willie invited Charlie on stage at a Dallas club where the owner had vowed never to book Pride. Willie kissed Charlie on stage that time. The shock effect worked and the club owner relented. There were still hotels and restaurants where Charlie was denied entry, but this tour did a whole lot to solidify his acceptance with the country audience.

Crash Stewart and Willie were pals as well as business associates. Crash would sometimes accompany Willie to his recording sessions with Chet Atkins at RCA's Nashville Sound studios. One time at the ranch, Crash gave Willie a few pointers about calf-roping, and when Willie successfully made a catch, Crash hollered, "That makes one in a row," inspiring the song *One In A Row*, which Willie wrote later that same day.

When Willie returned to full-time touring, Shirley suspected Willie was running around on her. In *Heartworn Memories*, Susie describes Shirley's behavior as becoming increasingly erratic, a condition brought on by excessive drinking and prescription drug abuse, as she fought off the grief and anger she felt imagining Willie's exploits. A series of car accidents led to a discovery of this situation and to her rehabilitation in a treatment center, but Shirley was correct in believing that her marriage was falling apart. For a brief period, she was replaced at the Ridgetop farm by a woman named Helen, a dancer Willie brought home after one tour, but Susie, Lana, and Billy hated this intruder and hastened her departure. All three children had bonded with Shirley, and they loved her as their 'mother number two'.

Sometime in 1968, Shirley discovered that Willie had fathered a child by someone by the name of Connie Koepke in Phoenix, Arizona. Reading this news from a hospital bill, which had been delivered along with the other mail that day, merely brought her fears into focus. Shirley left the Ridgetop farm to seek rehabilitation at her parents' home, to be replaced by Connie, Willie's third wife.

Willie had met Connie at a venue called the "21 Club" in Cut 'n' Shoot, Texas. He first spied her from the stage, then did what he'd always done when he was in a mood for a one night stand. "I turned to my steel player," Willie later told *Newsweek*, "and said, 'Get that tall good-lookin' blonde for me.' Like any good, obedient steel player, he came up after the show and said, 'Here she is.'" Once again, Willie fell in love, and Connie came along with him on the road at times, until she gave birth to their daughter, Paula Carlene and they were found out.

In 1969, with his life in turmoil and his records still not selling, Willie was still writing as passionately and frequently as when he first arrived in Nashville. One December day in the basement studio, Willie and Hank Cochran wrote *What Can You Do To Me Now?*, yet another song with plenty of double entendre meanings, which pretty much summed up what had been happening in his life. "I think that year I had four cars wrecked," Willie recalls in his autobiography. "I got a divorce. Decided to get married again. There was a lot of things goin' on that year, and Hank and I set down in the basement and we wrote *What Can You Do To Me Now?* The next day my house burned down."

What can you do to me now
That you haven't done to me already?
You broke my pride and made me cry out loud
What can you do to me now?

I'm seeing things that I never thought I'd see
You've opened up the inside of me
How long have you been doing this to me?
I'm seeing sides of me I can't believe

Someway, somehow, I'll make a man of me
I will build me back the way I used to be

Much stronger now, the second time around
'Cause what can you do to me know?

— *What Can You Do To Me Know?* (Willie Nelson, Hank Cochran)

The allusion to his less-than-successful recording career in Nashville is barely veiled here, though Willie never held a grudge. In 1978 he would tell *Chicago Tribune* columnist Jack Hurst, "that anti-Nashville shit has been overdone . . . . I made some records and they didn't sell, so it's easy for me to say RCA didn't promote them. Maybe they weren't good enough to sell. I've listened to some of 'em recently and I think that may be the case . . . . If I'd picked up my guitar and let 'em join in, I think I could have got a different feel on my records back then." Willie regretted hanging up his guitar to become a vocalist backed by an orchestra, as he told Michael Hall during another interview. "By the time I got to Nashville, they had already forgot about the guy and his guitar, and it was a guy and an orchestra. That's fine, I've got nothing against orchestras, but it so happens that I had a country band."

Without any prospect of a recording career in Nashville and with his Ridgetop home in ashes, Willie was ready to move his family band back to Texas. Willie called Crash Stewart. "He told me his house had burned down in Nashville," Crash recalls, "and he wanted me to find him a house near a golf course. Willie was heartbroken about losing his home, his belongings, and about 500 songs he had written, which were not yet published." During that tragic blaze, Willie rushed into the burning house and retrieved his guitar and a sizeable stash of pot, which was described in various publications as being 'Mexican', 'Colombian', and 'primo'. The times they were a changin' and soon Willie would be leading the way.

COUNTRY WOODSTOCK

After the Ridgetop fire, Willie pulled up stakes and headed for Texas. "I was ready to move somewhere anyway," Willie told Bill DeYoung, "and it just seemed like when the house burned, I didn't have any excuses anymore. If I'm gonna look for a new house, I might as well look for one back in Texas, because that's really where I felt I ought to go. First of all, I needed to go somewhere where I could take my band and play. I knew I could do it in Texas, New Mexico, Oklahoma, and Louisiana. I didn't have to travel that far, and I figured, 'If this is my retirement, I'm gonna enjoy it and be somewhere I want to be.' I think I had reached a point where I just said, 'Wait a minute. This is not working. I'm ruining my health, running around all over the world trying to do something that just ain't working.'"

After a career of too often being in the wrong place at the wrong time, Willie found himself some higher ground in Texas. "I think he was doing exactly what he wanted to do," Mickey Raphael suggests in the authorized video biography. "He really didn't plan to move out to Texas and, like, 'Let's get big!' He wanted to play in Texas. I remember he turned down the Rolling Stones world tour — I remember I was so excited about doin' that — but Willie said, 'No, I don't think I feel like leavin' Texas right now.'"

An idyllic interval on the eastern slopes of the west Texas hill country near Bandera, Texas, some 50 miles west of San Antonio, where he, his band, and their wives hung out together at the closed-for-the-off-season Happy Valley Dude Ranch provided Willie with some wide open spaces and the opportunity to stretch out and relax. Living in cabins, swimming in the resort pool, and playing golf on the 9-hole Dude Ranch course, they got back to basics. Away from the Music Row hierarchy with its highly systematized way of doing things, playing casual gigs where he and the band were free to experiment, Willie evolved both musically and spiritually. He became determined to record with his guitar in the mix and his road mates providing the backing tracks.

By this time, 'Willie Nelson and many others' included golf pro and promoter Larry Trader, who had spent many years working with Ray Price and veteran Texas promoter Tom Gresham. Gresham and Trader booked

Willie into the clubs in Texas on weekends, but both remember that Willie was a hard sell at first because the times were lean. On top of that, Willie let his hair and beard grow out, took to wearing a gold earring, jeans, t-shirt, and sneakers, which was a radical departure from the 'spic & span Willie' of previous years when he wore fashionable western cut suits, and, for a while when they were in vogue, Nehru jackets, always with a crisply pressed shirt and tie. When it was warm, he now wore cut-offs and sandals. He no longer distinguished between what he wore on stage and off stage — he was just Willie. No more clip-on ties, suits, and boots. They were all changing, becoming a band of gypsies. "We wasn't hippies, but we lived like hippies," Gresham notes in *Willie: An Autobiography*.

During the time spent at the Happy Valley Dude Ranch in Bandera, the band began to pull together. "Our shows were sellin' well," Paul English recalls in the video biography, "but our records weren't sellin' at all. So, Willie said, 'Well, we can go to Texas and work the beer joints.'" Bee Spears remembers that it took a while to establish themselves in the honky tonks. "People would come out to see him. We really built up a grassroots following. There would be maybe 25 or 30 people there. We would come back, and there would be, like, 50. It just slowly built up at the grassroots level. The attitude was, like, well, 'I like 'ole Willie but you sure can't dance to it'."

For a while, life was free and easy, and Willie had plenty of time for reading and meditation. He still owed RCA an album, but Nashville was out of sight, out of mind. When Willie got the call to return to Nashville to record, he wrote the material for YESTERDAY'S WINE rapidly, as if merely decoding messages he was receiving from another plane of existence. Spliced together on this concept album Willie's songs *Where's The Show* and *Let Me Be A Man* suggest he was at a spritual crossroads in his life and form a prayer for finding his way.

Explain to me again, Lord, why I'm here
I don't know, I don't know
The setting for the stage is still not clear
Where's the show, where's the show?

Let it begin, let it begin
I am born, can You use me?
What would you have me do Lord?
Shall I sing them a song?

I could tell them about you, Lord

I could sing of the loves I have known
I'll work in their cotton and corn field
I promise I'll do all I can

I'll laugh and I'll cry
I'll live and I'll die
Please, Lord, let me be a man,
And I'll give you all I can.

If I'm needed in this distant land,
Please, Lord, let me hold your hand.
Dear Lord, let me be a man
And I'll give it all that I can

If I'm needed in this distant land
Please Lord, let me be a man

— *Where's The Show / Let Me Be A Man* (Willie Nelson)

The opening lines of this album made it clear that the time in Bandera had been a time of change. This was a different Willie Nelson. Willie had been 'twice-born'.

Yes, there's great confusion on earth
And the power that is has concluded the following
Perfect man has visited earth already and his voice was heard
The voice of imperfect man must now be manifest
And I have been selected as the most likely candidate . . .

Yes, the time is April, and therefore you, a Taurus, must go
To be born under the same sign twice adds strength
And this strength, combined with wisdom and love, is the key

— *Do You Know Why We're Here?* (Willie Nelson)

As Tom Gresham has said, they "wasn't hippies," but in 1971 these opening words of Willie's fit right into the New Age demographic. He could not have known it when he penned the songs for YESTERDAY'S WINE, but this album would appeal directly to the soon-to-emerge long-haired cosmic cowboys and cowgirls of the 1970s. At the time of its release, though, RCA marketed this unusual album to traditional country fans, most of whom were puzzled by what Willie was talking about on the first cut. The study of astrology was on the rise, but it was not yet widely accepted in mainstream society.

By the time 'Shotgun' Willie was heard on the radio in the early 1970s, he had tranformed himself into a longhaired gypsy cowboy. While not the first 'cosmic cowboy' to show up on the scene, he had the highest profile of any of the progressive country artists at that time and he soon became their most likely candidate for the role of leader.

Willie's transformation had really begun back in the 1950s when he quit the Methodist church and became disillusioned with all Old South religious practices. After discovering the Aquarian Bible and the books on reincarnation by 'sleeping prophet' Edgar Cayce in the 1960s, Willie began to forge a personal system of belief and a code of conduct he still lives by. During the heady '60s, Zen Buddhism, astrology, something called 'transcendental meditation', and the rediscovered teachings of the ancient mystery schools led many people to once again envision both a deity and a program for self-realization not driven by fear and guilt. As Willie would write in his autobiography, "the constant struggle between good and evil is approaching another great climax in our lifetime. By good I mean your inner voice that comes from God — maybe you call it conscience — and by evil I mean negative thinking, materialistic, greedy attitudes that you know are wrong but can be reduced into acting as if you believe they are right. This is the Devil — to be overwhelmed by desire for things of the material world, to be swept under by negative thinking, to be selfish and petty, to use power and wealth to dominate others: this is hell and we make it for ourselves. Running alone in the dawn, this is the sort of thing I think about. It's nothing mysterious. People may think I'm mysterious, but I don't plan it that way. It all seems clear enough to me."

Authors like Edgar Cayce, Alan Watts, Carlos Castaneda, G.I. Gurdjieff, P.D. Ouspensky, Kahil Gibran, and Zen master Shunryu Suzuki were offering alternatives to the realm of Heaven and Hell and the war between good and evil in our behavior. Many 'baby boomers' like me had become alienated from the church, but rejected atheism with equal fervor as we sought a kinder, forgiving God, a deity who infused all Creation with love and peace. We also wondered why the god our parents had taught us about was always referred to as He. Perhaps god was not a patriarch, but rather a matriarch, a goddess — or perhaps the diety was male and female energies.

On a fictional beach in Kinky Friedman's mystery novel *Road Kill*, a fictional Kinky asks a fictional Willie Nelson, "What does God think of you out here doing nothing but smoking a joint and hitting golf balls into the sea?" Fictional Willie replies, "Oh *She* doesn't mind. She's always guided all my actions." Of course, these words emanate from the fervid fertile mind of Kinky Friedman, retired cosmic cowboy and former fearless leader of Kinky Friedman & the Texas Jewboys, who had ticked off a lot of people in Nashville with records like *They Don't Make Jews Like Jesus Anymore*, which Willie Nelson had produced for Kinky, and *Asshole From El Paso*, which Willie had not produced. Those words said on that beach are not exactly the gospel according to Willie, nor is the advice that this fictional She-God whispers in fictional Willie's ear, which is, "Fuck 'em if they can't take a joke." But there is some truth to Kinky's take on Willie's articles of faith.

As Willie explored these new notions of cosmic consciousness, he became interested in advanced mathematics and the new physics. "Scientists have identified the fundamental forces that govern all matter in the universe," Willie writes in his autobiography, "gravity, electromagnetism, nuclear energy, and so on. What they are looking for is an explanation that will bind all of these forces together into one force that controls all the laws of the universe. This one force is God. The scientists, not the preachers these days, are investigating the nature of God. We should be paying more attention to raising the consciousness of humans to know the truth of the divine law. Pretty soon scientists will prove it as reality. The law that I mean is that all is one, that every atom in your body was once in a star, that life is continuous and nothing dies, and that the law of Karma — what the scientists would call cause and effect — is as real as electromagnetism is real. The law is love. What puts the law of love into proper operation is the Golden Rule." Willie Nelson would be the first country artist to put his new age ideas and beliefs onto vinyl when he recorded the forward-looking YESTERDAY'S WINE album in 1970.

Willie and Connie had married in April 1970 in Las Vegas, and for a short while they lived in the rebuilt Ridgetop house, but with the RCA deal falling apart, Willie felt no compulsion to remain in Tennessee, and Willie Nelson and 'Many Others' moved again, this time to Austin to live there on a full-time basis. Bobbie Nelson was already in Austin and suggested it was a cool place for musicians to live. Willie found the relaxed atmosphere and the cross-pollinating musical influences to his liking. There was something happening in Austin. He also checked out Houston, where he had lived in the past, but Austin's 250,000 population seemed to live at a far more relaxed pace. During the 1960s, an influx of beatnik artists and folksingers, who held hootenannys at local coffeehouses in the University of Texas district, had fostered a spirit of permissiveness. Soon-to-be influential cartoonists like Gilbert Shelton were getting together with the soon-to-be famous Janis Joplin for sing-alongs in the student housing project.

By the time Willie and Connie settled there, hippie mural artists had decorated the walls of an arts center, an old National Guard armory, with the underground images of a whole slew of Austin artists, people like Shelton, Jim Franklin, Jack Jackson, and Michael Priest. These artists had gotten started by contributing to the *Texas Ranger* humor magazine, but their images had soon spread throughout the counterculture during the print media renaissance in underground newspapers and comics. The air was clean, and the Pedernales River, the artesian waters of Barton Springs, and Lake Travis made Austin a true oasis in every sense of the word. As described by Laura Joplin in *Love, Janis*, Austin is "located on the edge of the picturesque Texas Hill Country, Oxford on the Pedernales River."

In 1962, when Janis Joplin enrolled in courses at the University of Texas, she was merely one of a whole generation of rebellious youth who hit the college campuses that year during the Cuban Missile Crisis and the early stirrings of the Civil Rights Movement. Joplin's first 'group' was harmonica player Powell St John and guitar and banjo player Lanny Wiggins. This trio, calling themselves the Waller Creek Boys, played at poetry and music events organized by Ted Klein at venues like the Cliche coffeehouse on Guadalupe and hootenanny nights at the Student Union building. Janis was long gone by the time that Willie arrived, but throughout the 1960s, the local scene had benefited positively from the interaction between university students and locals. Joplin and others had kept the Bay Area-Austin connection open. She was in Austin again in 1966, contemplating joining a band called the 13th Floor Elevators, when she got the call to join Big Brother & the Holding Company in San Francisco.

In the spring of 1969, "Jerry Garcia got a pedal steel guitar to fool around with," *Rolling Stone* reporter Michael Landon notes, "and ended up commuting down to Palo Alto twice a week to play Nashville style in a little club. That group became the New Riders of the Purple Sage, and other Dead members sat in from time to time. All that country music got them singing, something for which they had not been noteworthy in the past, and hours of three-part harmony rehearsals got them back to acoustic instruments. Less noise made them less wired. All that ended up with the groove that made WORKINGMAN'S DEAD possible." For the WORKINGMAN'S DEAD album, Jerry Garcia told Landon, "Tom Constanten had just left to go his own way, and with his (keyboard) influence gone, we got back to being a rock & roll band, again, not an experimental-music group." With the West Coast's most influential psychedelic band getting mellow on a hybrid country music all their own, suddenly it was hip to try your luck with country rock, like ex-Byrds' Gram Parsons and Chris Hillman were doing with the Flying Burrito Brothers. The Dead had created a hippie anthem with *Truckin'*; the New Riders would come up with *Panama Red*, a country rocker about a charismatic doper, for the cosmic cowboys. So, when Willie hooked up with the youth of Austin, he tapped into a whole West Coast connection, and would soon become the link that helped some of the country rockers get recognition within the country music community.

Asleep At The Wheel had formed in West Virginia before migrating to San Francisco to record and perform their mix of satiric originals and Western Swing revival music. They soon relocated in Austin, where they called their sound "regressive country" in response to the term "progressive country," which New York critics had come up with. It is not widely known, but it was Willie Nelson who helped them break onto country radio. "I first moved to Texas on the urging of Willie Nelson," Ray Benson recently told *America's Music: The Roots of Country* author Robert K. Oermann. "I said, 'Oh, do you think we could work there?' He said 'Shoot, you could work four nights a week. Come on down.' The first six months I lived in Texas, I never left the border except to go to Louisiana and Oklahoma once."

The world would come to know Janis Joplin as a dynamic blues singer who burst onto the San Francisco scene during the Summer of Love with Big Brother & the Holding Company, but while in Austin she sang songs like *Careless Love* and *Black Mountain*, mixing gospel with traditional bluegrass, and digging on the music she heard in the eastside jazz and blues clubs. During these early years, Joplin was most influenced by yodeling country blues singer Kenneth Threadgill, who operated a country club in a converted Austin service station. In *Love, Janis*, she remembered Threadgill as "a great big man with a big belly and white hair combed back on top of his head. He'd be back [behind the bar], dishing out Grand Prizes and Lone Stars." She also remembered that, at the time, the only records on the jukebox in Threadgill's bar were by Jimmie Rodgers, the Yodeling Brakeman. The regulars were truck drivers and country people. The musicians Janis Joplin jammed with were black blues practitioners, folkies, bluegrassers, and country pickers. Fusions such as these made Austin into a hotbed of creativity. Threadgill would become a regular at Willie's outdoor events.

When they first arrived in Austin, the Nelson family lived in an apartment complex on East Riverside Drive. Then when Willie and Connie's second daughter, Amy, came along, they moved to a duplex in Lake Austin Estates. Willie, Connie, Paula Carlene, and Amy lived on one side. Susie and Billy lived on the other. Willie was seldom home. He was on the road playing the honky tonks. Or he was in New York, recording and playing Max's Kansas City club in New York, then trekking out to the west coast to play The Troubadour in L.A., and when RED HEADED STRANGER came out, he was playing arenas. But it was while he was in Austin that he got his momentum, playing clubs like the Broken Spoke, Big G's in nearby Round Rock, and Randy's Rodeo in San Antonio.

"He hit Austin with a bang," Darrell Royal, Willie's longtime friend, former football player, and coach of the University of Texas football team, recalls. "He really did. He hit it strong!" There were already a lot of venues for live music in Austin, which would soon become known as the "Live Music Capital of the World." The bands that were happening then were similar to the hundreds of bands that rally in Austin to this day for the "South by Southwest" music industry convention. They were young, experimental, and anti-establishment. No one could have predicted that it would be this young audience who would become as fascinated with Willie Nelson as his older, traditional country fans already were. "The crowds got bigger, they got younger," Mickey Raphael recalls, "but he didn't change anything. He was doin' the same thing, and I think the crowds kind of found him."

"Well," Willie explains in his autobiography, "I began to see a lot of young people, a lot of young guys, longhairs, comin' in to places I was playin' like Big G's in Round Rock, which is not normally where the hippies would go. So, I realized that there was an audience there, for what we were doin', in the young people. It had never been there before. It was always rock & roll or folk. Now, they wanted to hear some country music, and they were having a hard time finding a place that would welcome them in and let them listen." The venue where longhairs gathered for their concerts was called the Armadillo World Headquarters. Before Willie played there, this center of the arts, which was located in the refurbished armory that also housed the office of an off-the-wall organization of free-thinkers known as 'Mad Dog', had been booking a fairly wide range of performers, from sitar guru Ravi Shankar and the Austin Ballet to bands like Shivas Head, the 13th Floor Elevators, the Conqueroo, and Commander Cody. Country music was played in road houses and beer joints, many of which were off limits to hippies, but the times were changing. Next thing you knew, you had longhair cowboys. Willie — with his red beard, his hair held back by a bandanna, or braided into pig-tails, his single gold earring, blue jeans, and sneakers — fit right into the mix. "That was a big change," Bee Spears remembers in the authorized video biography, "as it was in the whole country. All the stuff goin' on with the Vietnam war and all that stuff. That whole era. That affected the music."

In the spring of 1972, some promoters from Dallas set up what was viewed as a sort of country Woodstock at a ranch 26 miles west of Austin. They called it 'The Dripping Springs Reunion'. This three-day festival was both an unprecedented success and a financial disaster. "The 60,000 fans got wet," Bill DeYoung notes, "muddy, and stoned, in that order, and the promotion men took a bath." Willie, there to perform, along with Coach Royal, who emcee'd, watched the proceedings with interest. He could see the potential for doing it again, and doing it right. That summer, Willie played the Armadillo for the first time. His August 12, 1972 performance was written up in *Rolling Stone* magazine. The Armadillo's Eddie Wilson was quoted as saying that "Willie Nelson is the Bob Dylan of country music." *Billboard* called the Armadillo World Headquarters "the first longhaired country music hall in the nation." One woman who attended the concert told *Rolling Stone* reporter Michael Bane that "people went fucking nuts. It was like going to church or something."

"People used to say, 'What's the Austin Sound?'" Ray Benson recalls. "I'd say, 'There ain't no Austin Sound, there's an Austin Scene.' We were all as different musically as you could be. Doug Sahm had his thing. Greezy Wheels, Marcia Ball, Willie Nelson . . . a hundred other groups. There wasn't anybody who sounded the same . . . . We were takin' the hippie thing and giving it this real Texas country slant." The laid-back Austin lifestyle was also an important contributing factor. "It was wonderful," Benson recalls. "We were always broke, and everybody wanted to get high and play music. There were many, many like-minded people. Willie was the father of the whole thing. He was the most successful. He was the oldest. And he was pure Texas. Willie was in touch with the establishment . . . he was also part of the counterculture. So, he had his feet in both camps." As time passed, Willie continued to open doors for counterculture groups. And when the cycle completed itself, he and Waylon would tour with the Grateful Dead.

Audiences in the armory were like audiences at Bill Graham's Fillmore Auditorium in San Francisco or the Retinal Circus in Vancouver — they filled the dance floor, but they were often sit-down-and-groove-on-the-music audiences. Of course, when they started boogieing, all hell broke loose. At Willie's picnics, things would get a whole lot wilder, but amid the pagan practices a harmony would be established. In September 1973, *Houston Chronicle* music critic John W. Wilson would write a story titled,

"Willie's New Tune: 'My freaks don't scare my kickers, anymore.'"

Wilson had been intrigued by seeing "redneck cowboys smoking reefers" at Willie's first Fourth of July Picnic. "It wasn't all that long ago," he wrote, "that Willie Nelson, too, had slicked down hair and was playing only country music clubs and events like the Texas Prison Rodeo. But that's all changed. Willie's been discovered by the Beautiful People in New York and freaks from coast to coast. And his old fans are still around. Getting the freaks and the kickers together hasn't been easy. 'There was a lot of fear on both sides,' says Nelson. 'The country crowd is discovering the freaks are just longhaired kids who also like country music, and the freaks are finding out that the kickers are just kids whose parents wouldn't let them have longhair. The thing they have in common is the music.'"

Jerry Jeff Walker, who had already written *Mr. Bojangles* and was hitting on the FM radio with cuts like Guy Clark's *L.A. Freeway* at this time, was already popular with the Armadillo audience. Right away, he could see that not only did Willie fit right in, he was bringing his traditional country fans along, as well. "The young people liked it," Jerry Jeff recalls in the authorized video biography, "because the songs cut right through. He played them with such straight convictions. It was amazing to pull into a gas station and have the owner of the station say he was going to the Willie show, too. I thought, old people dig him, too."

The success of Willie's first show at Armadillo World Headquarters led to Willie being booked onto college campuses. With his horizons widening, Willie invited Waylon Jennings down to Austin to share a date at the Armadillo. Their opening act was Commander Cody. "I had never worked the Armadillo before," Waylon recalls in his autobiography. "I thought it was a cowboy place. I looked through the curtains and saw that it was a rock & roll club. The Armadillo crowd was all young kids, longhairs, sitting on the floor. The smell of reefer hung heavy in the room. I was upset. 'Somebody find that red-headed bastard and get him up here!'"

When Willie did show up, Waylon's often-quoted line, "What the hell have you got me into?" did not faze him, although his "Just trust me" answer did not immediately convince Waylon at the time, either. But this was Commander Cody opening for them, not Led Zeppelin or Black Sabbath. Pianist George Frayne (the Commander) had recorded *Hot Rod Lincoln*, and they were becoming notorious for a number called *Seeds And Stems (Again)*, but lead vocalist Billy C. Farlow also sang Willie's *Family Bible* in their show, a song which they had recorded. They had a fiddle and a steel in the band. Once Waylon began his set, his fears were melted away by the warm response of the audience. Willie had been right, after all. "That whole thing," Waylon points out, "spread from Austin." In one interview, with Barbara Thomas, Waylon elaborated on what had gone down between him and Willie that night. "He said to me, 'Just trust me. If they don't go for it, you're goin' down with me.' I saw them, like an ocean of kids, man, who freaked out over our music, and I couldn't believe. Willie said, 'I think we've found something. I think we've found people who understand us and who believe in what we're doing, who like us and take us as we are, as people, and can relate to our music.' I think he was right."

OUTLAWS

Waylon Jennings and Willie Nelson first met in Phoenix in 1965 when Willie attended one of Waylon's shows. Willie had told his new friend, "If you want to make a living with country music songs, stay away from Nashville. They'll just break your heart." History shows that Waylon did not follow this advice. When his recording contract with Jerry Moss and Herb Alpert's Los Angeles-based A&M Records ended, Waylon signed with Chet Atkins, the newly appointed president of RCA Nashville, and he and Willie became label-mates. Waylon recalled the restrictions of recording in that era during an interview with Grant Alden in *No Depression*. "When we came to town, you had to use their studios, you had to use their songs, you had to record four songs in three hours. And that was no good. That was like cuttin' cookies."

Willie was able to break out of Nashville though, and Waylon would break the studio system a few years later. During Country Music Week 1971, Willie participated in a guitar pull organized by Harlan Howard, where he sang the songs he had written in Bandera and planned to record for another concept album with his band. Jerry Wexler of Atlantic Records was knocked out by Willie Nelson's new songs when he heard them at this guitar pull and told Willie he wanted that concept album to kick off his new country division. The enthusiastic Wexler said he had no problem with Willie using his band in the studio. Willie said, "I have been looking for you all my life." After a decade of being sugar-coated and smothered with Nashville strings and choirs, Willie was to get a chance to make the music he had always wanted to record.

Now signed to Atlantic Records, Willie recorded SHOTGUN WILLIE in New York. Producers Jerry Wexler and Arif Mardin flew Willie and his band to the Big Apple and supplied a hot horn section for the high energy sessions. Guests Leon Russell, Doug Sahm, and David Bromberg contributed some hot licks. Willie had busted out of the Music Row mold. He had his guitar and his band in the mix, and he was kicking out all the stops, really wailing on cuts like Johnny Bush's *Whiskey River*. In the lavatory of his New York hotel room before the first sessions for the album began, Willie did a little soul-searching and come up with a new song that he took right back into the studio to kick things off. It became the title track.

Shotgun Willie sits around in his underwear
Biting on a bullet and pulling out all his hair
Shotgun Willie got all his family there
Well you can't make a record if you ain't got nothin' to say
Well you can't make a record if you ain't got nothin' to say
You can't play music if you don't know nothin' to play

— *Shotgun Willie* (Willie Nelson)

While Willie had cut himself loose from RCA, signing with Atlantic to record SHOTGUN WILLIE in New York City, then PHASES & STAGES in Muscle Shoals, Alabama, Waylon was still with RCA, but over the years he'd slowly been gaining ground, negotiating better percentages and an ever increasing amount of artistic control. By the time Waylon recorded HONKY TONK HEROES, he had negotiated the right to use some members of his road band in the sessions at RCA's Nashville Sound studios. Liner notes author Roger Schutt, a Nashville critic who went by the moniker 'Captain Midnight'. noted that the presence of the Waylors in the studio was an important component on Waylon and Tompall Glaser's production of Billy Joe Shaver's songs. "Those crazy, wonderfully wild and beautifully talented Honky Tonk Heroes are just naturally a part of any music Waylon Jennings puts down these days. A lot went down with the recording of every song in this album. A lot of emotion — the kind of feelings that go unsaid and usually unmentioned." Jimmy Moore's photograph of Jennings, Shaver, and the boys in a honky tonk cluttered with amps, instruments, bar glasses and a cash register, everyone holding a glass of whiskey or a beer, was a radical departure from the rhinestone cowboy image that Music Row usually airbrushed together for their stars' album covers. Someone has just told a joke. There are smiles on these men's faces.

With Chet Atkins easing into his retirement years in the '70s, Waylon's business was handled by Jerry Bradley who suspected that he was out to sabotage country music. Before any of the executives had heard a single note, Waylon would get called into meetings where he would find himself defending a move he'd made the day before in the studio. But when Waylon got himself a New York manager, Neil Reshen, and Reshen got a look at the books and called the Nashville RCA execs whores . . . well . . . things began to change real fast. During a contract negotiation with Bradley, Atkins, and some of RCA's New York executives, Waylon walked out of the room to go to the washroom, but the suits thought he was walking out because he was angry. They'd heard he'd been talking to other labels. Reshen did nothing to dissuade their fears. In fact, he kind of fed the fire some extra fuel, telling them he was sure Waylon was mad as hell. He met Waylon in the hall outside the office and told him the RCA execs had caved in. When Waylon told Reshen he'd just gone for a piss, the wily lawyer said, it was a "$25,000 piss." Waylon had the contract he wanted, and a $25,000 advance.

After that, Waylon had a better picture of what you had to do. One time, when handed an advance check for his next album and asked what he planned to do with the money, Waylon told RCA he planned to start his own record label. By this point, they had no idea if he was serious or not. He did form his own production company to gain control over the money spent on his records. Before this, he'd recorded at the RCA studios and they'd simply chalked up the charges against his royalties. These charges could be pretty well whatever they wanted them to be. In 1982, Willie would respond to these shady practices by recording *Write Your Own Song* for the feature film *Songwriter*.

You're callin' us heathens with zero respect for the law . . .
Mr. Record Executive, why don't you write your own song.
An' don't listen to mine
It might run you crazy
It might make you dwell on your feelings for a moment too long
We're makin' you rich
An' you're already lazy
Just lay on your ass and get richer, and write your own song.

— *Write Your Own Song* (Willie Nelson)

Willie has cited so-called 'mechanical rights' as another dubious recording industry business practice. When a record began to sell well, the label would often replace the B-side somewhere during the sales period with a song to which they held the publishing rights, effectively cutting the artist's share in half. Yet another area where the artists were bilked out of their money was by booking agents and promoters. "I never figured out," Waylon wrote in his autobiography, "how I could owe the booking agency money after being on the road 300 days a year." But these agents with their "plaid jackets and shiny ties" had not anticipated the new kind of country audience that had been seen at Dripping Springs. Through Neil Reshens connections to the rock world, soon Waylon and the Waylors were playing Max's Kansas

City club in New York City, the Troubadour in L.A., and sharing a bill with the Grateful Dead. Once Willie got to know Neil, he asked Reshen to represent him, as well. The way Willie put it was, if they were going to be outlaws, they needed an outlaw lawyer, too.

In October 1973, Willie dropped into Nashville to lend a hand producing Waylon's first album to be put together under the independent WGJ (Waylon Goddamned Jennings) banner, but the two Texans soon moved on over to Tompall Glaser's Hillbilly Central building on 19th Avenue South for their sessions. Although Jerry Bradley feared this change of venue could put him in a hot box with his union engineers who had a contract locking RCA artists into using RCA studios, Waylon stood his ground, and with Willie's help, he recorded Willie's *Heaven And Hell* and *It's Not Supposed To Be That Way*. Then they dusted off a Waylon song RCA had rejected a few years back called *This Time*. When it was released, this song became Waylon's first chart-topper. "It was like the blind leading the blind," Waylon later told *Country Weekly*. "Willie and I had fun with it. If it ain't fun, we'll go somewhere else and play golf. Nowadays, making records is such a big pressure deal. They say, 'Do another take' and stuff. We never did anything like that. We just let the song carry everything. If everybody was into it, it would happen. If it wasn't happening, we'd quit for a while and do something else. We'd try another song and then come back to that one." Over at Hillbilly Central, Waylon's secret weapon was veteran songwriter, engineer, and producer 'Cowboy Jack' Clement. "When the magic was there," Waylon told Wendy Newcomer, "ole Jack would start dancing! That's what you look for — that magic moment. If that doesn't happen, you may have perfection but you don't have feeling." The way Owen Bradley had put it years before was, "Perfection can be dull."

When Waylon took the masters for the THIS TIME album to RCA, they initially refused to release the record in the face of union threats. Waylon didn't budge an inch. "This is all you're going to get," he told them. "I think greed broke them because they knew I was already selling records. And they knew it was a hit album. Finally, they put it out. They did lose their deal with their engineers and had to sell their studios. In fact, all of the labels had to sell their studios. That was the album that broke the system." When he followed THIS TIME with DREAMING MY DREAM, which was produced by Jack Clement, Waylon hit the top of the chart again with *Are You Sure Hank Done It This Way*.

Waylon and Willie were music biz revolutionaries long before they got labeled as outlaws. Their maverick behavior simply would not be reined in for all that long. When they broke out, they did it in style, in the process revitalizing country music. They were the first to insist that their record labels spend some real money promoting their albums. "Instead of beating his head against the RCA brass in Nashville," Bob Allen writes in *Waylon & Willie*, "he went to their bosses in New York. What happened there has become a very significant story in the country music business. It seems that one of the RCA heavies had a huge portrait of ex-RCA artist Willie Nelson hanging over his desk. 'You blew it with him, hoss,' he said. 'Now just don't blow it with me.'" With Willie's success in Texas staring them in the face, the RCA executives were at a disadvantage. "Waylon," Bob Allen notes, "left New York with the promise of the largest promotional budget RCA had ever granted a country artist."

While Waylon was going through these trials and tribulations with the RCA executives, Willie was creating RED HEADED STRANGER with the belief that the executives at his new label, CBS, had given him complete artistic control. "I found out later that they didn't," he told Bill DeYoung. "They just told me they did. It just so happens, on that very first album, they knew if they said 'no' then, then I was gone. So, they let me have it for a time, but then whenever they decided I'd had enough, they started rejecting my albums."

These confrontations were not the first time Texans and Nashvillians had come into conflict. In fact, the feud had been ongoing since the mid-1940s, since the first and only time Bob Wills had come up to Nashville to play the Opry. Already a huge star in the Lone Star state, Wills met his first opposition when the Opry managers told him he couldn't use his drummer. When Bob told the managers that if his drummer couldn't play on their stage, he'd rather go on home without playing, they agreed to let him have his way, but tried (unsuccessfully) to keep the drummer behind a curtain. As Willie continues the story in his autobiography, "Bob went on stage with his cigar in his mouth, they told him not to smoke onstage, and he walked off again. So far as I know, that was his one and only appearance on the Opry." Reportedly, Wills caused such a ruckus that one member of the audience had fallen out of the balcony. Bob's daughter, Rosetta Wills, notes in her book *The King of Western Swing: Bob Wills Remembered* that her father's 1945 visit to the Opry "defied Nashville's parochial proprieties. First, they arrived in a bus. They wore white, tailored western suits, white hats, and boots. The typical Opry musician drove an old car and dressed in overalls. As Minnie Pearl, who personally witnessed the phenomenon, said, 'He was way ahead of his time. People were awestruck. But as soon as he left town, every hillbilly act got a bus and western outfits.'" A similar confrontation took place a few years later when Ernest Tubb arrived to play the *Grand Ole Opry* with an electric guitar player in his band. This time the managers caved in completely, hillbilly music took a further step toward becoming known as country & western, and The Texas Troubadour hung around for the duration. His record shop and radio show became Nashville fixtures. For a while, beginning in 1964, Willie Nelson and Ernest Tubb co-hosted a television show.

For their attempt to free country artists from the dictates of the labels and to put the 'western' back into country & western music, Willie and Waylon soon were branded 'outlaws'. Waylon credits Hazel Smith, renowned Nashville publicist, for coming up with the term "outlaw music." According to legend, she coined the phrase when pressed by a deejay from WCSE in Ashboro, North Carolina as to what to call their music. Her inspiration came from Waylon's recording of Lee Clayton's *Ladies Love Outlaws*. At the time, Smith worked as publicist for Tompall's "Hillbilly Central" complex on 19th Avenue South and wrote a "Hillbilly Central" column in *Country Music* magazine. Journalists elsewhere had already begun referring to Waylon, Tompall, and friends as members of "the clique," and on November 17, 1973, journalist Peter McCabe had used the term "outlaws" and "the clique" in an article titled "Hard Living Is Trademark of this Musical Clique" in the *Miami Herald*. "They've been calling themselves the clique for some time now," McCabe wrote, "and certainly most of Nashville recognizes that they are a little apart from the mainstream. They are frowned on in some quarters, tolerated in others; you might say they are the 'outlaws of country music' . . . On a trip through night time Music City," he continued, "you just might run into all of them — Waylon Jennings, Billy Joe Shaver, Kinky Friedman, Tompall Glaser, Johnny Darrell, Captain Midnight, maybe Willie Nelson, plus assorted friends — in the Burger Boy, or Tiny Tim's, or Linebaughs, or, for that matter, anywhere that might have a pinball machine, or else they might be propping up Tompall Glaser's Lincoln Mark IV in the parking lot of any of the aforementioned establishments, passing 'round a bottle of Jack Daniels and waiting for the sky to turn gray before the dawn. Their noon is everybody else's midnight; raising hell is a way of life rather than an occasional pastime." Whatever this motley crew were called before January 12, 1976, whether it be "outlaws" or "a clique" or "progressive country artists," Jerry Bradley 'velcroed' the "outlaw" label onto them by releasing WANTED: THE OUTLAWS, featuring Waylon, Willie, Tompall, and Jessi Colter, their pictures displayed on a "Wanted" poster on the cover.

"I did the 'Outlaws' project at about three o'clock in the morning," Waylon later told Bill DeYoung. "A lot of those things weren't supposed to be released. Most of the tracks were 10-years-old by then." WANTED: THE OUTLAWS became the first country album ever to be certified platinum, and Waylon and Willie's *Good Hearted Woman*, which they had written together in 1968 during an all-night poker game, went Top 30 on the pop charts, held at number one on country charts for three weeks, and was named the 1976 CMA Single of the Year.

Willie seldom identified with the term but for years he faced interviewers' questions about being an 'outlaw'. In an interview with Alanna Nash published in 1988 in her book *Behind Closed Doors*, he was asked if he minded the label. "No, I don't care," he told Nash. "It was funny then, and, well, I think it's funny every time I read something where it says 'Willie Nelson, the outlaw'. But I guess it makes good reading for somebody." Nash wanted to know how it got started. "Oh, I don't know," Willie replied. "Somewhere between Tompall and Bradley, I guess. They thought it might be a good idea, and evidently it was. It caught on." In April 1979, Gail Buchalter, a reporter for the *Baltimore News American*, asked, "Do you feel you've been labeled with it or do you feel it's a justified term?" Willie responded, "Oh, maybe so. I don't know. I'm pretty cantankerous at times. The people who started out labeling 'outlaws', the outlaw movement, I think it had a lot to do with selling records. I think they could have started the campaign a little earlier. I think they could have gone back into Bob Wills and Ray Price and Hank Thompson. A lot of these guys preferred to stay in their own place and do it their own way and not conform to it. Usually, I don't consider myself anymore of an outlaw than Hank Williams was." Waylon would also cite Hank Williams' behavior as an inspiration to 'swarm', reminding people that ole Hank had once unloaded his handgun into a Nashville jukebox because it didn't contain any of his records.

While the "outlaw" label was a marketing ploy, Willie's friendship with Waylon was not fabricated by anyone. They were kindred spirits. "I don't know how two brothers could be any closer," Willie told one interviewer. "I love Willie," Waylon told Bill DeYoung. "He's like my brother of the road. And he's one of those type of friends that, when you've been apart for a long time, all of a sudden you look up and he's standing there. It's just a timeless friendship."

"We're friends, we fight . . . we have," Willie told DeYoung, "but we don't anymore. Back when we was on different kinds of drugs, we would fight." Waylon's long battle with cocaine addiction has been over-publicized.

Willie had an adverse reaction to it, a sinus condition that saved him from going through that. In fact, he's outspokenly against it. Perhaps, watching his close friend flirt with disaster has contributed to these feelings. However, their friendship survived through Waylon's worst years. "He don't try and change me," Waylon confided to DeYoung, "and I don't try to change him. Willie is the only true free spirit that I really know. I hear a lot of people say they are, but he really is. Now, there's other people say he's the most irresponsible person on Earth, and we're both right."

By calling their Nashville rebels "outlaws," Music Row identified these troublesome artists with the unruly world of excess. The New York press's designation "progressive country" was more accurate. Of course, Waylon and Willie contributed their fair share of legendary drinking stories to the mix. In his song *Me and Paul*, Willie set his close friendship with drummer Paul English to music. He also made reference to his days in Nashville being the "roughest." Released on the YESTERDAY'S WINE album before Willie left RCA, this overt reference to the difficult times he was having in Nashville would be his first public criticism of Music Row, but it wouldn't be his last. The second verse contains an indirect reference to marijuana, a reference that clicked with the youthful audience, but one subtle enough that his traditional country fans overlooked the transgression at the time. "Almost busted in Laredo / But for reasons I'd rather not disclose" was innocuous enough. The third verse, with the lines "We drank a lot of whiskey / So I don't know if we went on that night at all," along with the title track *Yesterday's Wine*, reassured Music Row that this album fell within the boundaries of acceptable behavior for a country artist.

In his book *Flashbacks*, Timothy Leary recalls that marijuana distribution during these years was carried out by enthusiastic "amateurs." Organized crime had not yet become involved. Songs like the New Riders of the Purple Sage's *Henry* and *Panama Red* championed the enthusiasm of these amateurs. Willie's *Me and Paul*, with its reference to the predilections of both rednecks and hippies, became a favorite in his shows. Johnny Bush's *Whiskey River*, from SHOTGUN WILLIE, became his set opener. And when Willie began hosting his own outdoor events, which became known as 'Willie Nelson's Fourth of July Picnics', Willie became a culture hero. Like Freewheelin' Franklin, from Gilbert Shelton's *Fabulous Furry Freak Brothers* comics, who was seen on t-shirts and posters quipping his phrase, "Dope will get you through times of no money, but money won't get you through times of no dope." Willie Nelson t-shirts and posters declared, "Where there's a Willie there's a way." Accepted by rednecks and longhairs, Willie would become a much-needed healer of the rift between the counterculture and the mainstream, which had grown dangerously wide during the anti-Vietnam years, splitting America in two.

After his first picnic at Dripping Springs he would become revered as a patron saint in Texas, inspiring the "Mathew, Mark, Luke, and Willie" slogan, which also began popping up on t-shirts. Still, staging a "country Woodstock" was a challenge. The promoters of the 1972 Dripping Springs Reunion had lost their shirts. Bill Graham, the masterful promoter who would graduate from his Fillmore West and Fillmore East venues to staging superstar tours with the Rolling Stones as his headliners, had lost his cool during the Woodstock Festival in upstate New York in 1968. He was not prepared for the hundreds of thousands of fans who showed up. Timothy Leary later described Woodstock as "a convincing demonstration of the swarming powers of the Baby Boomers. Half a million assembled for a weekend to form the third largest city in New York State. Instant metropolis! A hundred thousand LSD trips; two births, three deaths, none caused by drugs. Knowing the promoters, we were clued to the backstage greed, so we stayed away. The sharks were out in full force. The New York City police threatened to shut it down unless they were taken care of. Musicians and their agents maneuvered. The people fighting for control of the stage had no idea that the star of this show would be the crowd. The sheer numbers were awesome. Even more impressive was the gentleness of this Flower Power. Peace and Love was the theme of this event, which became the symbol of an era. Bill Graham saw what was happening and hated it. The movie *Woodstock* caught him at that historic moment tearing his hair, screaming with crazed eyes at this army of kids invading the grounds. The *little scumbags weren't buying tickets!* 'They're like those ants in South America,' he shouted to the cameras. 'The only way to stop them is dig trenches and set fire to them.'"

Three months after Woodstock, at the Rolling Stones' free concert at the Altamount Racetrack near Oakland, California, Peace and Love gave way to tragic violence when members of the Hell's Angels motorcycle club, hired as security, beat, kicked, and knifed the unfortunate few hundred fans who were crushed up against the stage as the crowd surged forward during the band's opening number, *Sympathy For The Devil.* Obviously, there was a lot of energy present with these outdoor gatherings. Someone had to steer that energy; it was no longer going to steer itself, as it had done at Woodstock. Tim Leary notes that while "Angels were diving from the stage, knives and fists flying," Mick Jagger had simply lost control of his audience.

"The Hell's Angel's riot," Leary continues, "culminating in the death of a bystander, produced moralistic editorials claiming that the decade of Peace and Hope had ended in aimless drug violence. The fact is that all the bad stuff occurred around the stage, the center of power, where the drug of choice was booze. I didn't see one person born after 1946 on the bandstand."

Sporadic violence had also marred the 1972 Dripping Springs reunion. "The crowd was a hostile mix of longhairs looking for their own Woodstock and traditional country fans who just wanted to get drunk," Ed Ward had written in *Rolling Stone*. "The truce was an uneasy one, broken by beatings of the longhairs by both the drunks and the security goons. I was standing back-stage talking to a short-haired guy who was wearing a golf cap. I didn't know who he was until Tex Ritter walked over and introduced him as Willie Nelson. I was properly embarrassed, but Willie just laughed about it. We retired to the shelter of an air-conditioned Winnebago to have a beer and talk . . . . Half a year later, he had long hair and an earring and was a cult figure in Austin rock clubs."

Preparations for Willie's first Picnic were done on a slim budget and took a grassroots approach. Posters designed and printed by the Armadillo artists would become collectors items, but ticket sales, Tom Gresham recalled, were basic. "We bought and bagged 20,000 tickets. Larry Trader, Billy Cooper, Gino McCoslin, and I set out to sell the tickets." SHOTGUN WILLIE had come out in late 1972, and with his appearance at the Kerrville Festival in May 1973, then the buildup to the July 4th Picnic, sales of the Atlantic Records album in the Austin area alone had surpassed everything he'd done everywhere else before. However, in staging an outdoor festival where longhairs and rednecks were both invited, he was taking on something that even hard-nosed rock promoter Bill Graham had botched.

The first Willie Nelson Picnic on July 4, 1973 could have turned out to be a gigantic disaster. The difference was Willie. He did not lose control of his audience. Willie not only survived his first outdoor event, he came out of it a hero. "I saw something that a lot of people didn't see," Willie told Bill DeYoung. "I saw a whole new audience out there. And the only difference between these guys and those guys is one of them has longhair and might smoke a little dope every now and then, and the other guy over here's got short hair and drinks rotgut whiskey. It was gonna be difficult for them guys to ever get together unless they had some common ground. And I knew what the common ground was. I knew that these same guys, who had hair down to their ass, loved Hank Williams. And I knew that this guy over here, who had just got through kickin' the shit out of some hippie, he loved Hank

Williams. So there was something wrong with this."

The Dripping Springs Reunion in 1972 had proven that the site just west of Austin was a good one with a natural concert bowl on the ranchland, but the promoters had not thought out the logistics for a three-day festival. Being new at this kind of thing, Willie planned a one-day event during the warm summer weather. "The reason I wanted to do it in July," he explained, "was because it was hot, and I figured that any kind of violence that might break out would be lessened by the heat. I figured if people smoked enough dope and drank enough beer, then they wouldn't want to fight. Especially if it was hot." Unlike the greedy rock promoters, who Tim Leary has noted were present at Woodstock and Altamount, Willie's motive for staging his picnics was not primarily to make money. "Some of them were big, some of them were just bombs," Ray Benson told Bill DeYoung. "He really wasn't making any money at all. He'd take his publishing checks and subsidize the whole thing." The benefit Willie did reap, as Bill DeYoung saw it, was that he "set himself up as the patriarch of the South's new counterculture."

As Tom Gresham put it, "Suddenly the Woodstock kids became the Austin kids. Willie came out of the Picnic a charismatic figure with an enormous audience." He really was on a roll. Weeks before the Picnic, the word was already out. As Waylon put it, "Willie had called a gathering of the tribes." Don Cusic, author of *Willie Nelson: The Lyrics*, describes the pre-Picnic situation. "In the spring of 1973 I moved to Nashville and landed in an apartment with Geoff, an Englishman who was a Waylon Jennings fanatic. Kinky Friedman had just moved out of the apartment, but there were 'Texas Jewboys' stickers all over the walls and one in the commode. Billy Swan lived upstairs, while the E-Z Method Driving School had its headquarters just below. The buzz in Nashville that spring was about a big concert planned in Texas for the 4th of July and organized by Willie Nelson. At this point the old-timers and the *Grand Ole Opry* had fallen out of fashion with the new breed taking over Nashville; it was Kris Kristofferson who was the hero, not Roy Acuff. Willie Nelson had a cult status; he had always been the insider's favorite, the songwriter's *songwriter*." Cusic, like so many other newcomers, was drawn like a moth to the flame.

The lineup for the first July 4th Picnic featured Kris Kristofferson, Rita Coolidge, Waylon Jennings, Doug Sahm, Tom T. Hall, Ray Price, Ernest Tubb, Billy Joe Shaver, Sammi Smith, George Chambers & The Country Gentlemen, The Threadgills, and Bobby Smith & his Country Blues. Leon Russell, who had recorded his country rock album HANK WILSON'S BACK, which would be released that summer on Shelter Records, was sometimes referred to in the newspaper stories announcing the event as Leon Russell; but other times, writers would refer to "a noted rock singer who is new to the country field — Hank Wilson." Russell had recorded his country rock album at Bradley's Barn in Nashville with a lineup that included Harold Bradley, J.J. Cale, Pete Drake, Grady Martin, Pig Robbins, and Buddy Harman. HANK WILSON'S BACK would become one of the most influential country rock albums of the decade. Kris Kristofferson had forged his reputation in Nashville as a songwiter, not a performer or recording artist. He was the author of *Me And Bobbie McGee*, a number 12 country hit for Roger Miller in 1969, and a number one pop hit for Janis Joplin two years later. Sammi Smith had ridden his *Help Me Make It Through The Night* to the top of the country charts in 1971. A native of Brownsville, Texas, Kristofferson had traveled the road never taken on his way to Music Row. A Rhodes scholar with a degree from Oxford University in England, and a helicopter pilot from his enlisted years, he'd worked as a janitor at Columbia Records in Nashville when he first came to town. Now he was riding high with his own number one country hit, *Why Me*, a cut that featured backing vocals by Larry Gatlin and Kris's new wife Rita Coolidge. Plus, he'd just finished filming *Pat Garrett & Billy The Kid*, Sam Peckinpah's western epic film, which also featured Bob Dylan, in Durango, Mexico. Although not listed on the poster, Charlie Rich was added to the lineup. While this was a superstar cast, to Willie they were merely the friends he had called to help out.

"The first picnic in Dripping Springs," Willie later told *Hustler* magazine, "was the biggest risk I've ever taken. Even though we had the best talent in the world there, there was still the possibility that nobody would give a shit, that there would be nobody there but us entertainers in the middle of a hot ranch in Dripping Springs."

Don Cusic hitchhiked from Nashville to Dripping Springs. "The sun was hot," he recalls in the 'Afterword' to his book on Willie's lyrics, "and the land was rocky and rolling and the people were heading into the concert like streams of water flowing to a pool. The music had started before I got there and it was after midnight when it finished. The emcee was Willie Nelson, a genial, relaxed, easy-going fellow who introduced acts and played a helluva show of his own."

"There were only three dirt roads leading into the ranch," Susie Nelson recalls in her book, "which was about five or ten miles off of 290. Helicopter shuttles flew the performers between Austin and the picnic. It was a good thing, too. Because they never imagined in their wildest dreams how many people were going to show up. The temperature hit 102 that day. Anywhere from 50,000 to 80,000 people paid $10 apiece — or at least a lot of them did — for the privilege of sitting on an overgrazed hillside while a hot wind coated them with caliche dust as fine as talcum powder and the hot Texas sun baked every bit of exposed flesh. And there was plenty of exposed flesh for the sun to work on." Susie was also intrigued by the mix of people, noting that she "couldn't believe" some of the "Texas society girls" with their lawn chairs, beer coolers, and their pre-rolled joints. "It was what they were wearing that got me. They had on skimpy halter tops, leaving a lot of white skin just begging for the sun to burn it. They had on short-shorts, panty-hose, high heels, and mascara. Just the thing for a concert in the middle of a cow pasture on a 4th of July in Texas." Waylon and his band were bug-eyed by how many women pulled off their bras and halter tops and flung them at the stage.

In his autobiography, Waylon recalls that at one point he and Willie rode a motorcycle onto the site. "Me and Willie, riding past five miles of backed up traffic, people hollering, car doors opening in front of us, flags waving, girls leaning off pickup trucks, frisbees flying, a different song from each radio as we zip along the shoulder." One Texas journalist would say they were all on their way to the "biggest honky tonk of their lives." There was an electric buzz of excitement in the air. *New York Times* music critic Patrick Carr, who had flown in to see what the heck was going on in Austin, would write an article that became widely syndicated titled, "It's So Progressive in Texas."

"This time," Ed Ward reported in *Rolling Stone*, "the longhairs weren't beat up. It was the watershed in the progressive country movement. Prominent state politicians mingled with longhaired kids. University of Texas football coach Darrell Royal had his arm around Leon Russell. Peaceful coexistence had come to Texas, thanks to Willie's pontifical presence. Two years later, for his 1975 picnic the Texas Senate declared July 4th 'Willie Nelson Day'. For that first 1973 picnic, he had to take out a bank loan to cover his losses — too many gate crashers — but he was *established.* Texas was *his*."

"It worked and it worked like a dream," Michael Bane wrote in his book *The Outlaws Revolution in Country Music*. "The event was, naturally enough, somewhat marred by snakebites, drug overdoses, over-enthusiastic security guards, lack of water, lack of parking facilities, and baking heat, but the children of Texas were hardy souls, and, in a way these little problems added to the thrill . . . . The kids of Austin had found their own definition of hip. Texas flags flew, rebel yells cut the soupy air, Willie presided with calm down-home regality."

Kris Kristofferson later remembered with a wry smile that, although a good time was had by all of the performers, Willie had sort of conned them all into coming out. "He said, 'Let's just you and me and Waylon, and . . . Loretta Lynn,' I think he said, 'have a 4th of July Picnic. We'll just split up the money' — but nobody split up that money." Willie seldom wanted to discuss the economics. He had pulled it off, and he was proud of it. "The sound was great," he recalls in *Willie Nelson: My Life*, "the people who were there really enjoyed it." He had approached the event as if it were a ritual, and the people had been drawn to the site as if by a magnet. "We sat up all night around a bonfire," he explained, "and waited till the morning of the Fourth of July. And when the sun started coming up and it started to get to be daylight, you could see the people comin' over the ridge carryin' their blankets and their beer coolers by the thousands."

"What Willie's picnic did," Jerry Jeff says, "it was kinda gettin' a chance for the people of the South to do something where the people of the alternative culture could come out in large groups. Lots of folks with long hair and wild moustaches. From Leon Russell to Faron Young, it made it a lot of fun to hear it all go together." "Rock & roll, soul people, and country people," Kris explains, "people who had a lot in common but didn't know it before that." Don Cusic, a convert after the first Picnic, began to be a regular visitor to Austin, dropping down whenever he had time off from his teaching position at Belmont University in Nashville. "Texas," he wrote, "especially the Austin area, was a magic place during the mid-1970s, and Willie Nelson performances there during that time were more than performances, they were events. I saw Willie play the Texas Opry House, at outdoor events, and in small clubs. It was always magic. And I also saw him perform in Nashville before a huge crowd at the Municipal Auditorium. Willie had returned a conquering hero; when he walked to the microphone with his guitar his first words were, 'Well, hello there. My, it's been a long, long time.' The crowd went berserk, screaming and cheering." Before that triumphant return to Nashville would take place, however, Willie would slug away at it in Texas where he drew crowds wherever he performed.

By this time, Willie could carry off the impossible simply because, as Mickey Raphael told *Rolling Stone*, "I don't think he ever has a bad thought." This 'changed Willie' had a lot to do with what he'd discovered when he'd returned to Texas. It had a lot to do with the success of his first Atlantic album SHOTGUN WILLIE, which despite the lack of airplay would sell some 200,000 records. But he'd undergone some powerful inner changes, too, as the 'far out' material on YESTERDAY'S WINE had shown. Also key to his peace of mind and his new-found ability to live out his positive visualizations was his marriage to Connie. Connie and Willie were friends. They didn't have the combative sort of relationship he'd experienced with Martha and Shirley. "It was a long time before I ran into any positive relationships with females," he told *Rolling Stone*. "Songs I'm writing now are less hopeless. I started thinking positive somewhere along the way." No doubt, reading books like Kahil Gibran's *The Prophet* and Edgar Cayce's books on reincarnation, which Susie notes were among the reading material he absorbed during the time spent at Bandera, and many other titles of a similar nature, had helped Willie realize his spiritual rebirth. By 1988, Tim O'Connor would note, "he was on the National Council of Theologians. He's read everything by every important writer. He's a statesman of sorts. If he wanted to be an evangelist of the Jim Bakker approach, he could raise so much money you could cover Texas eight times over with it, but that is the opposite of Willie's kind of message."

Now that family life was more harmonious, Willie and Connie's children, Paula Carlene and Amy, were a delight to him. He was also finding a way to relate to Susie, Billy, and Lana in their difficult teenage years. Susie, in her 1987 book *Heartworn Memories*, would remember that he reached out to her during a long drive they took together, singing her his new songs and old songs, and finding a way to bridge the generation gap. "We drove up to Denver and then turned around and drove back," she recalls. "We talked a bit, but mostly Dad sang. Dad knew I was having a lot of trouble figuring things out, and singing was his way of talking to me. Some of the songs he sang were from his yet-to-be-released PHASES AND STAGES album. 'Phases and stages, circles and cycles, scenes that we've all seen before — listen, I'll tell you some more.' It was a true concept album. It was about relationships — about divorce and finding the ability to live and love again. The first side tells the woman's story, side two, the man's. One song on the man's side of the record was written especially for me. I believe that, although I never asked Dad. But he really looked at me when he sang. 'It's not supposed to be that way; / You're supposed to know that I love you. / But it don't matter if I can't be there to console you.' That's how Dad always talked to us kids. In his songs. He only yelled at me once in my whole life. He would just sing and cry. And I cried, too, because I knew I was hurting him."

In October 1973, the Nashville Songwriter's Association welcomed Willie and Roger Miller into their Hall of Fame. Per usual, there was a Willie moment, as Susie Nelson notes in her book *Heartworn Memories*. "At the banquet, after the induction," Susie wrote, "Dad started singing his hits. You know Dad. Once he gets his guitar in his hands, it's hard to get him to stop.

Dad sang hit after hit after hit. The crowd just sat there, many of them probably realizing for the first time just how big Dad's song catalog was, and why he really belonged in the Hall of Fame. Finally, a voice hollered from the back of the room, 'Hell, Willie, what song *didn't you write?*'" The induction was recognition that everybody, even Willie, felt he deserved in 1973, and timely, too. Willie was just gearing up for the best years of his life.

In November, Willie, Waylon, Billy Joe Shaver, Sammi Smith, Darrell McCall, Kinky Friedman & the Texas Jewboys, Johnny Darrell, Asleep at the Wheel, Greezy Wheels, and comedian Don Bowman were all scheduled to play an Abbott Homecoming concert. Many of the acts would have to hightail it up the highway from the World Championship Chili Cook-off in Terlingua where they were booked on the previous night. "The problem is," reported Townsend Miller in a concert preview published in the *Austin American Statesman*, "that Terlingua is some 920 miles from Abbott." Atlantic Records had informed Miller that they would be filming and recording the homecoming. Typical of many of the twisted tales from Willie Nelson's life, the situation was even wackier than Miller could have possibly imagined. To begin with, "bright young area promoter Jim Martin," as Miller had referred to the organizer, had actually booked them onto what he called "The World's Biggest Show" in Terlingua, but "the site for this show was three miles from the 'World's Championship Chili Cook-off'." Willie and his band, along with Waylon & the Waylors, Leon Russell, and many others, found themselves outnumbering the small audience that night. Chili lovers, apparently, preferred to stay at their own event.

After they had performed at Terlingua, Sammy Allred, one of the Geezenslaw Brothers, rode toward Abbott in a Winnebago provided to Paul English by the Terlingua promoters. At daylight, they approached the Abbott site, where they were stopped by some men who were patroling the area in their pickups, armed with shotguns. The natives were restless and apprehensive, to say the least; they'd never experienced an invasion of longhairs, but they were pretty sure they were not going to like it. Someone from the Sheriff's department wanted Willie's signature on a piece of paper, stating "that anybody that sets foot on any property that ain't leased to the Abbott Homecoming Concert, it's okay if we shoot them." Abbott, they were learning, was not Austin. Once Willie arrived in one of the other Winnebagos, sanity prevailed, and the show started on schedule. Sometime during the afternoon, one of the acts, Kinky Friedman or Kenneth Threadgill, no one seems to be able to remember exactly who, set things back a bit when they married a young couple on stage during their set.

"Several thousand Texas cowboys jammed this tiny town," Kathrynn Gallagher reported in *The Nashville Tennessean*, "to help Willie Nelson and his friends put the 'western' back in country & western music. By noon the kids were piling into the farm Willie had rented for the occasion. They had seen the stained-glass poster with the halo-ringed cowboy hat announcing 'the PTA presents Abbott Homecoming: all-day singing and dinner on the grounds'. Kids rode by, joyously helmetless on motorcycles, ten-deep in pickup trucks, or clinging for dear life to the trunk of an overloaded car." Gallagher, used to the "hills, buildings, and smog always blocking the sky," found the setting picturesque. "The flat scrubland stretched out as far as the eye could see, with nary a streetlight nor a telephone pole to obscure the view. The sun went down in a blaze among mackerel clouds, and the moon and the evening stars came out to light the sky."

At dusk, there were some tense moments when the crowd started chanting Leon Russell's name. Leon, you see, was on the poster, but he wasn't on the bill. He wasn't even there. Michael Murphey appeased the crowd when he came out with his four-year-old son, just the two of them and his guitar, and calmed them down for a while with his songs. There was more tension when the power went down and they had to dig up several hundred dollars to get the generators started again. The crowd began turning ugly after that, yelling, "We want Leon!" and threatening to storm the stage. But Willie, who'd been off somewhere doing Willie stuff, came back in the nick of time to present Mamma Nelson with a dozen long-stemmed roses before he and his band cranked up the action. By the time they were done, the crowd had forgotten all about Leon Russell. They had got their money's worth, and more.

Willie's close friends will tell you that he has an uncanny sense of timing. Others have experienced it, as well. *Rolling Stone* reporter Ed Ward, for example, remembers well the night of Willie's first Fourth of July Picnic in Dripping Springs. "When the Picnic ended," he wrote, "at about four in the morning, and the 50,000 or so people that were there were jamming the two-lane highway back to Austin, I decided to find a back way out. I took off driving across the ranchland and, finally, miles away, found an alternative highway. But between me and that highway was a locked cattle gate. I was just revving up my Chevy to run the gate, when from out of the ghostly blackness a Mercedes came roaring up beside me. Willie got out, nodded hello, and held up a key. He unlocked the gate, smiled goodbye, and drove off. I don't know how he pulled that one off, but timing has been the key to his career. Right place at the right time."

PHASES AND STAGES came out in 1974, selling even better than SHOTGUN WILLIE, even though the singles didn't get a whole lot of airplay. This time he recorded in Muscle Shoals, Alabama. The second Atlantic album would sell more than 400,000 copies, and the critics were raving now. Baltimore *Evening Sun* music critic John Schulman called it "C&W's Answer To *Sgt. Pepper*." *L.A. Times* critic Robert Hilburn wrote, "PHASES AND STAGES is an important breakthrough. Not only is it a concept album deserving attention, but it, hopefully, will inspire other country artists to use more care and attention in the production of their own albums." George Kanzler Jr., writing in the Newark, New Jersey *Star Ledger*, wrote, "PHASES AND STAGES is one of those rarest of animals, a concept album that *works*. Not just a collection of songs, it's a complete story, told from two points of view about the breakup of a marriage and the resulting aftermath." Kanzler also pointed out that "a couple of songs" from the album "are surfacing on pop radio." Willie had begun to crossover. All of the reviewers praised the production by Jerry Wexler, citing the work of musicians like keyboardist Barry Beckett, guitarist Fred Carter Jr., fiddle/mandolinist Johnny Gimble, and drummer Roger Hawkins in particular.

Writing about the complexity of marital breakdown from both points of view was a departure from Willie's hurtin' songs of the 1960s. Surely, he was familiar with his subject. Robert Hilburn continued to praise the album's insight, writing, "the man's side opens with *Bloody Mary Morning*, a rousing, finely sketched portrait of a musician returning home from the adventures — including romantic — of the road. But he finds no one waiting. Suddenly, the loss sets in. In the album's finest song, one that contains much of the simple eloquence of Hank Williams' best work, Nelson sings: 'This is the very first day since she left me / That I've tried to put my thoughts in a song / And all that I can hear myself singing / Is that I still can't believe that you're gone.'"

It would later come out that *I Still Can't Believe You're Gone* was initially inspired by the tragic suicide of Paul English's wife Carlene English, but within the context of the storyline of PHASES AND STAGES, it worked very well. *Bloody Mary Morning* edged into the Top 20 in May, but stalled at number 17. *After The Fire Is Gone*, Willie's duet with Mother Earth vocalist Tracy Nelson, repeated this pattern later in the year. But, as good as his Atlantic albums SHOTGUN WILLIE and PHASES AND STAGES were, Willie still could not crack the Top 10 with his singles. Willie's gospel album THE TROUBLE MAKER hit the record stores, too, but it was issued on the CBS label because Atlantic's flirtation with country eventually ran into financial difficulties. When Atlantic dropped their 'experimental' country division, Willie found himself without a record label again.

Three months before the July 4th, 1974 Willie Nelson Picnic, the site was moved from the cow pastures of Dripping Springs to the Texas World Speedway, near the small university town of College Station, which Nashville journalist Chet Flippo would refer to as "a virtual sun-baked crater." Plans were massive. A crowd of 100,000 was anticipated, but no more than 25,000 actually showed up at the Speedway. "What they found there," Flippo wrote, "once they paid their $10, was a man-made oven. You could find shade only by standing in your own shadow. People who brought their own liquid refreshment were fortunate, for fresh water was as scarce as shade. The booze concessions were able to double their prices easily." What irked Flippo most, however, was the music. "When such country acts as Johnny Bush and David Allan Coe (and even progressive country groups like Tracy Nelson & Mother Earth, and Kinky Friedman & his Texas Jewboys) get bumped in favor of Rick Nelson, amateur singer David Carradine, and the bubblegum retread music of Spanky & Our Gang, the word 'country' becomes laughable. One reason for the rock emphasis was the presence of a tv crew from *Midnight Special*, the Friday night rock show. Once the tv cameras were rolled out, the audience was forgotten." Flippo had come to his first picnic with preconceptions as to what should not be, which was not the spirit of Willie's picnics. A few years later, a reporter from the *Star-Telegram* recognized this when she wrote, "If you wanted a seamless show, perfect sound, and a pattern of events that followed a set list, what on earth would you be doing at a Willie Nelson 4th of July Picnic? These events are for lovers of the moment, seekers of musical gems that sometimes could never be put on a set list." In 1974 Waylon Jennings fans were delighted that it took three sets for the tv guys to get it right.

Waylon had learned to go with the flow the previous year at Willie's first picnic. "Everything we did at Dripping Springs was wrong," Waylon noted in his autobiography, "and it didn't matter. Nobody paid to get in; the fences were being torn down. I'm singing *Bob Wills Is Still The King* and women are throwing their brassieres on stage. My band just went to pieces." Not long after the 1974 July 4th Picnic, Chet Flippo, now one of the converted, began to champion the 'outlaw' movement. "Helping spread the word," Waylon later wrote in his autobiography, "was Chet Flippo, who wrote reams of you-are-there copy for *Rolling Stone* and other alternative rock journals, a roving reporter inside Hillbilly Central."

Meanwhile, Willie quietly went about setting in place venues that would function year 'round. The first was a pool hall on South Lamar, which became known as 'The Willie Nelson Pool Hall'. Next came the acquisition of the Austin Opera House, a convention center, and an adjoining motel complex. Willie called this the 'Austin Opry House'. To get things started, Willie's old pal Zeke Varnon visited a local bank, parked the Mercedes outside, and went in to secure the loan for the pool hall. Once the bankers learned he was Willie's friend, there was no problem. The pool hall, with a tropical garden patio in back, proved to be a good hang out. Willie's daughter Lana became the bookkeeper. After a while, Ira and Lorraine took over the management of the pool hall, and Lorraine's chicken dumplings, served in the garden, became a favorite with the legions of youthful guitar pickers who showed up in hopes of meeting Willie Nelson. To acquire the Opera House, Willie partnered up with Tim O'Connor, a former club manager who had worked with Willie on several occasions. With only $10,000 cash and a note from Willie, Tim was able to secure a $1.6 million dollar loan. He immediately began renovations, turning a bar into an office and constructing a recording facility. The Austin Opry House soon became the premiere venue in the city.

With his third major label deal slowly going nowhere, Willie formed his own Lone Star Records. The initial inspiration came from some two-track tapes that Ira Nelson had salvaged from the ruins of the Ridgetop fire. Larry Trader had been reviewing them, sometimes re-spooling them because they were twisted and bent from the heat of the fire. More than one trunkful of tapes had survived from the cellar studio, song demos Willie believed he had lost forever, so the story goes. Lone Star began with Trader as president. Some of Willie's Ridgetop recordings were put out on the Lone Star Records label, along with some other Texas artists they discovered. While the events that followed the creation of Lone Star Records took Willie to such immediate heights that he was not forced to put out his own newly-created records on the label, the fact that he'd acted independently, and was poised to do so again, certainly provided food for thought to the major label executives in both New York and Nashville. If RED HEADED STRANGER had been released independently on Lone Star and become the monster hit it became, artists everywhere would be wondering what they needed the big labels for. In 1978, before Lone Star was dissolved, the label released two final LPs, Willie's FACE OF A FIGHTER and SIX PACK VOLUME I, which contain some of the best of the Ridgetop demos. Larry and Willie hadn't been all that savvy about selling records, but they'd had some fun with it.

Larry Trader went on to play an even more essential role when he and

Willie discovered that the Pedernales Golf & Country Club in Spicewood was up for sale. At the Pedernales location in Spicewood, Texas, Willie built his 'cabin', which has grown into a sizeable ranch house. He restored the fairways and greens, which had been long neglected, turned the club house into a state-of-the-art recording studio, repaired the condos, tennis courts, and swimming pool, and, eventually, built 'Luck', his western town movie set on an additional 750 acres across the road from the golf course. With these various projects ongoing, Willie gathered a team of people about him. With very little fanfare, and almost exclusively working within his expanding family, he was building his own small empire.

Willie's third 4th of July Picnic was held at Liberty Hill. Willie told interviewers that this event was designed to point out the difference between the Nashville sound and Austin music. "It's different, because there are different musicians doing it," he told the *Nashville Tennessean's* Lynn Harvey. "The Nashville Sound comes from sessions musicians, and they're outstanding musicians. But down here, we've got performing bands. It's just the difference between studio musicians and performing bands." Going back to the land, after the oven-like environment of the Speedway the previous year, appealed to Willie's audience, and they turned out in droves. "The 65,000 — mostly young people — that flooded the Texas cow pasture," Harvey wrote, "got what they came for. Beginning with Willie and his Family Band at noon, the music didn't stop until 5:00 the next morning. It was a day for Willie to present lesser known acts from his Lone Star Records, and for the crowd to see some big name performers — a 17-hour musical happening for $5.50 a head. After Willie came Floyd Tillman, then Delbert McClinton, Alex Harvey, Billy C [Cowsill], Milton Carroll, Johnny Bush, and surprise guest John Sebastian. All did their own music. Harvey sang *Reuben James* and *Delta Dawn*. Sebastian reached back to the days of the Lovin' Spoonful for *Nashville Cats*."

"Down here," Willie told Lynn Harvey, "everybody's doin' their own thing." Frisbees flew, a hot-air balloon took off, kites hovered, and parachutists dropped in unannounced. Picnic-goers were learning the wisdom of filling their beer coolers with Lone Star longnecks and lugging them onto the site, but the food and beverage concessions did a booming business, too. "As a late afternoon thundershower rolled over and the evening turned into darkness, the talent kept coming," Harvey continued, "Doug Sahm, David Allan Coe, the Pointer Sisters, the Charlie Daniels Band, Rita Coolidge . . . The crowd was up and down. Kristofferson mellowed them. Billy Swan brought them back with *I Can Help*. And finally, Willie Nelson, whose presence held it all together, came back again." No doubt, returning to the cow pasture and the one-day format also helped pull it together. "Nudity," Lynn Harvey noted, "which tends to be conspicuous and over-reported, made its contribution to the festivities — more among men than women. One Texas Department of Public Safety Official said that if people were arrested at the concert for nudity 'every jail between here and Dallas would be filled.'" The one tense moment came during the thundershower, which filled the canvas above the stage, collapsed it, and momentarily shut down the sound system. Lynn Harvey also noted David Allan Coe's impatience as he paced the stage during the interruption, waiting for power to be restored so he could go on. Coe, a firm believer in the outlaw identity, would soon become a more imposing menace to the clear-sailing of the progressive country movement.

While Willie didn't really identify with the 'outlaw' media hype, David Allan Coe not only claimed he'd created it, he sometimes slagged Waylon and Willie in his interviews. "Them radio people don't want real outlaws," Coe told Alanna Nash, "just somebody that looks like one." Coe, who'd first marketed himself as "the Mysterious Rhinestone Cowboy," long before Glen Campbell hit with the Larry Weiss song *Rhinestone Cowboy*, claimed that he was solely responsible for the 'outlaw' naming. "I think people are gonna find out in the '80s," he told Nash, "that the reason the term 'outlaw' music came about was because David Allan Coe was a member of the Outlaws Motorcycle Club, and he got up onstage at a Waylon Jennings concert with his Outlaws colors on, and his picture was taken by a photographer and was in every newspaper in the country. And that's how it started. David Allan Coe was the first person to ever use a phase shifter in country music. I was the first country & western person to be into theatrics and wear makeup and wigs onstage. I was the first entertainer to have semi-trucks to carry my own P.A. instead of just singin' on whatever they had in the house. I was the first one that cared enough about music to have my own lights at no matter what the cost. I was . . ."

Despite the ranting, Coe's stories of Nashville in the 1970s provide colorful snapshots of an era. "When I went to Nashville," he told Alanna Nash, "I had long hair. I was wearin' earrings. I had a beard — I was everything that they were against! And I could sing better than any one of 'em. And they resented me no end. And they did everything they could to keep people from hearin' me. A lot of other younger kids started comin' to Nashville — the Country Cavaliers, for example. They had hair down to their waists, you know? They never made it. Only a few filtered through. There's a few, like Kris Kristofferson, Mickey Newbury, but the majority of 'em fell by the way, man. And when I saw this last Country Music Awards show, and all them people were wearin' Levi's and cowboy hats, and dancin' like they do at Mickey Gilley's place, that just blew me away. Because three years ago, they would not let us wear our Levi's into the Country Music Awards."

At the 1975 Awards, Willie simply showed up in his t-shirt, jeans, and sneakers. Willie knew Nashville needed him more than he needed Nashville, so he had little to lose if by some unlikely circumstance they tossed him out into the Opryland parking lot. No one raised any fuss, and Willie played on into the night at Ernest Tubb's Record Store and other party sites.

The outlaw attitude and appearance soon had a bandwagon effect, as Coe describes. "And like everything that we stand for — Willie Nelson and David Allan Coe and Waylon Jennings," he told Alanna Nash, expropriating Willie and Waylon's friendship, "everything that we have built up to this point, them people have now taken it and said, 'This is ours.' Lynn Anderson is an 'outlaw' now. She's got an album out called OUTLAW IS JUST A STATE OF MIND. I mean, it's amazing to me, you know? I'm reading stories where it says Loretta Lynn was the first outlaw country singer because she sang a song about a pill. It's like whatever's fashionable at the time."

In 1943, Howard Hughes had advanced Hollywood westerns several forward-looking steps when he made *The Outlaw* starring Walter Huston as Doc Holliday and Jane Russell as the girlfriend of an outlaw who had become a nemesis to newly appointed sheriff Pat Garrett, a scenario that would later be reworked in Sam Peckinpah's *Pat Garrett and Billy The Kid*. Hughes' production was described as a "notorious western that tells the tale of Billy the Kid and the sexy dame who loves him." With a woman cast in a role that allowed her to do more than say "he went that-a-way" and flaunting her sexuality, the shoot-'em- up genre which glorified the outlaw became both believable and profitable. Just who made the first outlaw country record will probably remain clouded by the claims of conflicting personalities. In 1967, Bob Dylan had recorded JOHN WESLEY HARDING at Columbia's Nashville studios, a folk-rock album about a Texas outlaw from Hardin County. Dylan and Johnny Cash had teamed up for *Girl From The North Country* on Dylan's 1968 album NASHVILLE SKYLINE, which was far more country, even though it didn't springboard Bob Dylan onto country charts. He had also recorded the sound track for Peckinpah's 1973 film, often only using his acoustic guitar as the single instrument in the mix, which was both radical and innovative.

The Man in Black wrote and recorded *Folsom Prison Blues* in 1956 for Sun Records. In 1959, he hit the number one spot on the country charts with *Don't Take Your Guns To Town* on the Columbia label. Marty Robbins had huge hits that year with *El Paso* and *Big Iron* from his GUNFIGHTER BALLADS album. In the early '60s, Cash covered Jimmie Rodger's 1928 record, *In The Jailhouse Now*, and followed that up with *Busted*. Merle Haggard first heard Cash at one of his prison concerts while he was an inmate in San Quentin. Although always discreet about his two-and-a-half years of hard time, Haggard's first number one radio hit would be *I'm A Lonesome Fugitive*. He followed that up with *Branded Man* and *Mama Tried*, equally compelling tales of pathos and woe. Country songs about outlaws were old hat, really, and Waylon is quick to point out that their sense of 'outlaw' meant "standing up for your rights, your own way of doing things." In his autobiography, he wrote, "Bob Dylan sang 'To live outside the law you must be honest' in *Absolutely Sweet Marie*; the Shangri-Las liked their *Leader Of The Pack* 'good-bad, but not evil.' It's a common theme, dating back to Robin Hood and forward to Jesse James to Thelma and Louise. Most lawbreakers are common criminals. Bonnie and Clyde were nothing but a couple of idiots. So was Billy the Kid; you can look and see that he wasn't all there. They got attention by killing people."

Jennings could have been talking about outlaw wannabees Johnny Paycheck and David Alan Coe. Paycheck's sordid history of assault charges, B&Es, and passing rubber checks eventually led to the shooting of a man in a bar in Ohio in December 1976. For a few years, Coe, who once had a poster printed of his band with their bare butts mooning the Nashville establishment, boasted to reporters that he'd killed a man while in jail during the early 1960s. The Mysterious Rhinestone Cowboy was eventually confronted by a reporter from *Rolling Stone* who exposed this allegation as a much embellished jailhouse yarn with considerable appeal for homophobes because the justification for this 'murder' was said to be a reaction to an attempted jailhouse rape. "David Allan Coe is as good a songwriter as any of us," Willie told one reporter, "but he goes to extremes. He calls a lot of attention to himself at any cost. David Allan Coe reminds me of a white Muhammad Ali. Everything's carnival, circus ballyhoo, the old street hustle." Waylon, who had befriended Coe when the ex-con had first come to Nashville, commented, "he wrote a song called *Waylon, Willie and Me* at the same time he started taking potshots at us in interviews, saying that Willie and Kris have sold out, that I was running around wearing white buck shoes, and none of us was really an outlaw. I saw him in Fort Worth and I put my finger right up to his chest. 'You gotta knock that shit off,' I told him. 'I ain't never done anything to you.' 'They set us up,' he protested. 'You know I love you,

Waylon.' He showed me his bus. He'd painted it black: the grill, the bumpers, mirrors, everything. Just like my own Black Maria, with the ghost of Hank Williams inside. I couldn't stay mad at him for long." In 1997, David Allan Coe would still be welcome at Willie's July 4th Picnics, bringing the crowd to a hush with his strong, sparse rendition of *Please Come To Boston.*

Kinky Friedman, although as weird and wonderful as David Alan Coe, was cut from a different cloth, yet often rode the range with all of these outlaws during the 1970s, including an 11-month stint touring with Bob Dylan's Rolling Thunder Review. Born Richard Friedman in Rio Duckworth, Texas, in 1944, he studied psychology at the University of Texas in Austin before enlisting in the Peace Corp, where he found a vocation teaching the art of frisbee tossing to third-worlders as far away from Austin as Borneo. Returning to the U.S. just in time to get in on the beginning of the progressive country action, he formed Kinky Friedman & the Texas Jewboys, signing with Vanguard Records in Los Angeles where he was sometimes billed as the Frank Zappa of country rock. Friedman's earthy humor kept him from getting much air play on Top 40 country radio or gaining a substantial audience with the mainstream country audience, especially when he began releasing his satiric masterpieces *Asshole From El Paso, Ride Em Jewboy, High On Jesus,* and *Get Your Biscuits In The Oven And Your Buns In Bed.* No doubt, appreciation for his records and his stage shows was an acquired taste, and his most loyal fans were his fellow entertainers like Kris Kristofferson, Waylon Jennings (who produced one of Friedman's records), Ringo Starr (who recorded with Friedman), Bob Dylan (who helped Friedman by allowing him to release tracks recorded live off the floor of the Rolling Thunder stages), and Willie Nelson.

Kinky appealed to the earthier side of Willie, who speaks quite politely while taping interviews with journalists, but is known to be succinct to the point of bluntness when speaking off the record or in his autobiography, and hilariously funny and every bit as earthy as Kinky Friedman when among personal friends or ad libbing a line in a scene with a Hollywood actor like Robert Redford. Needless to say, these two men get along just fine when they find themselves in each other's company, and Kinky has become a regular at Willie Nelson's outdoor events. In 1978, Willie produced Kinky's record *They Ain't Makin' Jews Like Jesus Anymore*, and for many years, the two men have enjoyed a long-standing joke that they plan to record Ned Sublett's *Cowboys Are Frequently Secretly Fond Of Each Other* as a duet someday. Kinky and Willie seem to be the only people on this earth who have a "demo" of Ned Sublett, whoever he may be.

Willie Nelson at Woodstock '99, Rome, New York

LATE
SHOW

In the late 1980s, Kinky Friedman moved to New York City where he entertained at the Lone Star Cafe and began to issue a steady stream of mystery novels featuring a Jewish detective who is a failed country & western singer named Kinky Friedman, books with equally kinky titles like *The Love Song of J. Edgar Hoover*, *Armadillos & Old Lace*, *Greenwich Killing Time*, and *Elvis, Jesus & Coca Cola.* A compilation CD of the best of Kinky Friedman has sold more than 100,000 copies during the past decade, but Friedman, who has also contributed articles on country music to *Rolling Stone*, claims that he now considers himself to be an ex-country singer who is content having "finally found a vocation that doesn't require my presence." Not content with not entertaining for long, he has recently returned to performing in a duo known as Kinkajoo.

Kris Kristofferson is regularly included in all of the accounts of the outlaw revolution in country music, although he soon became sidetracked by his many feature film roles and a penchant for living on the wild side of life, but returned to the fold as a member of the Highwaymen in the mid-1980s. No doubt, his intelligent presence in Nashville during the late 1960s and early 1970s nudged the country music revolt along, as did his top-notch songwriting.

Willie saw beyond the outlaw controversy to a further truth. "The fascination with Texas," he told Ed Ward, "lies in freedom. Wide open spaces. The cowboy image, which is another form of freedom . . . it's very enticing to people living in places like New York City, Chicago or Los Angeles. I was taught since birth, that if you were from Texas, you could do anything you wanted to do because of opportunities. I'd heard those 'bigger and better' Texas brags all my life. I was reluctant to go out in the world and say those things myself because I'd heard 'em so much and I was sick of 'em. But the more places you go and have to compare to Texas, you realize those things ain't bragging statements. They're true."

When it was released in the fall of 1975, RED HEADED STRANGER was heralded as Willie's third concept album and his first masterpiece. He had been inspired to believe he was creating a film, rather than merely another concept album. He first got the inspiration for the album when he and Connie headed to Steamboat Springs, Colorado to do a little skiing, and get a little rest and relaxation from the scene that was beginning to swirl around him nearly 24-hours-a-day in Austin. Swirl so much that he'd been forced to build a high electric fence around the ranch on Fitzburgh Road just to keep out the weirdos and devotees who believed he could heal their ailments and disabilities, just by a laying on of hands. In his Mercedes, on the return trip to

Texas, Connie had a note pad in her lap, and was working on a list of songs with Willie that he might record for his next album. She mentioned a song that Willie was always singing to Paula Carlene and Amy before bedtime, the cowboy ballad *Red Headed Stranger*. "All of a sudden," Connie later told interviewers, "it was like a light came on in Willie, and we started talking right away about it being a concept album. Willie started mentioning other old songs he knew, like *Blue Eyes Crying In The Rain*, and he started outlining an album, noting where he could write a song to fill in the story."

"I used to be a disc jockey in Fort Worth when I first started out," Willie explains in the authorized video biography *Willie Nelson: My Life*. "Everyday at one o'clock I'd have a kiddie's show, and I'd play kids songs, Tex Ritter or whatever the hot kids songs of the day were. And I'd suggest to the mothers that they let their kids listen to this before they put their kids down for a nap. And the *Red Headed Stranger* had just come out by Arthur "Guitar Boogie" Smith. I thought it was a great song, so I played it every day at noon for the kids on the show, and I sang it at night for my kids. And they grew up listening to the *Red Headed Stranger*." The song, written by songwriter Carl Stutz and amateur poet Edith Lindeman, Bill DeYoung notes, "told the tale of a brooding rider who held a dark secret, riding from town to Western town, silently leading his dead lover's horse behind his own 'raging black stallion', and staring straight through anyone who approached him." Willie adapted the song to meet his own needs. "In his version," DeYoung continues, "the stranger was an idealistic young preacher who'd murdered his cheating spouse in a jealous rage and then went riding in search of redemption, haunted by the memories and deadened by the sin he's perpetrated. He added thematic links, he added Fred Rose's old *Blue Eyes Crying In The Rain*, as the rider thinks back on his deepest love. Eddy Arnold's *I Couldn't Believe* went into the narrative, and the old gospel standard *Just As I Am*."

Now the red-headed stranger
From Blue Rock, Montana
Rode into town one day
And under his knees was a raging black stallion
And walkin' behind was a bay
And the red-headed stranger had eyes like the thunder
And lips that were sad and tight
And his little lost love lay asleep on the hillside
And his heart was heavy as night . . .

So don't cross him, and don't boss him
'Cause he's wild in his sorrow
And he's right and he's hidin' his pain
Don't fight him, and don't spite him
Just wait 'til tomorrow
Maybe he'll ride on again

— *Red Headed Stranger* (C. Stutz and E. Lindeman)

"For the first time, Willie took on the production," notes *Waylon & Willie* author Bob Allen, "and the results are nothing short of magic. The album is built around an involved storyline of loss of love, adultery, murder, and, finally, redemption. It is like a Greek morality play acted out against the metaphors of the old West and the music of Texas." As Michael Bane, author of *The Outlaws Revolution in Country Music*, commented, "it was Willie's first attempt to combine his own and other writer's material into a cohesive story. Using some of his own songs, some old and new material from other writers, and some newly-written musical fillers, he created both a modern cowboy movie and a classical morality play set in the Old West so real that you could almost taste the trail dust and the whiskey."

Tom Carter, writing in the *Tulsa Daily Herald*, noted, "a favorite is the Hank Cochran composition *Can I Sleep In Your Arms*. The tune, written to the melody of Red River Valley, was a memorable hit for Cochran's wife Jeannie Sealey. Nelson's rendition, however, is much prettier. He has a feel for the song that comes across on the mellow, close harmony during the chorus. Another highlight is *Just As I Am*, the old hymm sung weekly from Fundamentalist churches to Billy Graham crusades. Performed by Bobbie Nelson, the rendition accounts for a thick sound played without gimmickry or hint of Floyd Cramer, a trait almost unheard of on a contemporary country keyboard."

While reviewers marveled at his mastery in adapting songs like Hank Cochran's *Can I Sleep In Your Arms* into the storyline, Willie was nonchalant about his efforts. "It didn't take any time at all," he told Bill DeYoung. "It all sort of fell together as they do, in a scary way, when you got something going for you at all, you just start writing. To put in *Blue Eyes Crying In The Rain* at that point, I didn't think about it for a month. It was there. It had to go there." Recording the album at Autumn Sound in Garland, Texas was simple, clean, and efficient. Just Willie and his Family Band — Willie on guitar, Bobbie Nelson on piano, Jody Payne on electric guitar, Mickey

Raphael on harmonica, Bee Spears on bass, and Rex Ludwick and Paul English on drums. Phil York was the engineer. They recorded the first day, overdubbed and fixed blown lines the second day, and mixed on the third day. Total cost $12,000.

The danger of such efficiency, Willie has pointed out, is that "if they [the label executives] see you only spent $20,000 on an album, you probably get dumped. They'll put out your record, but they won't promote it." The illogic of this is explained by the way record company executives produce $200,000 albums so they are motivated to spend even more money on the album just so they won't 'lose' money. There's not much motivation to sell a $20,000 album. Wisely, Willie also recorded most of the material that would become THE SOUND IN YOUR MIND, his second CBS album, during the week spent at Garland, bringing the overall cost up to $20,000. Harmonies on the Garland sessions were done by a handful of friends, the Geezinslaw Brothers, C.J., David Allan Coe, and Jody Payne. Tom Morrell dropped in to lay down a couple of pedal steel overdubs. The simplicity of both of these albums would appeal to record buyers, once Willie got them past the corporate red tape.

When the CBS executives in New York heard the masters for RED HEADED STRANGER, Willie faced the same resistance he and Waylon had always faced at RCA. "They thought they were demos," he has recalled. Waylon was present in Bruce Lundvall's New York office, along with Neil Reshen, when the master tape was wound onto the reel-to-reel machine. After listening briefly, Lundvall wanted to send them down to Billy Sherrill in Nashville to have them "sweetened with strings." They convinced Lundvall to go with what Willie had done. Billy Sherrill was opposed to releasing the album — indeed, opposed from the start to signing Willie to the label — but Rick Blackburn, the newly appointed vice president of CBS Records Nashville, was willing to go with what Willie had delivered. "We got that for $12,000," he recalls in the authorized video biography. "Willie wanted it put out, as is, and off RED HEADED STRANGER came a song called *Blue Eyes Cryin' In The Rain*. That's the song that launched his career."

Willie's delivery of Fred Rose's 1940s song seemed to be the perfect antidote for everyone's blues in the '70s, Willie's first number one record on the charts. While Willie had not yet become a country superstar, still playing to small audiences, his peers recognized that something special was going on. "I saw Willie at the Troubadour in 1975 just after RED HEADED STRANGER had come out," Emmylou Harris recalls. "There was this amazing undercurrent that was rolling across the country just after that album came out, but he was still playing relatively small clubs, which is what the Troubadour was. You could just see the love . . . he was bringing something so good out of the people, all the girls in front of the stage, and people reaching out for him." "It was just Willie and the guitar," Kris Kristofferson marvels. "That was it. That broke down so many barriers in one record. Classical simplicity. And it still tears me up." "It's the song, but it's more Willie's performance of the song," Emmylou emphasizes, "that takes it to what I feel is sort of a spiritual realm. Sometimes you can take a secular song, and a secular subject, and just take it somewhere else. It think Willie has the ability to do that, too."

Willie's theory is that Columbia put it out knowing that if it stiffed, they had him by the short-hairs on a four-year contract. It didn't, and for a while he encountered less resistance. Still, it was never easy dealing with people who always felt they knew better than what he or Waylon had done in the studio. People who maybe had a college degree in management or marketing but did not know squat when it came to music, couldn't even tune a guitar let alone play one, would tell them they should add stuff or lose stuff. In 1995, Willie told Michael Hall, "in order to do things the way you want to do 'em, you've still got to fight everybody from the top to the bottom, or from the bottom to the top. And that's never going to change. The guy who's puttin' up the money is going to want it his way."

As a result of the RCA concept album WANTED: THE OUTLAWS, Willie, who had waited 13 years to re-enter the Top 10, would find that *Remember Me*, his Columbia Records follow-up to *Blue Eyes Crying In The Rain*, was competing with RCA's Waylon & Willie duet *Good Hearted Woman*. In March 1976, *Good Hearted Woman* hit the number one spot, while *Remember Me* made it to number 2. That summer, Waylon and Jessi hit number 2 again with *Suspicious Minds*. In September, Willie would score another number one with Lefty Frizzell's *If You've Got The Money I've Got The Time* from THE SOUND IN YOUR MIND, the second album he had recorded at the jingle studio in Garland. *New York Times* critic John Rockwell would dismiss this release, writing, "it doesn't seem to be one of Nelson's more distinctive efforts, for all its passing charms," but *Billboard* would name it their country album of the year. When the nominations for the 1976 Country Music Association awards were announced, Waylon and Willie were up for several awards, including CMA album of the year for WANTED: THE OUTLAWS. They would win three awards for Vocal Duo of the Year, Single of the Year, and Album of the Year. "Call them outlaws, call them innovators, call them revolutionaries," Chet Flippo wrote in the album's liner notes, "call them what you will. They're just some damn fine people who are also some of the most gifted songwriters and singers anywhere."

Willie Nelson was quickly transcending the 'outlaw' label and becoming an "institution" in his own right, as a writer for *Country Style* magazine reported in September 1975. "In the good old days before he became an institution, Willie Nelson used to play down-at-the-heels honky tonks where the management strung chicken wire in front of the stage to protect the performers from flying beer bottles. Willie has gotten big since then, and it's been a long time since anyone threw a beer bottle at him, at least while he's performing . . . . Not long ago, he was playing a concert before a wildly approving audience in Wichita Falls, Texas, and a young lady threw her bra onstage. Willie didn't even notice . . . . At one point it seemed the audience might storm the stage and hug Willie to death, but Willie just kept singing and playing the guitar." After the Wichita Falls show, this *Country Style* reporter asked Paul English if all the crowds were like that. "I'm afraid so," English replied with a sly grin.

The article went on to describe Willie Nelson's many brushes with death, with Paul English playing devil's advocate and providing the color commentary. There was, of course, the oft-told-tale of the time Willie's old bus had careened out of control down a long freeway grade. "It was a run-down 1946 model bus," Paul told *Country Style*, "and the drive shaft broke, and caused the brake lines to go out. Suddenly, we were barreling down the freeway at 75 mph. Imagine that, in a 17,000 lb bus. Willie and some of the rest of us were at the back of the bus playing poker. Somebody ran to the back of the bus and said, The brakes are out, what should we do?' And Willie said, 'Deal the cards!'" This calm acceptance of circumstances proved fortuitous because the driver successfully stopped the bus by running it into the curbs, and they continued on their way as hitchhikers, making it to their show on time. Then there was a gun battle that he'd walked away from, when one of Susie's husbands initiated a drive-by shooting, firing several rounds of .22 calibre bullets into Willie's house, then came back for more, but was met by irate father, Willie, who brandished some heavy artillery himself, weaponry which eventually defused the situation, but not before quite a few shots had been fired, some of which seemed to have hit the car and punctured the young man's tires. Police were called, but Willie made light of the event to the investigating officer, suggesting those tires seemed to have picked up some lead . . .

And there was the oft-told tale of the time Willie and friends were en route to a show and dropped into Happy Shahan's 'Alamo City' ranch in Bracketville, Texas, where John Wayne had filmed *The Alamo*, just to say hello. Disaster struck as their light plane came in for a landing. Shahan, always eager to generate a little publicity, radioed the press that Willie Nelson's plane had gone down, but before the cameras arrived, Willie had walked away from the wreckage. He was found drinking a beer. "Dean Martin had once landed a jet there," Paul English explained in *Country Style*, "and we didn't think we would have any trouble landing. But when our plane hit the road, the right wheel broke off. It dropped the wing and spun us around. The plane nosed over and the tail came up over. 'Put your hands on the roof and brace yourselves,' Willie shouted. We had our hands up, the plane was demolished, but we crawled out. It didn't hurt anybody at all." "Nothing scares me," Willie told *Country Style*, "I haven't been scared in a long time."

As time kept on slipping away, it was said that Willie could perform miracles. Per usual, Willie sought a middle ground when questioned on these subjects. "The people who have me depicted as the guy who can do no wrong," he told Marina Nickerson, "I know better than that. And the ones who say I'm the most terrible guy in the country . . . I know better than that, too. I lie somewhere in between." As early as 1968, people like Tom T. Hall had alluded to the possibility that Willie Nelson might have some heavy-weight reincarnations in his past. Freelance interviewer Bill Littleton had mentioned to Hall that some people were saying that if William Shakespeare were alive today, he'd be writing for television, but that Littleton himself believed the Bard would be writing country songs. "Well," said Tom T., there are a lot of people, and I'm one of them, who think Shakespeare is alive today, only we know him as Willie Nelson." Ray Bachar, writing in *Country Style*, saw Willie as "the Pied Piper of country music's progressive branch," a "non-conformist who seemed to glory in his role as a maverick" who "nonetheless earned the grudging admiration of the establishment . . . . Even those whose toes he had stepped on admitted he was a genius."

In 1978, Willie hired Mark Rothbaum to take over his management and Jim Wiatt to act as an agent to advance his cause in Holloywood. Rothbaum was a former record label employee looking for a break. Wiatt was equally inexperienced but thought he might be able to interest a film company in a script that had been developed for RED HEADED STRANGER. At first, the film people were more interested in hiring Willie Nelson to play music than they were in talking to him about making films. So Wiatt set up a show for a private party some HBO executives were hosting, for a modest fee of $70,000, but couldn't believe his ears when Paul and Willie insisted they be paid in cash before stepping on stage. This was HBO . . . Time Life, what chance was there that the check he held in his hand was going to bounce? Guns had become a necessary collection tool, especially when Willie began hauling in $20,000 per night. Highway robbery was not just the title of a country song, Waylon had learned, when he'd lost a truckload of equipment to hijackers. As Susie Nelson notes, "getting paid wasn't always the easiest thing to do, considering some of the clubs where they played. Upon occasion, Paul (English) or Johnny (Bush), even Dad sometimes, had to use a little of Colonel Colt's contract enforcement technique to collect their fee. Of course, that's just part of the traditional way of doing things in some Texas circles."

Lists compiled of the top acts in the country music business had now begun listing Willie at the top of the pay scale along with Dolly Parton. They were both said to warrant fees of at least $50,000 per night. Willie had come a long, long way up the food chain from the days when he first hit Nashville and celebrated upon receiving his first $50 per week advance from Pamper Music. Where fame and fortune had gone to some country boys' heads, and their wardrobes had gone from Levi's to rhinestone studded costumes, Willie seemed headed in t'other direction, wearing t-shirts, jeans and sneakers, and turning to the people who had helped him get to the top rather than turning his back on them, recording tribute albums to his heroes, and, eventually, recording albums *with* some of these artists. His first move in this direction was to record an entire album of Lefty Frizzell's material, which he followed with a tribute to Kris Kristofferson. Both LPs would yield Top Ten hits.

The release of Willie's tribute album to Lefty Frizzell was delayed by Lefty's untimely death in 1975, and released in 1977. By the time that the duet album WAYLON & WILLIE was released, some of the critics who had once championed these outlaws as underdogs, now saw them as superstars to be put down for cashing in on their outlaw image, but key critics like Robert Hilburn identified the duet album as a blockbuster with plenty of crossover potential. "Country music is filled with excellent singers and songwriters, but inconsistent record makers," Hilburn wrote in the January 24, 1978 edition of the *Los Angeles Times*. "There's so much fan loyalty in the field that record companies have found you can just surround hit singles with equally designed filler. But Waylon Jennings and Willie Nelson have come up with an exception. Titled simply WAYLON & WILLIE, the RCA album is a gloriously consistent exercise that finds two of country's premier talents working with a stand-out batch of tunes. The arrangements are a touch plain, but there is a rousing evocative edge to the LP that makes it one of the best country albums of the 1970s. The song *Mammas Don't Let Your Babies Grow Up To Be Cowboys* is a classic, celebrative work in the freedom-searching, independent modern country stance first popularized through such early Kris Kristofferson tunes as *Me and Bobby McGee* and *Sunday Morning Coming Down*." Hilburn revealed that RCA exec Jerry Bradley had, once again, instigated the album when he instructed the RCA art department to design the album cover long before he'd even mentioned it to his artist. "I put it on a credenza behind my desk," Bradley told Hilburn. "When Waylon came into the office last August to talk about some new projects, I showed it to him and he liked the idea."

Some critics began to complain that Willie Nelson was no longer releasing entire albums of originals, but Willie often pointed out that he had written so many songs in those early years because of personal turmoil, "an awful thirty years of negativity" and a couple of mismatched marriages. Those times were past. "I don't write as much as I used to," he told one reporter. "I think it has a lot to do with hunger. When you are hungry, you write a lot more. Once you get a song written, there's always a good feeling about it, but from the beginning to the end, songwriting is not that much fun. It's really a lot of work. It's something you have to make yourself do, and, really, I think having a little success is dangerous to a songwriter — because he gets to thinking that, well, he doesn't need to work. The bills are paid this month, so he doesn't write. Hungry songwriters are the best ones, I think." When pressed on this issue by a writer from the *Milwaukee Journal*, who wanted to know if all of this meant that Willie was writing fewer songs, Willie wondered if putting so many of his top notch songs on each album in the past had been the smartest thing to do. "I've put out 33 of my albums. At an average of 10 to 12 an album that eats up material pretty fast. I still have some new material of my own that I want to put out, but I'll never again, I don't think, put 12 good songs of my own on one album. I think it was a horrible mistake that I made because now there are 300 of my songs back there that didn't sell nuthin'. I should have put one of my songs and nine of somebody else's."

Despite these complaints, Willie's reputation as a songwriter was still on the rise. "The songs he writes appeal to all kinds of stars — Elvis Presley and Aretha Franklin, Lawrence Welk and Ray Charles, Frank Sinatra and Dolly Parton — at last his own voice is finding its audience," Al Reinert in the *San Francisco Chronicle* noted. "Last year, Nelson sold more records nationally than Bob Dylan or three out of four former Beatles. In the past two years, Nelson has won a whole hat-full of awards, including a Grammy for *Blue Eyes Crying In The Rain*, joined Waylon Jennings on what may have been the biggest grossing tour in country music history, appeared on NBC's *Saturday Night Live*, and filled the Santa Monica Civic Auditorium with exactly the same show he's been doing for a decade at the Palamino Club in Los Angeles and truck stops all over the South. Nelson's newest album WAYLON & WILLIE went gold, made one million in retail sales in just a couple of months, and he currently has three songs on the national country charts, including the number one *Mammas Don't Let Your Babies Grow Up To Be Cowboys*, and *Georgia On My Mind* from the forthcoming STARDUST album. After 30 odd years struggling on the road, Willie Nelson has suddenly become the most popular singer in the United States."

It was a remarkable turn of events from the early 1970s when Willie and family had left Nashville because his house had burned to the ground; Willie had been fully prepared to accept that he was going back to Texas to retire from the record business. But after 10 years of struggle and strife in Nashville, life had just gotten better every day they spent in Texas. The music scene in Austin had seemed to bloom around them. New opportunities had kept popping up, and Willie kept seizing the day. Willie seemed to have friends just about everywhere, including Don Meredith, the ex-football star and broadcaster on ABC's *Monday Night Football.* The show, Susie Nelson notes in *Heartworn Memories*, was giving wives across the nation one more reason to hate the NFL. But Don Meredith was captivating the football audiences with his Texas twang, and he developed the habit of singing '*Turn Out The Lights*' whenever the winner of the game was apparent. He'd finish by saying, What's the matter? Don't you know about Willie Nelson?'" "Turn out the lights, the party's over," for those who did not know, is the opening line of *The Party's Over*, Willie's set-closer, a song written before he moved to Nashville.

In 1976, Willie had another fan in an influential position when newly elected President Jimmy Carter sat down behind the desk in the oval office to assume his official duties. And on September 13, 1978, Willie made his White House debut, performing for a gala reception held for 500 members of NASCAR, the National Association of Stock Car Racers. A few days before the engagement, Charlie Williams, head of Willie's Nashville publishing office, fielded calls from curious reporters. "When I asked Willie what he'd be wearing," Williams routinely quipped, "he said he hadn't picked out which t-shirt he would be wearing, but he had decided on a headband." When Willie hosted his own charity marathon, his long-distance running exploits became front-page news. It was said that President Carter selected his athletic footwear according to advice he received from Willie Nelson. *People* magazine reported that, according to the image makers, that's Bach and Beethoven being piped into Jimmy Carter's study as he labors over affairs of state, but just as frequently he's tuned in to Willie Nelson."

Willie had helped the Carters out during the election, staging several benefits. The Presidential couple were just returning the favor. "Willie Nelson is a favorite performer of both the President and Mrs. Carter," White House spokeswoman Claudia Townsend told the media. "When he appeared at the Meriweather Post Pavilion near Washington six weeks ago, they both left Camp David to attend his performance and enjoyed it very much." President Carter, arriving by helicopter at the Howard University campus en route to the show at the Meriweather Post Pavilion, had been greeted by a small gathering of school children and had told them he'd come to hear Willie Nelson and Emmylou Harris. When Jimmy and Rosalynn entered the venue the concert was already in progress, but the 12,000-strong audience gave them a warm round of applause. "Willie wailed *Georgia On My Mind*," *People* magazine noted, "which brought the toe-tapping Prez onstage. ABC reporter Ann Compton in an aside to the *People* magazine correspondent commented, 'Jimmy and Rosalynn behaved like two teenagers on a Friday night date, whispering and holding hands.'" In 1980, Willie would sing the national Anthem at the Democratic Party National Convention, but even this Willie endorsement could not save the "Peace President" from going down to defeat in the November election.

Willie had learned that things often worked out better if he could not be found during the days leading up to the picnics, a plan that worked equally well in the days afterwards. He sometimes hung out in Hawaii while the smoke settled and the damages were assessed. Sometimes it took years for things to sort themselves out. While the Texas State Senate had blessed Willie's Fourth of July picnic in 1975, complaints were filed against the promoters in 1976. The 1976 'bicentennial' picnic, billed as "the nation's largest annual music event," was dogged by poor weather, seven stabbings, two rapes, and mounting losses. Willie did not plan a picnic for 1977. "A lot of people were relieved to hear we weren't going to have picnic this year," Willie remarked.

In 1978, a July 3rd, 4th, and 5th engagement at the Texas Opry House saw Willie testing the waters once again, and in 1979 at the newly-acquired Pedernales Country Club, Willie revived the picnic. "I've always wanted a golf course where I could decide what the pars would be," Willie told James Albrecht from *Country Style* magazine. With an estimated crowd of some 20,000 on hand, the event was smaller than in past years. "I think the lawsuit hurt us," Willie confided, "people didn't know whether it was really off or on until a few days before the show." Per usual, a thousand or so members of

Willie's extended family, friends, and guests were on hand and made good use of the backstage area, featuring a restaurant, tennis courts, and swimming pool, which provided some relief from the sweltering 90-degree heat. There was no such relief for the fans seated on the neglected fairways and greens of the nine-hole golf course.

Albrecht noted a heated discussion between an older woman and an ardent young Willie devotee. "'It just don't make sense to me,' argued the woman. 'Why would anyone buy a golf course and then park cars all over it? I just don't understand it.' The young disciple laughed into his draft. 'Whaddaya think?' he yelled, jumping to his idol's defence. 'You think Willie's just gonna leave this place a mess? Naw, Willie'll fix it up. He ain't gonna throw a picnic then let the place go to hell. Not Willie. Willie ain't like that,' he shouted, his voice now rising above the chatter of the other Nelsonites. 'I mean, I sleep, eat and breathe Willie Nelson. Willie's just, uh, just . . . I love the guy. He's . . . Whoa!' he stopped himself, noticing his praises creating something of a spectacle. 'I better watch it,' he laughed, downing the last of his brew. That's after midnight talk.'"

"As soon as the picnic is over," public relations man and manager of the Cooder-Brown band, Buster Doss, told *Music City News* reporter Lee Rector, "clean-up will begin and Willie is going to put the golf course back into condition." The buzz was that he had already spent $250,000 just getting the facility ready for the July 4th weekend. "Now," Willie told Rector, "we have a permanent site for the event."

After opening the show at noon beginning with his trademark *Whiskey River*, Willie sought shade beneath an old oak tree, spent several hours signing autographs, took a dip in the Olympic-size swimming pool, and then at dusk introduced Ernest Tubb, the Texas Troubadour. Tubb's set drew a 15-minute standing ovation. Willie closed the show, which went on well past midnight. "I didn't hear of no stabbings," Buster Doss told Albrecht, during the after midnight talk, "in fact, this might have been the closest thing to what Willie wanted to do when he started having picnics way back — just a good gathering for fans and friends and a chance to expose good talent." The *Austin American-Statesman* reported that "Travis County Commissioners had billed Willie Nelson for about $3400 in country expenses incurred" during the July 4th event, which seems entirely reasonable for the policing costs, overtime for county jail employees, the Pedernales Volunteer Fire Department, and clean-up crews. A far more civil response than Willie had received in past years, and the monies were deducted from the $5,000 bond he had posted.

The next day, July 5th, Willie Nelson arrived at Ceasar's Palace in Las Vegas in time to don his blue jogging pants and get in his daily 5-mile run before taking the stage in Circus Maximus. "Las Vegas, like Texas, was Willie Nelson's," Lee Rector noted in *Music City News*. "Billboards, advertisements on taxi cabs, sported Willie Nelson's face and promoted his week at Ceasar's Palace. His Vegas show opened at 9:00. Don Bowman (who had also been at the picnic) came out with 10 minutes of comedy . . . And then, unpretentiously and without fanfare Willie and Family ambled on stage, right and raw, just as they were the day before in Texas. As the opening strains of 'Whiskey River take my mind, don't let her memory torture me . . .' echoed out into one of Las Vegas' biggest show rooms, a grand Texas flag unfurled behind Willie Nelson and band. 'Someone told me this is Ceasar's Palace,' Willie announced to a house full of his friends during a short break between medleys, 'I can't believe it myself!'"

AUSTIN CITY LIMITS

By 1979, when he appeared in his first Hollywood film, Willie Nelson had become known to the world at large as an American hero. His image was as familiar as the pope, heavyweight boxing champion Muhummad Ali, Reggie Jackson, Clint Eastwood, Paul Newman, the Fonz, Archie Bunker, and most of the world's political leaders, including Margaret Thatcher, and if he'd decided to run for public office or become the dictator of the western world, there would likely have been little opposition at the time. But Willie had just found his rhythm, there was more to be done, and more music to be made, and what Willie set in motion had a way of keeping on. Take, for example, the PBS television show *Austin City Limits*.

In 1974, when Austin PBS affiliate KLRU-TV moved into a new high-tech facility on the University of Texas campus and decided to make a bid to establish a syndicated network show, Willie was drafted by the Armadillo's Mike Tolleson, along with B.W. Stevenson, to tape a segment for the pilot show. Stevenson hadn't drawn all that well during his taping, and Bill Arhos, founder of the show, recalls that "it looked like we had a party where half the guests had failed to show up. Willie's house was full, however, and he played some licks not even his band had heard before. At one point, during *Bloody Mary Morning*, Jody Payne (the electric guitar player) stopped playing and walked over to look at Willie's hands in wonderment. Not having heard any of these artists before, I was stunned by what I was hearing." This pilot show featuring Willie Nelson & Family was so good that the station got the nod from the network to go ahead. Over the years, the live music format with none of the usual host personality interference has set new standards for the presentation of music on television. "We've made a little history," Bill Arhos modestly wrote in 1999 in the preface to *25 Years of American Music: Austin City Limits*, "and probably for the first time chronicled a new form of music on videotape. I personally think it had a profound effect on the Nashville Sound because this music, this progressive country was, indeed, progressive, the star shone no brighter than the lead guitar or the bass or the drums, because the sidemen were liberated to play as they know how to play, and it didn't much matter what their discipline was. It was blues, bluegrass, country, and more, all rolled into one, and as distinctive as rap."

The show's familiar theme song, *London Homesick Blues*, with the lines "I wanna go home with the Armadillo / Good country music from Amarillo to Abilene / The friendliest people / And the prettiest women you've ever seen" was penned by Lost Gonzo Band leader Gary P. Nunn. The show was blessed by Willie, who put his all and everything into that pilot. *Austin City Limits* aired in 1975 and is still going strong. Over the years, patron saint Willie Nelson has made many appearances. Some of the best have been the guitar pulls or songwriter nights where Willie has shared the stage with the likes of Rodney Crowell, Lyle Lovett, and Merle Haggard. Without his help, some very good artists like Gatemouth Brown, Jerry Jeff Walker, and Billy Joe Shaver, to name only three out of dozens, might never have received national television exposure.

When *Austin City Limits* first showed up on television screens across North America, people from all walks of life tuned in to view Asleep At The Wheel and Bob Wills' Original Texas Playboys. Bob Wills had died the year before in 1975, the year that U.S. troops had evacuated Saigon and the South Vietnamese government had surrendered. We had lost a lot. While disco pulsed in tinsel-town clubs with deejays spinning records and putting musicians out of work all over the western world, the one consistently bright spot on the television dial was looking forward to a weekly injection of live music from Austin. Rusty Weir, Townes Van Zandt, Clifton Chernier, Flaco Jimenez, Ry Cooder, Augie Myers, Doug Sahm, Marcia Ball, Greezy Wheels, the Charlie Daniels Band, and Jerry Jeff and the Lost Gonzo Band were all highlights that year. When Vassar Clements came to town, I attended his show and found myself at a private party where he played from midnight until dawn, a thermos of coffee by his side for fuel, and a dozen local musicians sitting in and jamming everything from *Orange Blossom Special* to Dylan's *You Ain't Goin' Nowhere*, making up new verses when they ran out of old ones. If I hadn't seen Vassar on *Austin City Limits* that exhilarating night of music would not have happened for me.

Willie Nelson made his second *Austin City Limits* appearance on the first show of the 1977 season, along with former Mother Earth lead singer Tracy Nelson. Knockout shows by the Amazing Rhythm Aces, the Earl Scruggs Revue, Jimmy Buffett, Gatemouth Brown, Delbert McClinton, Guy Clark, Steve Fromholz, and the Dirt Band followed during that second season, and videophiles were madly taping each weekly enactment of the live action. Not being so inclined, I settled for checking out the records these people had made. As the years passed, many people's collections began to include recordings by Vassar Clements, Gatemouth Brown, Steve

Goodman, and other artists heard and seen first on the show.

The difference between Austin and Nashville, as Willie has suggested, was the difference between live players and session players. The live music scene in Austin has attracted many talented people over the years, including Ron Cote, a Canadian recording engineer who got his start working with Billy Cowsill in Vancouver in 1979. Cote soon migrated to Long Island, New York to mix a Doug & the Slugs record at Kingdom Sound Studios and hung around for five years working with Joan Jett, Eddie Jobson, Blue Oyster Cult, and Aldo Nova at many of the area's top facilities like the Power Station, Electric Ladyland, and the Hit Factory. After spending a year on the road in the U.S. and Europe with the hard rock bands Blue Oyster Cult and Aldo Nova recording live material, Cote was asked where he'd like to mix a live album and some radio shows. He chose Dallas Sound Laboratory. Cote remembered Billy Cowsill's enthusiastic endorsement of the live music scene in Austin. So, with a ticket to mix anywhere in North America, he chose Dallas because of its proximity to Austin, and eventually found himself recording artists like Leon Rausch, Stevie Ray Vaughan, and Willie Nelson, in both Dallas and Austin.

"I missed a turn somewhere," Ron recalls, "on my way to Dallas and ended up in Austin that first night. I walked around and went into a little blues bar, and, right away you could feel that there was something in the air, an air of creativeness in that city." Cote already had some gold records to hang on the walls at Dallas Sound Lab, but there would soon be more of them. "Between the four of us," he recalls, "me and Rusty Smith, the owner Russell Wittaker, and Johnny Marshall, we put together a multi-million dollar facility, and we ended up with a lot of clients. Mostly it was Texas acts, but there would be bands flying in and out from the West Coast. There were always people coming in from Austin. I started listening to some of this acoustic stuff, and I said to myself, 'This is really good music!'" After five years of recording hard rock, this exposure to blues and country was like a breath of fresh air. Ron Cote didn't know it yet, but he was just gearing up for a meeting with Willie Nelson.

"Between the Dallas rock guys, the San Antonio jazz guys, and the Austin blues and country guys, we had a great mix of music going on there. One week, this band rolls in to do a week of demo sessions and check out the studio, to see if it was any good," Ron remembers with a smile. Again, he didn't really know who 'these guys' were, but it turned out that Stevie Ray Vaughan & Double Trouble were the hottest act he'd recorded up to this point in his short but eventful career. "Russell came in one day and told me I had the Stevie Ray Vaughan album project, working with Richard Mullen, who had produced their first two albums. Stevie was the best guitarist that I had heard, so I knew this was something special. But I still didn't know, really, who this guy was. Then somebody told me he had just done some tracks on David Bowie's LET'S DANCE, so I was getting the full picture. And the sound stage facility next door was renting out space to all these bands who came in to set up their stage shows for tours, guys like Jimmy Page would drop over to the studio when Stevie was there." When Stevie Ray Vaughan brought in a full P.A., Cote had to stretch some, because P.A. equipment in a recording studio can be a nightmare, but coping would lead to the discovery of the facility's secret weapon, the world's biggest echo box.

"We miked everything and ran it through the big P.A. System they brought in," Cote recalls, "and they had a big sound. As soon as we did that, well, they started feeling good." Used to the concert situation, these musicians fed off the volume, which they could feel in their bodies. "For another month," Ron recalls, "there was just lots of jamming. Lots of vodka. Lots of late nights. Lots of jamming. They were jamming their old songs from other albums like *Cold Shot* and *Pride and Joy*. And it got so I knew who they were, I knew their sound, and what they wanted. Once you settle them in, and they are getting what they want to get, they don't want to see you. They don't want to know you are around. I did three albums with Stevie. Two studio albums and a live one. We were there in the studio for about eight months with that first one. We had guys like Bob Dylan comin' in to jam. There were some famous people coming up from Austin, but I don't remember names. That project with Stevie really helped me out a lot. I learned a lot," Cote says.

Next on his slate were a series of music videos for the charity anthems that came along, where all the stars got together to raise money for good causes. The studio in Dallas was right next door to this big sound stage, and we had all these lines running back and forth," Cote explains, "so, we got hired to do this big project they called 'The Texas World Reunion' featuring all the people from Texas. Everybody who was a star in Texas was coming in. I think we might have had 40 or 50 people, and we had 'em all set up on risers, all set up as a choir, for the start of the project. Leon Rausch was involved. Dusty from Z.Z. Top was involved. Willie was involved. Ken Sutherland was the producer. And there was a buddy of Willie's, that was involved. Together, they had written and arranged this song. That turned into a really neat kind of party as we recorded all of them singing together.

"This whole complex, which was huge — with four sound stages — the whole idea was, like, bring Hollywood to Dallas, and Dallas Sound Lab was part of this complex. Across the back hallway was a post-production facility, and there was a marketing, merchandising facility. Everything that had to do with making movies. We were just making music. The neatest thing about this complex, which was about a block long, was that between our half of the building and the other half of the building, there was this hallway that ran the whole length of the block. We had speakers set up all along the hallway, and mikes set up all along the hallway, and 60 percent of the reverb that's used on the Stevie album is this hallway. So, we stayed away from synthetic reverb. And we had this big empty room next to us that was as big as a gymnasium that was all wired up with speakers and mikes as well. So, that was kind of unique, which is something that Willie kinda grooved on.

"Willie had a solo part to do. He came in, sat down, and we set up, and he did his thing, and I added some reverb to his voice. And he's singin' away, and he stops, and he snaps his fingers, and makes some noises, and he says, What *is* that reverb? That's just great. I like it. Where can I get it?' And I said, 'Well, it's our hallway.' I took him out the back door and showed him the hallway, and he just stood there and said, 'This is amazing!' He went and got his acoustic guitar, and went out in the hallway and sat out there for 10 minutes and just played it. And then he came back in and did his thing and then he split. I was just, hey, Willie Nelson likes something that I did. That was pretty cool! After that, a lot of country guys started showing up, wanting to check out the hallway . . .That was something that I had picked up on while I was in Vancouver and Billy and I had experimented with some speakers in a big empty room we had next to the Water Street studio in Gastown."

These technical insights were the sort of discoveries that became critical in the days before sequencers and computer mixing. "I'd take their sound, their voices," Ron Cote confided to me in hushed tones, "and I'd send it out to the echoey room or the hallway at Dallas Sound Lab and, depending on the distance the microphone was from the speakers, this would dictate how much decay and how much echo came out of this. So, it would come back on those microphone lines and I would just blend this to the right levels (with the in-studio feed)." During his 10 minute meditation with his Martin guitar out in that hallway, Willie Nelson, no doubt, came to his own conclusions.

During the 1980s, the production on Willie's albums perked right up. At the 'Cut and Putt' studio in Spicewood, which was designed by Chips Moman and built by Larry Greenhill, Willie would have a state-of-the-art facility with a 48-track digital mixing console, a situation conducive to the live playing and improvisation that Austin musicians were so good at. Greenhill, the chief engineer, speaks of the relaxed atmosphere at the studio — sessions usually begin at 'dark thirty', which is half an hour after it is too dark to play golf. "This is mainly the result of the outdoor activities such as golf, tennis and swimming in the large dog-shaped pool," Greenhill told *Mix* magazine. "In the studio, Willie has chosen his own personal spot, which looks out over Lake Travis and the rolling hills. A typical Willie session might consist of the usual vocal and guitar overdub. For the vocal a Neumann U87 is used in conjunction with a Tube-Tech compressor; this chain is then patched directly into the Tascam DN-800 digital multitrack. Willie's guitar, 'Trigger', is normally run through an old Baldwin amp and miked with a Neumann KM84 through a Neve 1099 mic EQ. This is also patched directly to the input of the digital multitrack. Monitoring and headphone mix is accomplished through a Tascam M700 40-input automated console."

For Ron Cote, his meeting with Willie Nelson was like an encounter of the third kind. He began to spend his weekends in Austin whenever he could. With Stevie Ray Vaughan, he worked at the recording studio that Willie's nephew Freddy Fletcher managed in the Austin Opry House complex, equipped with a monitor screen so the engineer could see the musicians playing or jamming in the Opera House. He also became a volunteer at some of the tapings of *Austin City Limits*. "In Austin it was always fun," Ron recalls. "We didn't always go there to work, but we always had fun. We always went to the studio that Richard Mullen owned, and there was always jamming going on. Somebody was always showing up. There was no tape, just a party. Guys would come down there at two o'clock in the morning, after a nightclub, and they'd break out their stuff and they'd jam away until all hours of the night. You would have blues guitar players mixed in with steel guitar players, fiddlers, country singers; you'd have this incredible mix of players! Out of all the music situations I've been in, this was the true form, the true heart. These boys in Austin had a respect for each other, and they sat down and they knew how to give and take. It wasn't like they were playing music. They were talkin' to each other! You know, a guy would play a lick, and the steel guy would play a lick back, and someone would get carried away, and someone else would throw something in there that would cause that guy to back off and give the room back to guy he'd stepped on — there was never arguing."

For the fifth season of *Austin City Limits* in 1980, Willie Nelson was part of just such an event, appearing on the first "Songwriter's Special," a guitar pull with Hank Cochran, Whitey Schafer, Floyd Tillman, and Ray Price. Willie and the producers had taken a page out of the Nashville songwriter's book and adapted it to the television medium. It worked incredibly well, and the following year Willie Nelson, Hank Cochran, Whitey Schafer, and Floyd Tillman were back to reprise the guitar pull along with Red Lane and Sonny Throckmorton. In 1982, Willie Nelson and band returned for a show which also featured Guy Clark. Willie would continue to return throughout the years. He is always welcome in my living room.

3

STARDUST

Where many recording artists have latched onto one good thing, and milked it until the dairy ran dry, Willie Nelson was not content to sit on the 'outlaw' country approach for very long at all. Nor was Connie Nelson, Willie's third wife, willing to suffer the same indignities that Martha and Shirley had suffered when Willie rode off into the sunset in a station wagon or a band bus, leaving his wife of the moment at home to wonder what new young honey he was snuggled up to. Wisely, Connie decided that living at the center of Willie's cyclone at the ranch on Fitzburgh Road could only lead to disaster. Her solution was unique — Connie set up her own household in Colorado where she could ski and bring up their children in a less chaotic environment.

Now that the band had their own bus, and the crew another, Willie often felt most at home on the *Honeysuckle Rose*. He would sometimes stop by the hotel rooms — which now had to be registered in someone else's name or he would have been badgered, bothered, and bewildered — to wash his jeans and t-shirts out in the tub, and then rendezvous with his bus driver, Gator, to spend the night at some remote beach location where no one in the world knew where he was. To facilitate his solicitations of a film deal with Hollywood producers, Willie had acquired a condo in Malibu, California, which is where he met Booker T. Jones, the producer who would help Willie realize his vision of recording an album of long-forgotten standards.

Willie had written a few classics himself, songs like *Healing Hands Of Time*, back when he was still coming to terms with his divorce from Martha and his new marriage to Shirley. This song represented a turning point in his songwriting. In the lyrics, forgiveness and acceptance replaced the all-too-familiar country ethic of lovin', cheatin', hurtin', lyin', which he had reworked in the effort to keep the situations and people in his songs human, adding twists and dimensions not normally heard in country music. With this song, he turned the spotlight onto the healing process and the intriguing mystery of time, already evoked in *Funny How Time Slips Away*. When asked by some interviewers what his favorite song was, Willie would sometimes refer to *Healing Hands Of Time*, citing the way the lyrics dealt with a negative situation positively.

They're working while I'm missing you
Those healing hands of time
And soon they'll be dismissing you
From this heart of mine

They'll lead me safely through the night
And I'll follow as though blind
My future clutched tightly within
Those healing hands of time

— *Healing Hands Of Time* (Willie Nelson)

Willie had learned through his live shows and concept albums just how eagerly people wanted to hear good old songs like Fred Rose's *Blue Eyes Crying In The Rain*. Now, he sought to record a whole album of similar gems, but entertained no illusions of becoming the next "Sinatra." He realized both his limitations and his strengths. "George Jones," he later told Michael Hall, "is, as far as I'm concerned, the best country singer that ever lived. Merle Haggard and those guys can sing circles around me as far as being country singers, but I enjoy singing country music, and I can do it. I know all the songs, and I can play them all on the guitar. But I also enjoy hearing jazz, and I enjoy blues and I enjoy gospel and bluegrass, I enjoy the big band sounds of the Dorsey Brothers and Sinatra. And I tried to dabble in all those other things. I'm limited in some ways, but I try to watch it and not get beyond my limits."

Unlike some superstar entertainers, who endeavor to keep a goodly distance from their competition, Willie regularly welcomed fellow artists like George Jones onto his stages. He was not afraid of comparison, and, in the 1980s, would hit new heights in a series of duets with the best in the business, including Jones. The Possum's set at the 1976 Fourth of July Picnic in Gonzales, Texas, had triggered widespread acknowledgement of his ability to distil the essence of honky tonk in his unique vocal style and wring every drop of emotion out of a hurtin' ballad, acknowledgment from the mainstream press, including *Rolling Stone*. That Independence Day show had also become indelibly etched onto Doug Sahm's memory. As 'Sir Doug' told me, "one of the greatest moments I ever had was at one of Willie Nelson's Fourth of July Picnics — George was up on stage — there was Willie Nelson, Waylon Jennings, and Jerry Jeff, and me, and our mouths were wide open! If there ever was a guy who is respected by his peers, it's George Jones."

Willie Nelson would record duet versions of *I Gotta Get Drunk* and *Half*

A Man with the Possum, working with Jones' producer Billy Sherrill, who had once opposed Columbia signing Willie but was now fully aware of Willie's talent as a vocalist. During that session, George Jones had some difficulty with Willie's phrasing. To break the ice, Willie said, "You know something, George, I wrote that song for you in the '50s." Jones quipped, "Hell, Willie, I tried to find you once because I wanted to record *Crazy*, but I couldn't find you." As the session progressed, George was still having difficulties. "How the hell does Waylon sing with you," he asked. "I'm used to singin' right on the note. I could do two lines during one of your pauses." Not long after this session, George Jones would begin his rehabilitation at the Hillcrest hospital in Birmingham, Alabama, and Willie Nelson would ascend to the pinnacle of the country music world when the Country Music Association named him their 1979 Entertainer of the Year, a popular yet not widely anticipated win over stiff competition from fellow nominees Kenny Rogers and Barbara Mandrell. This acknowledgement had seemed to surprise Willie at the time, although he had shucked his trademark t-shirt for a freshly pressed western shirt before attending the show, which some observers took to indicate that he at least had a hunch. In 1980 and '81, George Jones would be named the CMA's top male vocalist. They were just two good ole boys from Texas who loved to sing, and during the 1980s the whole world loved to hear both of them do it.

Willie Nelson was also eager to work with the top production people in the record making business whenever an opportunity came along. "I was living in L.A., in an apartment right underneath the apartment of Booker T. Jones," Willie reminisced in a recent chat with *Digital Interviews*. "He was married to Rita Coolidge's sister, at the time, Priscilla. He and I hung out together a lot, and the more I got to know him, the more I realized that this was the time to do the STARDUST album. I'd wanted to do those songs for a long time, but I just didn't find the right producer and arranger. I knew that in order to do songs like that, I would need someone in there who knew everything there was to know about writing and arranging. Booker T. was the guy I felt could do it. Sure enough, he was the guy."

As a member of the famed Stax Records rhythm section along with Steve Cropper, Donald 'Duck' Dunn, and Al Jackson, Booker T. Jones had backed some of Atlantic Records and Stax Records best artists, including the great Otis Redding, Wilson Pickett, Sam & Dave, and Rufus Thomas, and, during the 1970s, had produced and played on several top notch Rita Coolidge albums. "We got together a few times before we went into the studio, Willie and I," Jones recalls in *Willie Nelson: My Life*, "and we sat a few nights just with guitars and keyboards and messed around with the songs. I had no idea what Willie would really be like in the studio, but I found out real quick that he was fast. We got the tape rolling and we got everything on tape pretty quickly. After we had the final mix; and we left the studio, I listened to it; then I listened to it again. Then, after we got home, I listened to it *again*, and I just felt that it was a winner."

"We've worked together a lot," Willie would later tell *Mix* magazine. "He did the STARDUST album, which has sold more records than anything I've ever done. All those songs in there were favorite songs of mine. Fortunately, Booker T. Jones was around to produce it. We got together, and it's still the best album that I ever made. I thought that the STARDUST album was a good idea, but, again, the record label didn't like it." Rick Blackburn recalls that he thought Willie was way off the mark at the time. "I think that idea is crazy," he told Willie. "Look, you're a good writer; you need to stay fresh with your material. I don't think that a project like that is going to have any impact whatsoever." This response was not too much of a surprise to Willie. He'd seldom been encouraged by label guys in the past, and he wasn't going to let a little thing like Rick's lack of enthusiasm deter him from his plan to go into the studio with Booker T. Jones.

"I couldn't see how it could miss," Willie reminisces in the authorized video biography, because it had ten songs on there that were my favorite songs, but, besides that, they had sold millions and *millions* and millions of copies to the people back in the '30s, '40s, '50s, '60s and '70s. And a lot of the young people that I was singing to had never heard these songs, and I knew they would like them because I knew they liked music, and it's impossible to like music and not to like *Stardust*."

"I can remember playing the tape," Blackburn recalls, "and he just sat there. And I thought to myself, maybe he's right . . . . The album went on to sell five million, at the time. I don't know what it's up to now. Even back then, Willie had a strong sense of who he was and he wouldn't compromise. Sort of 'take me like I am or don't take me at all.' So, we just put it out, at his insistence. We just followed him. We knew he'd take us somewhere." Once the Columbia Records executive bought into the Willie way, Willie and the label did, indeed, travel a long, long way together during the next 15 years. It seemed like Willie Nelson had horseshoes up his ass, all night long, and every day, too, because when he hit his stride, the record-buying public seemed to want every album he cut. Sure there were some they bought less than others, but with a double live album with his Family Band, and then a double album with Leon Russell, rolling out of the pressing plants, for the first time since he'd begun recording, Willie Nelson and his record label seemed to be on the same page — and staying on that page for more than the initial few weeks when he was being wooed into signing a contract.

"If you believe in luck," Willie told *Mix* magazine, "I'm the luckiest guy alive. I have a saying that I'll take credit for: 'Fortunately, we are not in control.' That's really the truth. We can sit around and think what we'd like to happen, but if we have to *make* it happen — it's impossible. You just have to believe that it is going to happen — fortunately, we are not in control. If you get out of the way and let it happen, most of the time it will. We get in our own way more than anybody else does." Letting it happen had led to Willie meeting and befriending Booker T. Jones. Before this, it had scarcely seemed likely that Willie Nelson would become a popular 'crooner' of such classics as *Stardust*, *Midnight In Vermont*, and *All Of Me*, and have number one country hits with *Blue Skies* and Hoagy Carmichael's *Georgia On My Mind*, yet this is precisely what went down in 1978. In *Willie Nelson: My Life*, Willie explains, 'Great songs are great songs no matter when they're written." Even though some of the Columbia Records people who worked the record were not exactly sure what they were going to do with *Sunny Side Of The Street*, once they started humming the tune it was a whole lot easier to think positively in their day-to-day activities. Many simple tenets of the gospel according to Willie Nelson suggest looking on the sunny side, "accentuating the positive," as Johnny Mercer had once put it. If you did that and believed that things could get better, problems seemed to melt away. John Lennon once said, "There are no problems, only solutions." The way Willie's fans voiced it was, "where there's a Willie, there's a way."

"It worked like a marketing dream," Rick Blackburn recalls. "The older demographic loved the songs even if they didn't like Willie, and the young demo, they liked Willie, and they thought he wrote every song, so he couldn't go wrong. Willie had figured it out. That was a pivotal album for country music. It opened up a whole new audience." Blackburn has called Willie a "prophet." Before long, Rick was the head of the CBS Nashville operation.

"Willie had vision," Blackburn later told Bill DeYoung. "You gotta listen to him. I encouraged it, because Willie was a lot of things to a lot of people. I never really thought that hurt him all that much. Willie was everywhere; Willie had an appetite to do all kinds of music. He'd bring you so much, and then you'd sit down and talk about what made sense. The product just flowed all the time, in rough states. But good roughs. Would that fly today? It depends on the artist. Willie would sort of be what you've got Garth Brooks to be, now. You had hits, and then you had Willie. We were selling four or five million records back then. That's a lot!"

Working with Leon Russell worked out well, too. Their association went back a long way to the sessions for Liberty Records in the early 1960s. Leon had also played on the first Atlantic sessions in New York, and, after that, he became a regular at Willie's 4th of July picnics. Leon even married his wife at Willie's home. "He is a giant among men who lives inside a quiet down to earth understanding," Leon once described his friend.

In the summer of 1979, Leon Russell and Willie Nelson's version of Mae Axton and Tommy Durden's *Heartbreak Hotel* became Willie's 7th number one on the *Billboard* country chart. Many people, myself included, wore out their copies of that vinyl record, playing it until it sounded so scratchy you knew the needle was going to start skipping all over the grooves. Some of us went out and bought the double LP again — and wore that one out as well. Side one begins with "There's a muddy road ahead, detour!" and just does not let up. Willie and Leon testify on Hank Williams' *I Saw The Light* and leave Elvis and everybody who ever sang *Heartbreak Hotel* before this behind in their dust. *Let The Rest Of The World Go By* is a pit stop for a brief second-breath before they launch into *Trouble In Mind*, with Bonnie Raitt onboard playing her slide guitar and Maria Muldaur contributing significant vocals. Side two begins gently with Cole Porter's *Don't Fence Me In*, moves on to *The Wild Side Of Life*, Gene Autry's *Riding Down The Canyon*, then *Sioux City Sue*, before landing squarely on an extended version of *You Are My Sunshine*. The other disc in the double album package, the one people weren't wearing out, was Leon playing all the instruments and Willie singing, but without Willie's Family Band the live feel just wasn't there. The songs were, though, and it was great in 1979 to hear *Tenderly*, *Far Away Places*, and *Stormy Weather*. These road hogs were in their element as Side Four ends with Willie and Leon grooving on the lyrics to *One For My Baby And One More For The Road*.

Meanwhile, RCA was releasing a steady stream of Willie's tracks, something old, something new with Waylon, and then came the all-time low for RCA reissues, this time Willie's songs but his voice overdubbed in all the wrong places by Danny Davis and the Nashville Brass — which wasn't exactly Herb Alpert & the Tijuana Brass or Chuck Mangione. But Willie smiled through all of it, and when asked to contribute to the liner notes, complied.

A reporter from *Rolling Stone* once asked Willie if he felt that he had beaten the system or made it work for him. "I think I kinda let it work for me," Willie responded. Had he permanently altered the Nashville system? "The big change," Willie said, "now that we proved that country albums can sell a million units, naturally they're gonna try and figure out how that's done. These guys just didn't know that audience was there. That's what happens when you sit behind a desk a lot." On the road playing the beer joints, then the bigger clubs, and by 1978 the arena shows, Willie and band knew what people wanted to hear, knew what was going on in their lives. "We were out on the streets trying to make it against all these people who were in their offices," Willie told another interviewer. "They'd stay in their offices all day expecting people to call 'em up and tell 'em what was going on in the music business. You can't do that. You gotta get out in the streets and find out, what people are into . . . but, you know, they were in charge."

Of course, the road life would eat you up if you didn't have a survival strategy, which in Willie Nelson's traveling medicine show meant outright chaos, most of the time, although someone named Beast usually fed you one hot meal a day, whether you needed it or not. "This organization runs on confusion," Paul English observed. "Nobody has a title. Everybody is too busy helping everybody else." T. Snake, known to journalists as someone they had to 'go through' to get to Willie, would tell them, "one thing we've all learned from Willie is that very few decisions have to be made immediately. If you just let things slide, they'll usually sort themselves out." When a journalist finally got to speak with Willie, he would probably have heard the familiar Willyism, "as long as it's fun, we'll do it, when it stops being fun, we won't do it," several times. "I think the biggest thing I've learned from bein' around Willie," Paul English told a reporter from the *Orlando Sentinel*, "is to always be positive. Willie never wants people around who are negative about things. He doesn't care who you are or what you are up to; long as you are positive about it." The power of positive thinking as it was practiced by Willie Nelson and his entourage allowed them all to float through entire zones of negativity, although you had to watch out for Willie because he could be accident prone on occasion, just when you least expected him to be. They were a most unlikely crew for a most unlikely country superstar.

In *Road Kill*, Kinky Friedman provides an interesting snapshot of Willie's security chief, L.G., as he boarded the bus one rainy morning in Abbott. "In a matter of moments Willie and his sister Bobbie were aboard the bus, followed quickly by the large, tattooed form of L.G. With L.G. standing behind them, Willie and Bobbie looked like little gingerbread people, inherently good, almost magical, and somehow it seemed fragile beyond words and music. Then the door closed. Then the bus began to roll. Then we were on the road again." For many years, the enigmatic L.G.'s formidable presence would ensure Willie Nelson's easy passage wherever Willie went.

Three years after the Texas State Senate's declaration designating July 4th as "Willie Nelson Day in Texas," Willie was commissioned as an honorary Texas Ranger and an Admiral in the Texas Navy. Souvenir dollar bills were circulated with Willie's photo above the Latin script *E. Pluribus Willie*. And the gospel according to Willie' was popularized by the slogan "Matthew, Mark, Luke and Willie," which became a fast-moving souvenir item when printed onto t-shirts. Next came the cover of *Rolling Stone*, then President Jimmy Carter invited Willie to play at the White House, where Willie recalls in his autobiography sitting on the presidential roof with an discreetly not-named White House aide, a longneck beer in one hand and "a fat Austin torpedo" in the other. What Olympus was left to climb? Well, there was Hollywood, and Willie had been telling people he'd conceived of the RED HEADED STRANGER album as if he were making a movie.

Now, spurred on by his new friends, actors Jan Michael Vincent and Gary Busey, Willie turned toward movie-making in a serious way, working with writers like Bud Shrake and Bill Wittliff to create a film script and make a deal with a Hollywood film company. At first, they concentrated on *Red Headed Stranger*. After some negotiations with Hollywood corporations, they also began developing the property that would become known as *Songwriter*. In Willie's mind, he saw someone like Robert Redford playing the 'stranger', but he had seen himself playing a part in the movie, too. Next thing he knew, he walked into Billy Sherrill's house and staring him in the face was the famed actor of blockbuster movies *The Sting* and *Butch Cassidy and the Sundance Kid*. "He was trying to get some country singers to do a benefit for his Citizens Action Committee, I think he calls it," Willie told *Look* magazine. "That was the first time I met Bob Redford and he and I hit it off pretty good. So, we flew out to California together. And he asked if I'd ever like to get into the movies. I said, sure, I could do it."

WILLYWOOD

The Electric Horseman starring Robert Redford and Jane Fonda turned out to be the perfect vehicle for Willie Nelson's big screen debut, although film director Sidney Pollack was surprised when he got a call from Willie Nelson. Next thing Pollack knew, Willie was in his production office. Willie did not exactly audition for a part in the film, but he was persistent, and Pollack agreed to create a role for the singer at the last minute, expanding the character of Wendell, Sonny Steele's (Robert Redford's) manager. "'I'd like to be in that there movie with Robert,' he says," Pollack recalls with a smile in the authorized video biography. "I said, 'Oh, ah, it isn't always that easy, Willie.' I was real worried about whether he was going to be able to handle this. But he had a real odd aptitude, immediately, like he has in his singing, for a kind of honesty. And, other than a little bit of uncertainty, the very first shot, as to how this new-fangled process was going to work, he was okay." Pollack had met Willie once before, when the director and Redford had been scouting scenes for a film in Nashville and had dropped by one of Waylon Jennings' recording sessions. He had not been a fan of country music at the time, but was intrigued by both singers, and remembered that Willie had told him about having placed a couple of scripts with Universal Pictures.

In the movie, Willie (Wendell) does appear somewhat tentative when he and Redford (Sonny) pause before entering a bar in a Las Vegas casino. His opening lines are not remarkable as he instructs Redford, saying, "Don't tell no jokes, don't lift up nobody's dresses. Okay?" Left to improvise once they are seated, Willie insured his future Hollywood career by coming up with the most memorable one-liner in the movie. "I don't know what you're gonna do," Willie ad libs to Redford, "but I'm gonna get me a bottle of tequila, one of them little Keno girls that can suck the chrome off a trailer hitch, and kind of kick back." Redford cannot believe what Willie has just said. Willie (Wendell) sits back in his chair with a smirk on his face. "He improvised a lotta lines," Pollack reminisces, and he had us hysterical! I don't think the rating board, and there was a rating board then, understood the line, or they'd never have let it go. I mean, I don't think people knew what it meant."

Willie had probably said the line or something similar to Ray Price or Johnny Bush or Roger Miller in real life right there in Las Vegas. Willie knew Las Vegas inside out. He was said to hold both the record for the *least* money paid for a show in the Golden Nugget and the most money paid for a show in the Golden Nugget. Long-time pal, Bernie Binion, a promoter Willie had worked with way back when, just happened to be one of the major players involved in transforming the barren wastes of Nevada sagebrush country into a gambling Mecca, tourist oasis, entertainment capital of the world. At ease on the set, Willie became a breath of fresh air for the actors and crew of *The Electric Horseman*; they'd never heard nothin' like Willie before, certainly not ad libbing into their camera lenses.

Although he played only a supporting role, his acting was larger than life, and Willie had marquee billing, a co-starring credit along with Valerie Perrine, beneath top-billing for Redford and Fonda. His fans loved it. Willie and Hank Cochran scored the soundtrack and co-wrote *So You Think You're A Cowboy*. And the release of the soundtrack album, featuring Willie Nelson, shortly after the movie began playing in theaters, helped make Willie's cinema debut a success. For a solo version of Ed Bruce's *Mammas Don't Let Your Babies Grow Up To Be Cowboys* and Sharon Vaughan's *My Heroes Have Always Been Cowboys*, Willie and Sidney Pollack went into Richey House Studio in Nashville. *My Heroes Have Always Been Cowboys* became Willie Nelson's eighth number one hit on the *Billboard* country chart.

Sparked by this instant notoriety, Willie became a hot Hollywood property, and while contractual stalemates kept delaying the production of the initially proposed film script of *Red Headed Stranger*, he appeared in several other films. The first was *Honeysuckle Rose*, a short story that had been crafted into a screenplay by Carol Sobieski, Bill Whittliff, and John Binder, all of whom, no doubt, had Willie Nelson's life story in mind as they wrote and re-wrote the material, converting the original story manuscript into a shooting script. Willie played Buck Bonham, a wayward country singer with a beautiful wife (played by Dyan Cannon) at home, and a burgeoning romance on the road with a young female vocalist (played by Amy Irving) who soon joins his band. The media became convinced that Willie and Amy (who was living with film director Steven Spielberg at the time) were having an even hotter romance off-camera than the obviously steamy romance they were having on camera. Willie isn't telling. More to the point, Amy Irving and Susie Nelson became friends during this time and Amy became a source of support for battered wife Susie, as she relates in her book *Heartbroken*

Memories. Both Dyan Cannon and Amy Irving turned out to be pretty good at singing a country song, which seemed to surprise most critics. Key to the success of this production were live performances by Willie Nelson and Emmylou Harris, filmed at the Convention Center Arena in San Antonio in a concert setting.

This was Willie's first starring role, but even more significant to note was the fact that, even though Sidney Pollack produced the film and Jerry Schatzberg directed the action, Willie Nelson had begun to absorb the film-making process, co-opting hundreds of friends, associates, and fans into the production. Eventually, he would build his own western town and call it 'Luck Texas' in order to cut production costs. "The tiny hill country town of Fischer, Texas, population about 10," *Country Style* magazine reported, "will never be the same. For three weeks in October it was the location set for Willie Nelson's first starring movie. About 150 local residents were cast as extras in the eight million dollar Warner Brothers production. Other Nelson disciples came from hundreds of miles away to get a chance at being in Willie's film and many of Willie's own children, grand children, and members of his musician's families were also used as extras."

No doubt, spreading the action around, as well as sharing the fame, only increased his popularity in hill country. But wasn't this the way things should be done? So many so-called 20th century icons forgot the folks back home once they'd tasted a sip of big city success, but not Willie. He was happy just being there and doing that, evidenced by the photos taken by still- photographer Rick Henson, which accompanied the "Behind the Scenes of Willie's *Honeysuckle Rose*" story in the magazine. Sidney Pollack was quoted as saying, "Willie is a natural." Willie, per usual, provided colorful quotes, too. "Acting's not hard," he said. "Saying lines in a movie is like singing without a melody. I enjoy it, as long as it doesn't interfere with my music, I like to dabble in it now and then." Emmylou reportedly missed the boat when it came to a starring role only due to her pregnancy, but shone in her musical contribution. Willie's skinny on the plot, as told to journalist Linda Cain, proved interesting to some readers, considering how blatantly biographical the plot really was. "It's about an aging band leader on the road with his band," he told Cain. He has a wife and family at home. His guitar player retires and so his young daughter is hired to take his place. She and the band leader end up having a May to December affair. It's a pretty good story. Of course, things like that never happen in real life; it's all strictly fiction."

But the most remarkable aspect of the film was, once again, the music, and, in particular, two new Willie songs, *On The Road Again* and *Angel Flying*

Too Close To The Ground. Sidney Pollack relishes the telling of the tale of the time he and Willie were seated side-by-side on a 747 flight and Pollack mentioned they might just need a theme song. "What do you want it to say?" Willie wanted to know. "Oh, something about being on the road," Pollack replied. Willie nonchalantly wrote the lyrics to *On The Road Again* on the spot, scribbling them on an envelope, and read them aloud to Pollack. It had taken him all of 10 minutes to come up with them. "He sat on the plane and he started scribbling," Pollack recalls in *Willie Nelson: My Life*, "and then he said, 'What do you think about this?' and he reads, 'On the road again / I just can't wait to get on the road again / The life I love is makin' music with my friends / And I just can't wait to get on the road again. What d'you think?' I said, I don't know. What about the music?' And he said, 'Oh don't worry about that, I'll get the music.'"

This song would become the most identifiable lyric Willie Nelson ever wrote, synonymous with the Willie experience. Those memorable lines, "like a band of gypsies, we go down the highway, we're the best of friends, insisting that the world keep turnin' our way, and our way . . . is on the road again," would romanticize just what Willie & Family were up to out there in their Silver Eagle buses driving until the dawn while most people were at home snuggled beneath the covers. "Bob Dylan and Willie Nelson," Kinky Friedman writes in *Road Kill*, "have been like spiritual bookends for the musical and possibly mystical, if dusty, shelves of my life. They both know what it's like to be gypsy kings. They also know how deafening and spirit-grinding loneliness can be once you've been the king of the gypsies. I look up to both of them for wisdom and advice even though they're both shorter than anyone except Paul Simon."

Angel Flying Too Close To The Ground was overshadowed in the moment, yet it was also one of the most remarkable songs Willie Nelson had ever penned, melding his deep spiritual beliefs with those of a love song, in the process creating a tender sense of aching for the rare, elusive, fleeting moments of intimacy we sometimes share but cannot hold on to forever.

If you had not fallen
Then I would not have found you
Angel flying too close to the ground

And I patched up your broken wings
And hung around for a while

Trying to keep your spirits up
And your fever down

And I knew someday that you would fly away
For love's the greatest healer to be found

So leave me if you need to
I will still remember
Angel flying too close to the ground

— *Angel Flying Too Close To The Ground* (Willie Nelson)

Ernest Hemingway had sometimes managed to capture a similar bitter-sweet angst amid the tortured machismo of his best novels. Here, Willie avoids male chest thumping altogether, and offers a haunting glimpse of our human condition. *Honeysuckle Rose*, taken from a Bob Wills standard, was the original title; however, during the months of pre-production, the title was changed first to a Willie Nelson title, *Sad Songs And Waltzes*, then a Leon Russell title, *A Song For You*, and then returned to the original title before being released. Considering that Willie's bus has been named the 'Honeysuckle Rose' for years, the Wills' title seems ultimately appropriate.

With this starring role in the movie *Honeysuckle Rose*, Willie had stepped up a level into the pantheon of Hollywood celebrities who were familiar household names known round the world. Journalists were penning stories with titles like "Willie Nelson a Movie Natural" and "Willie Nelson Gets the Acting Bug" and "Country Goes Hollywood." Willie Nelson would be rumored to be involved in no less than eight film projects, said to be in the front-running for a starring role in a film version of the hit Broadway musical *Best Little Whorehouse In Texas*, which had seen its origins in a magazine article by Texas writer Larry L. King. Rumor also had it that Willie would play opposite either Jane Fonda or Dolly Parton, but when Willie went to New York to audition, he didn't click with the producers, and the role was given to Burt Reynolds. When John Travolta hit it big in *Urban Cowboy*, Willie's country spirit had become pop culture.

A dramatic role in *Thief*, a well-received made-for-TV film about a modern day Robin Hood (James Caan) who runs afoul of Mob controllers, and another as Red Loon in the true story drama *Coming Out of the Ice* were followed by an announcement that Willie Nelson would star in *Barbarosa*, which roughly translated meant 'red beard'. Bill Wittliff had written the script, and Gary Busey, who had portrayed the life of Buddy Holly on the big screen, had been selected to co-star. This role was a natural for red-headed, red-bearded Willie Nelson. Celebrated film critic Leonard Maltzin gives it a favorable pat on the back in his *Movie & Video Guide*, three stars plus a blurb stating, "Nelson is fine as a legendary, free-spirited outlaw constantly on the lam, with able support from Busey as country boy who becomes his protege. Solid western, flawlessly directed by Fred Schepisi." Willie Nelson wasn't exactly an orthodox method actor, but he did have a certain appeal, as Gary Busey observes in the authorized video biography. "Willie doesn't act, he reacts to situations he's in, in a most positive manner, no matter what situation he's in." Cradling a guitar on his knees and thrusting forward his open palms, Busey adds, "he comes to you with his heart out like this."

Despite his friend's glowing endorsement, critical favor, and fan approval, the distributors torpedoed the production, much to many people's amazement, including Willie Nelson's. Patsi Cox delivered a scathing put-down of the Hollywood system in an article for *Rocky Mountain Country* entitled, "Whatever Happened to Barbarosa?" with the informative subtitle, "Willie makes his third film and Universal leaves fans holding the popcorn bags." "Univeral Pictures would have to be crazy," Cox wrote, "to fall out of love with a Willie Nelson movie, but that's just what the good folks in Hollywood did when they shelved *Barbarosa.* And if you're one of Willie's faithful who's been waiting around to buy a ticket, forget it. When the film premiered in Denver, it was well received by fan and critic alike. Even those attendees who came away with reservations about the singer-turned-actor walked away ready to buy a 'Red Headed Stranger' t-shirt and a bandanna. But Universal's handwriting was already on the wall, and *Barbarosa* producer Paul Lazarus knew it. Lazarus later admitted to a Denver writer that he believed that the studio was scrimping on promotion, and placing misleading — if not outright bad — advertising in those areas where the film was to open. (One such ad is said to have completely ignored the film's comic aspects and featured only a few shoot-em-up ride-em-to-the-ground scenes, which had little to do with the actual storyline.) Willie himself has alluded to a strange agenda by which Universal had sought to lure him away from his lucrative recording contract with Columbia. Go figure.

Willie has played dramatic roles in some 25 feature films and made-for-television releases, often bringing as much or more benefit to his family and friends as to himself. Literally hundreds of people benefited every time the Hollywood crews pulled into town. For example, Rosetta Wills and her husband Michael were initially invited to a record release party of a tribute album Willie and others had put together for original Texas Playboy, Jesse

Ashlock, but soon after this, Rosetta and Michael found themselves at one of Willie's film shoots in Luck, Texas, as she recalls in her biography of Bob Wills, Willie's first hero. When Willie arrived on the set driving one of his golf carts, she met him face-to-face for the first time, and as the hours slid slowly past, she learned more details about the filming that was taking place concerning a reunion recording of Willie's first Nashville band, the Offenders, produced by Willie's daughter, Lana. "At least a hundred extras had shown up for this mysterious filming of Lana's creation," Rosetta notes "possibly a movie about a fictitious C&W star or a documentary about Willie's life or perhaps a music video for CMT. Pianist Floyd Domino, who had helped lay down some tracks in the studio, said, I heard it's for CD-Rom. Oh, well, who knows? It's a Willie thing.'" In 1983, Willie Nelson fans saw him appear the Hollywood production of *Hell's Angels Forever*, in which a squadron of WWII bomber pilots continue their daredevil activities riding Harley Davidson motorcycles long after the war has ended.

Sports journalist turned novelist, Bud Shrake, who had been working with Willie on pitching the *Red Headed Stranger* script to Hollywood since the late 1970s, came up with a another script, *Songwriter*, which was conceived in the late 1970s but not produced until 1984. The film had been in the making for five years at least, as Willie told *Country Style* in 1979. "There's another one comin' up," he said enthusiastically, "it's *Songwriter*, which is about the music business in Texas and road play, and the crooked dealings and the rip-offs in Nashville, and in the publishing companies and record companies and with the agents and the promoters. I guess we're gonna get everybody mad at me." Universal Pictures was said to have picked up an option on the property, although Waylon Jennings, the first choice to play opposite Willie, had already been replaced by Kris Kristofferson. When *Songwriter* was released by Tri-Star pictures, there were a lot of uneasy people on Music Row, but nobody needed to have worried themselves overly because once again the plot was highly autobiographical. Rather than point fingers at specific villains, the writers satirized the entire country music business, which was already known to be riddled with self-serving hustlers.

As Doc Jenkins, Willie plays a singer-songwriter, retired from touring, who becomes ensnared in the sleazy dealings of ex-Chicago gangster, Rodeo Rocky (Richard Sarafian), camouflaged in the hokey guise of a Music City manager slick enough to sign Doc up to a one-way-street publishing deal that is likely to last for the next 100 years, especially if Rodeo Rocky's enforcers have their way. Doc panics, but in the back of his whiskey-addled party-hardy mind, amid all of the self-preservation moves he's been making at his

Music Row office and recording studio, including double billing his clients by producing *and* playing all the instruments on their records himself, he has a plan. His one ace in the hole (as unlikely as this seems) is that he still himself holds a management contract on his old pal Blackie Buck (Kris Kristofferson a.k.a. a real-life Waylon). Kristofferson is convincing as a burned-out country rock star — he simply plays himself. Doc sets fire to his Nashville complex and moves back to Austin, showing his human side by visiting his children and his ex, inveigling his way back into her presence by impersonating a vacuum cleaner salesman. The only details not based on the life and times of Willie Nelson are minor.

Doc's scam is as devious as Rodeo Rocky's plan to use contractual law and muscle to exploit Doc's songwriting talent. Doc has in mind setting Rocky up for a fall, suckering him with the irresistible lure of someone younger, sexier, and perhaps even more talented than he is. Lesley Ann Warren is convincing as a flaky chick singer dependent on being stroked constantly by her ego-building boy friend, played by Mickey Raphael, but really is no more than a lush who sips from her flask of liquid courage before every set she sings. If Doc can convince his nemesis that this tart — her name in the film is Gilda — has written hits for herself and Blackie Buck, he just may pull this off. Rip Torn eclipses everything he'd ever done up until this point in his already many-splendored acting career as a scuzzy yet benign promoter who is used to having things his way with gullible performers like Gilda until he finds himself outdistanced by Doc and Blackie. Willie and Kris turn a blind eye as Rip robs the box office at gun point, his perk for going along with their con. Chuckles all round as they pull it off. And we are left to believe that Doc will reunite with his wife and children. Amen. The gospel according to Willie. And one of my favorite feature films of all-time.

HALF NELSON

Meanwhile, in real life, Willie and Family Band were still on the road. Once when they played Las Vegas, the band added a little something special to highlight Willie's performance of *Angel Flying Too Close To The Ground.* "Bee was in a bar in one of the casinos," Mickey Raphael recalls, "and he met this guy whose dad was the rigger who flew *Peter Pan* (with Mary Martin)." Bee Spears continues the story, explaining, "we were talkin' about it, and he said 'How would you like to fly in *Angel Flying Too Close To The Ground?*' We were just talkin' about it; I thought it was just bar talk, so, I said, 'Sure, I'll do it.'"

"That night," Raphael relates, "they put him in this little harness, this little rig." When the song came up in the set-list, Bee slipped backstage and got hooked up. Their timing was perfect. "I came out just exactly on his solo," Bee recalls. "He started his solo and I came flying out and the crowd went crazy." The incident was captured on video and included in the authorized video biography, *Willie Nelson: My Life*. The bass player really does look like he is flying, flapping his arms, none too gracefully, of course, but slowly, languidly . . . but as he is swung out over the audience, he begins to tip and flip. Of course, the audience loved all of these antics . . . and Willie, well, he just didn't get it because everything was a little over his head, so to speak. In response to the cheers coming from the audience, he graciously responds, "Well, thank you very much." At this stage, Mickey recalls, "Bee is about 15 feet overhead, flying back and forth across the stage, and he is nervous and he doesn't have his balance right, so he's upside down; he's really not so graceful." As Bee adds, "Willie looked up and he looked around and he thought he was killin' 'em. But he really didn't know what was going on. He told me later on, he said, 'I knew I was doin' good, but I knew it wasn't *that* good.' I flew over his head a couple of more times and finally they lowered me down and I said, 'Honey, I'm home.'"

By this time the Family Band had two drummers, with Billy English or Rex Ludwig joining Paul English on a second set of traps, and two bass players, with ex-Flying Burrito Brother Chris Ethridge joining the troupe. When Grady Martin began touring with them, joining Jody Payne on a second electric guitar, there would be three lead guitar players because Willie played a lot of the solos himself. More players didn't necessarily add up to the music being louder, it just became more layered and intricate. With their three Silver Eagle buses, one for Willie and Bobbie, one for the band, and one for the roadies, a truck for the equipment, and a huge following of friends with backstage passes wherever they roamed, they came to resemble a country version of the Grateful Dead.

When interviewer Alanna Nash alluded to their growing cult status while asking how the troupe had been assembled, Willie replied, "Kinda strange. Most of 'em just kinda showed up. Jody Payne, for instance, turned up one day to play with Sammi Smith, who was on the show with me. Bee Spears showed up one day to take over for somebody who went into the army. So, I haven't really had a lot to do with it. Mickey Raphael I met (in 1974) at a football game in Dallas. Darrell Royal was givin' an after-the-game party, and we were all sittin' around playin' music, and there was this harmonica player who was just playin' fantastic, so we played together that night, and a few days or weeks later, I did a benefit over in Lancaster, Texas, and Mickey showed up with his harmonica. He's been with me ever since." Bee Spears had only been 18 years old when he'd come on board, and Willie was like a second father to him. L.G. (Larry Gotham) would head up security for the organization until the summer of 1999.

Paul Axthelm, writing in *Newsweek* in 1978, painted this portrait of the band. "The family begins with the band, ranging from Willie's piano-playing sister Bobbie, 47, down to the 26-year-old Mickey Raphael. Then there are the traveling crew members with the strange names and ways that have inspired Texans to call their leader the 'Damon Runyon of the Southwest'. Poodie Locke, the road manager, exists chiefly for moments like the one last month when President Carter visited backstage at a Maryland concert — and someone said, on cue, 'Who's that guy with Poodie?' T. Snake (that's his whole name), whose main function is keeping track of where Willie is, wears t-shirts that say, 'I don't know where Willie is.' Beyond that, the circle widens."

"Willie's got the highest-paid staff in country music," Paul English, told Axthelm, "but a lot of us have worked for nothing in the past and we'd do it again for him if we had to. I love Willie, because he's taught me tolerance. The only time I get impatient is when someone takes advantage of him or says something unfair. Like when there was a rumor he was packing a gun. That got me mad. Everybody knows *I'm* the one with the gun."

Despite the apparent sameness of Willie's shows — he always began with *Whiskey River* and he always finished with *The Party's Over* — Willie never played the same show, even though he may have played same set list every night. "Our show is a lot of improvisation," he told Alanna Nash. "Basically we know the songs, we know the chord progressions, and we've got some head arrangements going. But as far as who's gonna do what, and what notes we're gonna play, we don't really know. I think that makes it more interesting. Everybody looks forward to working that night, because they don't have any idea what they're gonna do."

Willie loved life on the road during these years. "I enjoy doin' it," he told Alanna Nash. "If I didn't play music, if I wasn't allowed to play music, I'd probably get physically sick." And when Nash wondered, "What does that do to your private life?" Willie quipped, "Well, of course, I haven't had one of those in years." "He wants to stay on the road all the time," Don Bowman told *Country Style* magazine. "The only reason he doesn't is because some of the rest of us start gettin' strange. All he ever wanted to do was for people to listen to his songs, and, for 15 or 20 years, he couldn't get hardly *anybody* to listen. But now, they're just bustin' their ass to listen. So, shit, he's sure as hell gonna play!"

The night life did take a toll on Willie's body, though. Out jogging on Mauii one day, he suffered a collapsed left lung, and spent some time in an island hospital, which prompted him to quit smoking cigarettes and lose some 30 pounds. He was befriended by Hawaiian elders or "old Kahunas," as he has called them, medicine men who lived in seclusion on the volcanic slopes of remote mountains. The only other guys out there were ex-Vietnam vets, who Willie also befriended. The healing procedure administered by the Kahunas was accelerated by ingesting four nuts from a candlenut tree, which sped up the expulsion of 50 years of accumulated poisons from his body. This cleansing brought back Willie's strength and prepared him for the treatment these medicine men would begin next — working on Willie's longest standing aggravation, his back injury. Meditating on a mountain top in the Hawaiian Islands helped clean out the cluttered accumulation of years and years of struggle and strife on his way to discovering a path to a positive way of being. This period of re-birth prepared him for the challenge of the events that lay ahead. Willie returned to the mainland a changed man in glowing health.

After recording WILLIE NELSON SINGS KRISTOFFERSON, which yielded the Top 5 hit *Help Me Make It Through The Night*, Willie embarked on a series of duet albums. For FAMILY BIBLE, Willie teamed up with sister Bobbie to deliver a smorgasbord of old time Methodist hymns and gospel songs dating back to their earliest days playing music together in Abbott. He next cut SAN ANTONIO ROSE with his former employer Ray Price, and their duet version of Bob Wills' *Faded Love* became a number 3 hit on the country charts in the fall of 1980. SOMEWHERE OVER THE RAINBOW followed in early 1981. With mandolinist Paul Buskirk, fiddler Johnny Gimble, and guitarist Freddy Powers on board for cuts like *I'm Gonna Sit Right Down And Write Myself A Letter*, *Mona Lisa*, and *Over The Rainbow*, this jazzy set of standards was swingin' country with plenty of hot licks, a winning combination as the album immediately went gold. Albums with Johnny Bush, Roger Miller, Webb Pierce, and Hank Snow were payback time, but each had its own special moment.

When Willie Nelson settled into the studio with Merle Haggard, the two would hit a sweet spot similar to the Waylon & Willie days. Their duet of Haggard's *Reasons To Quit* edged into the Top 10 and then *Pancho and Lefty* climbed to the top of the chart, Willie's 13th number one. The country classic *Pancho and Lefty*, which Emmylou Harris had included in her shows and on her LUXURY LINER album, was written by Houston fixture, Townes Van Zandt, a candidate for the most under-appreciated songwriter of all time, but his song almost was not recorded by Willie and Merle. According to Susie Nelson, Lana, a friend of Townes Van Zandt, interrupted the musicians as they were packing up to leave and pitched the song to her father. Haggard has said he doesn't even remember recording the track at the time, yet his vocal is certainly there. Willie has said that he thought that Van Zandt had Pancho Villa in mind, which is why he liked it right off the bat. But Townes has said otherwise, relating that it just blew in the window one day and he wrote it down. Lana would produce an award-winning video of the song.

This collaboration with producer Chips Moman, who was already familiar with the studio at Pedernales, having supervised the installation of the gear, was a perfect fit for the Hag and ole Willie. Moman and Nelson also worked on the project at the producer's own facility in Nashville, which made for a nice blend of Texas and Tennessee flavor. Players included ex-Memphis pianist Bobby Wood, who'd played with Elvis and Aretha Franklin and was also a hot songwriter at this point in time, having recently penned the Top 10 hits *He Got You* for Ronnie Milsap and *Half The Way* for Crystal Gayle. Grady Martin, who'd played on everybody's made-in-Nashville records dating back to Johnny Horton's *Honky Tonk Man* and Marty Robbins' *El Paso*, also contributed to the sessions. Willie and Grady had first met during the Nashville sessions for his 1962 Liberty debut AND I WROTE; Grady would be in the Family Band until he retired from the road in the 1990s. Considering that Leon Russell had been the musical director for the

L.A. sessions for AND I WROTE, Willie had some *Old Fashioned Karma Coming Down* in those days, a notion that he would fashion into a song of the same name and into a Top 10 hit in 1983 when it was released as a single from the TOUGHER THAN LEATHER album. Add guitarist Reggie Young and the tight rhythm section of Mike Leech on bass and Gene Chapman on drums to Mickey Raphael's mournful harmonica and the PANCHO AND LEFTY album sported an all-star line-up. Willie had burned very few bridges over the years and he was still meeting new musicians at every turn in the road.

Guest appearances on albums by other artists added to the Willie Nelson legacy, and by 1995 would number several hundred tracks on more than 120 albums. Highlights from these guest appearances include a duet with Steve Fromholtz on *A Rumor In My Own Time*, a guitar track on Emmylou Harris' *Green Pastures*, a legendary performance on Chet Atkins' *Chet's Tune*, and collaborations with Bobby Bare, Rattlesnake Annie, Mary Kay Place, Jerry Reed, Johnny Rodriguez, Don Johnson, Jerry Jeff Walker, Boxcar Willie, Joni Mitchell, and a version of *Blue Hawaii* for the sound track of *Honeymoon In Vegas*. The biggest record for Willie Nelson in the 1980s would not be a duet, though, but his solo recording of Johnny Christopher's *Always On My Mind*, a re-tread from an Elvis record that songwriter Christopher had drunkenly pitched to Merle Haggard during preparations for their duet album, lurching onto one of their Silver Eagles with a tape of the Elvis cut of his song clutched in hand. After they had a listen, the Hag said, "Aw, that's not for me, Johnny." Willie, who'd been listening, quietly told Christopher, "That's for me," and pocketed the tape. Willie had ears in those days.

The ALWAYS ON MY MIND album featured the same lineup of musicians as the duet album with Merle Haggard and boasted a Waylon & Willie duet version of Procol Harum's *A Whiter Shade Of Pale*, as well as Paul Simon's *Bridge Over Troubled Waters* and a cover of Barbara Mandrell's recent hit *Do Right Woman, Do Right Man*. All of which represented a departure from the STARDUST album approach. *Always On My Mind*, Willie's 11th number one, was a monster smash that crossed over into the Top 5 on the pop charts and sold half a million singles. The album went on to sell more than four million units. What is even more remarkable about this era is that RCA released Waylon & Willie's *Just To Satisfy You* a week after Columbia released *Always On My Mind*, and the duet followed Willie's single all the way to the top, his 12th number one. There they were, Waylon and Willie, leaders of the pack seven years after their first duet success with *Good Hearted Woman*.

Willie kept on playing golf and recording music with his friends, artists like Faron Young, Johnny Lee, Jackie King, and Billy Walker. When Willie contributed a track to an Ernest Tubb tribute album, he was just paying his respects. "I *like* to record albums with my friends," Willie told Bob Allen. "It's a lot more fun that way, and I always thought we were supposed to do it that way. The way the music industry is set up though, the ones that can sing have their own bands, and there's only one singer to a band. That's not fair, because that way the singers don't get to sing with each other. Ray [Price] and I have known each other for years, ever since I was in his road band. We haven't kept in constant communication for all those years, but sometimes we'd end up in the same town together playin' different clubs. We ran into each other a while back up in Lake Tahoe and played some golf together. We decided it would be fun to make a record together. It was just another one of those cases where we kept running into each other and decided we wanted to pick and sing together. Haggard lives up there, not far away, you know. He comes up and hangs out with me and plays fiddle and guitar whenever I'm up that way." Ray Price has a similar fondness for Willie. "Willie has always been a close friend, quick to pay back anything I've ever done for him. But the only reason I think Willie likes me is I'm the only guy he can beat in golf. Despite his prowess in golf, over the years I've been able to teach him quite a bit about the art of fishing." That time back in the 1960s when Willie killed one of Ray's prize fighting cocks because that rooster was killing Shirley's laying hens had been forgiven many times over.

With his duets proving to be popular, Willie embarked on a whole-hearted attempt to 'go global', seeking out Julio Iglesias as his next vocal partner. The ex-Real Madrid professional soccer goalie had turned the misfortune of a crippling car accident and subsequent partial paralysis into a money-making machine as an internationally acclaimed recording artist and entertainer who would sell more than 100 million albums world-wide before his popularity waned. In an effort to crack the North American market in the early 1980s, Julio had begun to pitch himself as a modern-day Valentino, crooning English-language ballads laced with a svelte Latin accent, and had already made some inroads on the *Billboard* charts with Cole Porter's *Begin The Beguine*. "Julio Iglesias was the biggest thing in the international market," Rick Blackburn recalls. "We had him on CBS International. I didn't know him, but he had a house down in Florida. So, Willie set out to find him, and did." Julio and Willie recorded Hal David's *To All The Girl's I've Loved Before*, which was not by the longest stretch of the imagination a country song, but the song hit the top of the country chart and became a Top 5 pop hit that sold a million 45s.

A second Nelson-Iglesias duet, *As Time Goes By*, the theme song from the classic Bogart-Bergman film *Casablanca*, failed to repeat the same success at radio when released from the Booker T. Jones produced album WITHOUT A SONG. Jones and Nelson had enjoyed a good run with their STARDUST approach, but their versions of Johnny Mercer's *Autumn Leaves* and other old gems proved to be no longer in demand at the record mart, and the title track stalled at number 11 on the *Billboard* country chart. However, Steve Goodman's *City Of New Orleans*, first made popular by Arlo Guthrie during his *Alice's Restaurant* days, from the CITY OF NEW ORLEANS album, proved to be a winner with everybody when released in the summer of 1984, Willie's 15th number one. Of special note to Willie's fans was how trim and fit he looked these days, especially in t-shirt and swimming trunks seated pool-side with Booker T. at the Pedernales Country Club in a photo reproduced on the album sleeve for WITHOUT A SONG.

The next well-known artist to step up to the microphone with Willie Nelson was Ray Charles, known simply as 'The Genius'. For Ray's 1984 duet album FRIENDSHIP, they recorded Troy Seals' *Seven Spanish Angels*, a soulful, melodic, story song. The duet begins with Ray Charles singing:

He looked down into her brown eyes
And said, "Say a prayer for me."
She threw her arms around him
Whispered, "God will keep us free."

They could hear the riders comin'
He said, "This is my last fight.
If they take me back to Texas,
They won't take me back alive."

There were seven Spanish angels
At the altar of the sun
They were prayin' for the lovers
In the valley of the gun . . .

— *Seven Spanish Angels* (T. Seals and E. Setser)

Willie's part was pure outlaw all the way as if he were reciting a scene from one of Louis L'Amour's novels:

She reached out and picked the gun up
That lay smokin' in his hand

She said father, "Please forgive me,
I can't make it without my man."

And she knew the gun was empty
And she knew she couldn't win
But her final prayer was answered
When the rifles fired again.

When the battle stopped
And the smoke cleared
There was thunder from the throne
And seven Spanish Angels
Took another angel home . . .

Brother Ray gave testimony as to Willie Nelson's special genius when he said, "he has this uniqueness. When he sings one note. Not two. One. You *know* it's Willie Nelson. And that's what captivated me. It was nothin' but pure fun. I mean just genuine fun. There was no hang-up, no hassle, no nuh-thing! Willie just went into the studio and sung it, and then he said to me, 'Okay, you got it.' And that was it." Willie Nelson and Ray Charles had a whole lot of fun together singing these bleak, tragic, yet transcendent lyrics, elevating the deaths described as if they themselves were angels welcoming the desperado and his lady as they passed through the pearly gates. Willie Nelson's duet career on Top 40 country radio had reached a zenith. *Seven Spanish Angels* by Ray Charles and Willie Nelson would be Willie's 16th number one.

In May 1984, the two artists shared the stage for a five-song set at the Austin Opry House, performing *I Can't Stop Loving You*, *Seven Spanish Angels*, *Angel Eyes*, *Georgia On My Mind*, and *Mountain Dew* for a sold-out house on hand for the taping of "The Willie Nelson tv Special," which also featured Willie Nelson and his Family Band, with special guest jazz guitarist Jackie King joining in on two numbers. Predictably, there were stories to tell. Willie mentioned to the Opry House audience that the night before this, he and Ray had rehearsed, and then they had gone over to Ray's hotel room and played chess. Naturally, someone wanted to know who had won. "Well, he won," said the red headed stranger, "but the next time, we're gonna turn the lights on." After his duet with Hank Williams' ghost on the HALF NELSON album, Willie would find himself smiling when his pals kidded him, saying, "Willie had to do it, he'd sung one with everybody else."

Since his childhood Willie had dreamed of being a singing cowboy of the black & white silver screen era. Gene Autry, Tex Ritter, Rex Allen, Roy Rogers . . . those kinda guys. During the 1980s he would make several western movies, including a critically acclaimed made-for-tv account of Jesse James' final days, costarring Kris Kristofferson, Waylon Jennings, and Johnny Cash, as well as the less remarkable *Where The Hell's Gold* and an even less remarkable remake of *Stagecoach*.

In August 1983, Willie, Connie, Paula Carlene, and Amy were featured on the front cover of *Life* magazine, a healthy family who lived in a compound in Colorado "like some utopian hippie clan," as reporter Cheryl McCall would later note in *Willie: An Autobiography*. McCall was intrigued that Willie had just bought Connie "a candy red Ferrari GTS 308 for Christmas." From all accounts, a consistent picture of their more than a decade and a half of marriage emerges. Connie had her 'thing', skiing, but she put family life before everything else. Her children deserved an opportunity to grow up in a normal environment, not the hectic, topsy-turvy world of show business. Connie chose Colorado and nested there. Willie was welcome when he arrived and missed when he wasn't there, but life went on. For many years they were a happy couple with a fulfilling home life — when Willie was home. Connie accompanied Willie to Maui and other vacation spots, but she just didn't hang out with him on the road, in the studio, or when he was doing his 'thing', playing a whole lot of golf and even more music. While their marriage didn't last forever, when they were together, Willie was happier than he had been with Martha and Shirley, although he would always have a soft spot in his heart for both of his exes and all of his children. He would sometimes share his cabin in Spicewood with Lana. Lana, Susie, and Billy were in and out of his life, and most of the hurt they'd felt during his rocky marriages with Martha and Shirley was forgiven, although there were scars that would never completely vanish. As the family grew in strength and size, Willie's assessment of his parental performance would improve. For a guy who was away a lot, he hadn't done as badly as he'd once thought he had. Willie soon found himself surprised by an avalanche of grandchildren descending on him in the morning as he awoke.

FARM AID

Mavericks, one and all, Johnny Cash, Waylon Jennings, Willie Nelson, and Kris Kristofferson became the Highwaymen in 1985. "Four for the price of one," as Cash often put it. The world's most dangerous quartet first worked together when the Man in Black was putting together a CBS Christmas Special, scheduled for production in Montreux, Switzerland, the home of the Montreux Jazz Festival, and a picturesque alpine setting in the 1984 yuletide season. Willie, Kris, and Waylon were his special guests.

Things got off to a predictably unpredictable start at the initial press conference. Just off the jet, Waylon, asked by a journalist why they were doing their Christmas Special in Switzerland, quipped, " 'Cause that's where the baby Jesus was born." They got along well, off stage as well as on, although John later said he was just getting to know Willie at the time. Some hotel room guitar-pulling put an idea in their heads that maybe, someday, they should record something together.

The situation came together without a whole lot of planning or plotting when Waylon and Kris dropped by a Nashville session that Chips Moman had put together for John and Willie, a duet for one of Cash's albums. Moman had been the sound tech for the tv show in Montreux, and remembered how they'd all liked Jimmy Webb's song *Highwayman* at the time of their guitar pull in Switzerland. Being that they were in the right place at the right time, the producer recorded the four of them singing that song and several others. Before they knew it, they had an album, a tour, a number one hit with *Highwayman*, and were being sued by the *Michael Rowed The Boat Ashore* folk group who had recorded in the 1960s as The Highwaymen.

Their collective experience in the trenches over the past few decades — more than 100 years if you added it together — had weathered them all, and by the 1980s coming up with a solution that put a smile on everyone's face was no problem. A benefit show, with the original Highwaymen coming out of retirement to open for the new configuration, did the trick. The tracks Chip Moman had produced had a cutting edge, especially numbers like Kris's *Desperados Waiting For A Train* and John's *Big River*. Willie's friendship with Waylon Jennings, Kris Kristofferson, and Johnny Cash would never diminish. When you made friends with Willie, it was for better or worse for the duration.

Over the years, Willie Nelson's Fourth of July picnics evolved from wild extravaganzas into smaller, mellower events, and, for several years, would find a home in Luckenbach, Texas, made famous in song by Waylon Jennings, a postage stamp-size town that had, as a frontier trading post, survived the Commanche uprisings. The picnic also evolved one stage further into a benefit show for American farmers.

Benefit shows had become a staple in the rock music world ever since George Harrison's 1971 "Concert for Bangladesh" in New York. The concert was made into a feature film and the live music was released on a double LP. Eleven million dollars was raised. In 1984, Irish rocker Bob Geldof put his career with the Boomtown Rats on hold while he organized two fundraisers designed to help famine victims in Ethiopia. The first of these brought a number of U.K. artists together to record *Do They Know It's Christmas*, a song Geldof wrote with Ultravox's Midge Ure. This single, featuring the likes of Paul McCartney, Boy George, Paul Young, Phil Collins, Sting, George Michael, U2, Spadau Ballet, and Duran, Duran, sold two million records in less than two weeks as it zoomed to the top of the British charts. All proceeds went directly to famine relief. Geldof took it upon himself to supervise the distribution of food in Africa, a personal touch that went a long way when it came to insuring the relief supplies got to the people who needed them. Geldof next took his fundraising activities to the United States where he linked up with people like Quincy Jones, Michael Jackson, and Lionel Richie for a similar benefit recording.

Meanwhile, at a February 1985 recording session, organized in Toronto by Bruce Allen and Maureen Jack under the banner 'Northern Lights', the first fund-raising anthem, *Tears Are Not Enough*, was cut. Written by David Foster, Jim Vallance, and Bryan Adams, this anthem was recorded by a 'cast of thousands', including the 1985 NHL allstars, members of the Second City television cast, Tommy Hunter, Alan Thicke, Gordon Lightfoot, Neil Young, Oscar Peterson, Joni Mitchell, Bruce Cockburn, Anne Murray, Corey Hart, Bob Rock and Paul Hyde of the Payola$, Loverboy, Rush, Rough Trade, The Band, and many other prominent Canadians. The record was played so often on Canadian radio stations that it became as familiar as the national anthem itself. The music video was equally ubiquitous. A lot of money was raised, food and other survival items were purchased and put on board ships, and some of the relief packages became the first documented cases of the 'Shanghai' process when off-loaded in Africa.

The next fund-raising anthem, also instigated by Bob Geldof, was even more grandiose. Forty-six major artists collaborated to form the one-time supergroup 'U.S.A. for Africa'. Michael Jackson and Lionel Richie penned the fundraising song, *We Are The World*, featuring solo lines from (in order of appearance) Lionel Richie, Stevie Wonder, Paul Simon, Kenny Rogers, James Ingram, Tina Turner, Billy Joel, Michael Jackson, Diana Ross, Dionne Warwick, Willie Nelson, Al Jareau, Bruce Springsteen, Kenny Loggins, Steve Perry, Daryl Hall, Huey Lewis, Cindi Lauper, Kim Carnes, Bob Dylan, and Ray Charles. *We Are The World* sold four million records and hit the top of the U.S. sales and airplay charts in the spring of 1985. In July, a billion and a half television viewers tuned in via satellite to twin concerts staged at London's Wembley Stadium and Philadelphia's JFK Stadium. Headliners like Mick Jagger, The Who, Phil Collins, Madonna, Paul McCartney, Queen, Led Zeppelin (with Phil Collins and Tony Thompson replacing original drummer John Bonham), David Bowie, U2, Black Sabbath, and Geldof's Boomtown Rats performed for 16 hours to nudge the fundraising total over the $100 million mark. Numerous spinoff anthems and benefit albums followed, which led Geldof, now a global celebrity with a bestselling autobiography, to remark that *We Are The World* sounded too much like the "Pepsi Generation."

Willie Nelson was not on the show, though, shuffled out of the mix during the struggle for primacy among the principal players, a development lamented by Geldof in his book, *Is That It?* Willie watched the proceedings of 'Live Aid' on a television set in a Holiday Inn where he saw Bob Dylan struggle to keep it together despite the bad monitor mix he was getting, finish up with his classic *Blowin' In The Wind*, and say, "It would be nice if some of this money went to the American farmers," before leaving the stage. The artist formerly raised as Robert Zimmerman had merely been speaking from the hip, so to speak. Geldof was incensed, calling Dylan's actions "the biggest disappointment of the evening" which showed "a complete lack of understanding of the issues." No doubt, Bob Dylan had his reasons.

Willie Nelson heard Dylan clearly and wondered if maybe there might not be a way to help the American farmer. While touring, Willie had heard tales of woe from farmers, tales of being foreclosed upon. Sometimes, he would subtly drop a few hundred dollar bills on the ground, then bend down, say, "Oh, I believe you dropped something," and hand them to the needy farmer. On more than one occasion, he pulled out his checkbook and wrote out whatever amount was needed to stave off this latest family disaster. But his pockets were not deep enough to help all of the farmers, thousands of them each year, who were losing their farms. When Illinois Governor James Thompson caught wind of Willie's concern for the farming community, he called Willie and proposed the idea of a 'farm aid' concert, then helped him secure the University of Illinois football stadium in Champaign, Illinois, as a site for the benefit concert in 1985.

The plight of the American farmer had been voiced way back in 1927 by silent film star, comedian, and sage Will Rogers, who wrote in his diary, "the poorest class of people in this country is the renter farmer, or the ones that tends to the little patch of ground on shares. He is in debt from one crop to the other . . . Out in the wide spaces where *Men are Men and Farms are Mortgaged*. Where the Government has showed them every way in the World where they can borrow Money and never yet introduced an idea of how to pay any of it back. Where women are women and only get to go to town when they have to go to endorse a Note with their husbands. If your crop is a failure and you don't raise anything, why you are fortunate. Because it costs you more to raise anything than you can sell it for, so the less you raise, the less you lose, and if you don't raise anything you are ahead." Following the boom years that came with World War II, the situation for the family farmer worsened. Every year hundreds of thousands of farmers lost their spreads. By the time Willie Nelson and co-founders John Mellencamp and Neil Young launched Farm Aid the situation had become even more desperate.

Television executive Paul Corbin remembers the day Willie Nelson called him in 1985 and said, "I wonder if there isn't something that we can do for the farmers." Corbin became executive producer to the Farm Aid telecasts, bringing with him vital support from TNN and CMT. At first, Nelson, Mellencamp, and Young sought a tribute song similar to the *We Are The World* model created for Bob Geldof by Lionel Richie and Michael Jackson. Neil Young's *Get Back To The Country* addressed some of the issues — it became his only Top 40 hit on the *Billboard* country chart when it was released in the wake of the first Farm Aid concert — but it was not exactly an anthem, and Neil didn't enlist a cast of thousands when he recorded it. Willie offered his song *Farming For A Living.*

> *When you're farming for a living*
> *And you make your living from the ground*
> *And you take it to the banker*
> *And it ain't enough to go around*
>
> — *Farming For A Living* (Willie Nelson)

The song that eventually became an anthem for farmers was not written until 1992 when Bob Dylan sent Willie Nelson a melody and a single line, the germ that would grow into *Heartland*. During the recording session, Dylan sang along on the choruses.

There's a home place under fire tonight in the heartland
And the bankers are takin' my home and land from me
There's a big achin' hole in my chest now where my heart was
And a hole in the sky where God used to be

My American dream
Fell apart at the seams
You tell me what it means
You tell me what it means

— *Heartland* (Willie Nelson & Bob Dylan)

In 1985, during one of his first interviews as a grassroots spokesperson for the American family farmer, Willie told *Music City News* reporter Neil Pond, "I made all my money as a kid working on farms. "I've known about the problems of the farmer for a long time because I am, to a certain extent, a rancher. I lost $8,000 last year feeding cattle. The problem is the farmer is not getting enough money for his product. Everything has gone up around him except what he's getting paid. His income has got to be brought up. He was talked into planting more than he could sell, talked into it. These are all individual cases, of course, but they were encouraged by our government to do it back in the '70s, to plant all they could, and they had a world market for it. And all of a sudden, because of embargoes, there were surpluses and a big debt." Willie was always ready with a case history, a story of a beleaguered farmer he knew. "Another guy, he went to borrow $5,000 and his banker said, 'Sure, take $15,000, everything is wonderful.' And then they bring up his land value, appraise his land for enough to justify the loan, and all of a sudden land values drop and his loan comes due and the old banker is not the same guy who was there a year ago. And the new banker says, 'I'm sorry, we have a new owner now, and we have to take your land.'"

Nevertheless, Willie held high hopes for Farm Aid. "Everybody is behind it," he told Neil Pond. "It's one of the first times I've seen all of America behind anything. Young, old, it doesn't matter; male, female, everybody is behind this farm issue because I think everybody realizes how important a farmer is to the American way of life." With the concert only days away, Willie reported, "Everyday something real positive has been happening to keep everybody's enthusiasm going. So, I'm not the least bit sorry we started preparing when we did. Things went really well from the start. The fact that it sold out in two and a half weeks surprised everybody. I think it stunned everybody that it turned out this successful."

Neil Pond provided the setting for his interview by describing Willie's office at the Pedernales Country Club. "His desk, with inlaid rope trim and a hand-carved cowboy scene on the front, is cluttered with newspaper clippings, memos, and scribbled phone messages," Pond noted. "A trophy case behind him holds family portraits, framed snapshots and a few personal mementoes. A steer skull, painted in the red, white and blues of the Texas state flag, hangs overhead. At the door is a colorful head-to-toe Indian headdress encased in protective glass. This is where Willie Nelson holds court." Neil Pond was also on hand at Farm Aid to report on the proceedings. "An audience of some 80,000," he wrote, "endured rain and chill to enjoy 15 hours of music by some 60 major performers. The largest gathering ever of American musicians for a single-day event, Farm Aid to this date has raised upwards of $15,000,000 in pledges, corporate sponsorships, ticket sales and concessions. The brainchild of Willie Nelson, who initially enlisted the support of John Mellencamp and Neil Young, the marathon concert was broadcast live by TNN. Concert-goers were treated to a feast of non-stop entertainment. Willie Nelson began the day with *Whiskey River* and closed the show 15 hours later with the same."

U.S.A. Today reporter Nanci Hellmich hung out back stage throughout the proceedings, where she had access to everybody, from Joni Mitchell to Arlo Guthrie, Brian Setzger to Kenny Rogers. Joni Mitchell, who had of course written the anthem *Woodstock*, was quoted as saying, "I'm sceptical by nature about most things, but I came here to help." Arlo Guthrie made reference to Woodstock, commenting that "Woodstock was a commercial venture that ended up having more significance than it was meant to. This is going to end up being larger than Woodstock in significance if the cause keeps going." At Farm Aid George Jones' *Who's Gonna Fill Their Shoes* was the closest thing to an anthem. The Possum was in great shape, although he had a little difficulty reading an announcement from a cue card, a detail not as widely reported as were incidents like the awkward moments Loretta Lynn and band spent during a three-song medley trying to figure out what song they were playing, and a full set of sour harmonies from the Beach Boys. Most of the music was great and everybody backstage had themselves a big old time.

"Debra Winger, in white pants tucked into suede boots, showed up with two bodyguards and boyfriend Nebraska Governor Bob Kerrey," Nanci Hellmich reported. "Dancing backstage, she wouldn't talk to photographers, saying only that she was there to 'show my support.' On stage, she introduced the Blasters and the Charlie Daniels Band." While watching their 12-year-old daughter Amy rockin' to the beat of Foreigner, Connie Nelson confided to Hellmich that "the greatest misconception about Willie is that he's a hippie, that he doesn't take an interest in anything besides performing and music, but he cares deeply about things. Maybe this will show that to people. When Willie's home, everything's normal. He's not a performer. He's a husband and a daddy."

After the initial enthusiasm, the figure said to be raised settled in at $9,000,000. Farm Aid II in August 1986 was a mere shadow of its former self in terms of funds raised, although some 75 acts performed at the Manor Downs racetrack in Austin on July 4th. Willie's picnics had become merged with his fundraisers. VH-1 broadcast the event for 17 hours. Fifty thousand people passed through the gates, but a mere $1,000,000 was said to have been donated to the cause. A dozen years down the road at Farm Aid '98, Harvest of Hope, staged in Chicago's Tinley Park, Neil Young was still appealing to the audience, "If you like this next song, send your money." After *Heart of Gold*, he continued his pitch, "I don't want to be the doomsday guy, but you have to understand how big and out of control things are getting." John Mellencamp was up for his set, dressed in black, and electrified the 20,000 people gathered in the park, as did Steve Earle and the Del McCoury Band with an acoustic set of bluegrass. Beach Boy Brian Wilson sang sunny California surf music but never got warm enough to shed his parka. Willie sang with everyone and teamed up with Daniel Lanois to showcase songs from TEATRO. "We created Farm Aid," he told reporters, "as a way that everybody could help keep farm families on the land. We hope that people will see how desperate the situation has become for farmers and that they will be inspired by their stories and by the generosity of the artists who have donated their time." Soni Sonefeld from Hootie & the Blowfish laid it out plain and simple: "Every time I play Farm Aid, I go home and pray there won't be a necessity to play it again next year."

By September 2000, 15 years after the first Farm Aid benefit, conditions for the family farmer had not improved. "It was bad when we started," Willie said. "It's worse, now." While the organizers had increased public awareness, petitioning the lobby-plagued Congress and Senate had proven to be fruitless, and legal entanglements had often stalled the dispensation of the money raised at benefits, not unlike the problems faced by George Harrison and Apple Records back in 1971. Most of the $11 million for the flood and famine victims in Bangladesh was not put into use until six years after the fact. More than once, the I.R.S. had been active in delaying these proceedings as an ongoing examination of Apple Records held up the delivery of the Bangladesh proceeds to the needy victims, with the result that hundreds of thousands — if not millions — may have died. In 1978, a check for the remaining $8.8 million was finally delivered to the United Nations UNICEF agency, long after the initial crisis. When he began staging the Farm Aid benefit concerts, Willie Nelson also found himself being scrutinized by the I.R.S.

While Willie had been working on the first Farm Aid benefit, his *Red Headed Stranger* film was at last produced. "Dressed in pithy black from head to toe," Nancy Williams reported in *Music City News*, "Willie Nelson gravely exchanges vows with Morgan Fairchild. All is most decidedly not well, though, for even as Willie leans over to kiss his blushing bride her eyes stray to the face of her ex-lover, standing in the back of the room with other guests. The wedding is actually the opening scene of *Red Headed Stranger*, a movie Willie has waited 10 years to film; written and directed by Bill Wittliff, who has also authored or co-authored scripts for *The Black Stallion*, *Honeysuckle Rose*, *Barbarosa* and Sissy Spacek's *Raggedy Man*." That October, Willie visited Nashville to cut the ribbon on a special exhibit of his personal memorabilia at the Country Music Hall of Fame.

While you might have expected Willie Nelson's heightened profile from these highly publicity events to have sparked record sales, the 1983 album releases TOUGHER THAN LEATHER and PANCHO AND LEFTY would be the last Willie Nelson records to be listed in the Top 40 on *Billboard* magazine's top-selling album chart. Although filled with great music, albums like ME AND PAUL, THE PROMISELAND, and the duet compilation HALF NELSON all sold slower than during Willie Nelson's heyday, the eight years following the release of RED HEADED STRANGER. Not even a duet with Neil Young of Young's *Are There Any More Real Cowboys* sparked significant record sales. The party was over, so to speak, and the tough times had just begun. In the final years of the decade, with an Internal Revenue Service investigation ongoing, his marriage with Connie falling into disrepair, and a youth movement at radio beginning to push veterans from the Top 40 charts, Willie Nelson found himself besieged on all sides. The death of his son, Billy Nelson, who had lost his will to cope, was a devastating blow. This period of turmoil was reflected in his music, as Willie suggested in song on the

ISLANDS IN THE SEA album . . . *There Is No Easy Way (But There Is A Way)*. Whereas some entertainers would have thrown in the towel, accepted the fact that at 50-something they were over the hill, and retired from public life, Willie Nelson seemed to find a second wind as if he were a marathon runner who had merely slowed his pace in order to build up steam for the final leg of the race.

NOTHING I CAN DO ABOUT IT NOW

In February 1989, Fred Foster and Willie Nelson took up where they had left off back in 1964 when that purple ink fouled up that full-page *Billboard* advertisement and the deal they had cooking together at Monument Records went sour. They kicked off the sessions for their first album together with a little golf down in Spicewood, where they recorded the first of two songs written by Beth Nielsen Chapman that would become Top 20 hits. Nothing I Can Do About It Now would roll out onto tape as if Willie had written the lyrics himself, echoing many tenets of his philosophy, which he had leaked out over the years as if they were truly the gospel according to Willie — verse and chorus and song — along with the many, many Willie Nelson stories that had become part and parcel of the folk culture of North America and the emerging global village.

I've got a long list of real good reasons
For all the things I've done
I've got a picture in the back of my mind
Of what I've lost and what I've won
I've survived every situation
Knowing when to freeze and when to run
And regret is just a memory
Written upon my brow
And there's nothin' I can do about it now

I've got a wild and a restless spirit
I've got my price through every deal
I've seen the fire of a woman's scorn
Turn her heart of gold to steel
I've got the song of the voice inside me
Set to the rhythm of wheel
And I've been dreamin' like a child

Since the cradle broke the bough
But there's nothing I can do about it now

(chorus)
Running through the changes, going through the stages
Comin' round the corners in my life
Leavin' doubt to fate, stayin' out too late
Waitin' for the moon to say good night

And I could cry for the time I've wasted
But that's a waste of time and tears
And I know just what I'd change
If I went back in time somehow
But there's nothing I can do about it now

I'm forgiving everything that forgiveness will allow
And there's nothing I can do about it now

— *Nothing I Can Do About It Now* (Beth Nielsen Chapman)

Knowing when to "freeze and when to run" described Willie Nelson's situation so well that many fans, myself included, simply thought that Willie Nelson had written this song. Of course, when we checked out the credits on the insert card, we discovered the true author of the song and marveled that someone else could write so meaningfully and emotionally from Willie's point of view.

With Willie's own *Mr. Record Man*, *I Never Cared For You*, and *Is The Better Part Over* added to Nielsen Chapman's ballad *If My World Didn't Have You*, the album had considerable continuity, although not the narrative drive which characterized his greatest albums. The title, A HORSE CALLED MUSIC, came from a Wayne Carson-penned track and graphically presented the record buying public with a singing cowboy image of Willie Nelson. In August, *Nothing I Can Do About It Now* hit into the Top 40 and eventually climbed all the way to number one, Willie's last chart-topper, his 20th overall, if you included his eight number one hit duets with Waylon Jennings, Leon Russell, Merle Haggard, Ray Charles, and Julio Iglesias.

Beth Nielsen Chapman would go on to write songs like *This Kiss* for Faith Hill and herself record *Sand and Water* on the Warner Bros. label, a song that has also been performed by Sir Elton John, but writing *Nothing I Can Do About It Now* for Willie Nelson is still one of the highlights of her career. "More than anyone else," Beth told me, speaking from her home in

Nashville, "I was listening to Emmylou Harris and Willie Nelson's records in the late '70s and early '80s, and that is what made me really gear some of my writing toward country music. Aside from that, I don't consider myself a 'country' songwriter, I just consider myself a songwriter. I was mostly influenced by Hoagy Carmichael and those kind of songwriters from the '30s and '40s. After that it was the singer-songwriters of the '70s. But basically I've always been a junkie for whoever is really saying something. It doesn't really matter what musical genre it is. As that would change from one place to another, I would go and find it. That's when country radio was playing Emmylou Harris and she introduced me to a whole world of songs. Some of them are country songs, it's a very broad field — everything she's recorded."

Beth continued, "It's the same thing with Willie. He's a great artist and he just makes everything come through his filter, and it creates this other way of showing that song. You know, in itself, *Stardust* is not a country song any more than *This Kiss* is a country song. It's just that recorded by that artist, it becomes that style. Willie totally transcends the country style. He's got his own style. He should have his own section in the record stores. Willie just sort of carved his own terrain. He went through so many changes and came out from under that early stuff as who he was — with his braids and with his music — and with those braids, he goes and does these amazing classic recordings. He was my hero!"

At that time in 1989 when Fred Foster asked Beth for a song, she had only written one hit with Don Schlitz for Tanya Tucker called *Strong Enough To Bend*. "It went to number one," she recalls. "And it was nominated for song of the year. And it was a very exciting time for me. At the time I got this phone call from Fred Foster, Willie's life had gone through these *big* shifts. He was in the process of getting a divorce. He had fallen in love with the woman who is now his wife. Many, many shifts, and I just think he wasn't in the writing mode. And he and Fred were talking on the golf course one day, and Willie said, 'Why don't you find me some songs? I'll do some outside songs. Why don't you find out who wrote that *Strong Enough To Bend*? I like that!' So, Fred calls me up and he says, 'I'm producin' Willie Nelson and would you consider writing a song?' For a songwriter, of course, this was the 'dream call' of your career. You bet I'll write a song for Willie Nelson! And I hung up the phone, and I thought, 'how am I going to write a song for the guy that wrote *Crazy*?' I mean, at that point in my career the idea that he would even hear it was just such a dream. So, I thought, 'I'm going to write a song that I can be proud of, and I'm going to send it in, and that'll be enough for me.' Just that I got a call, and I did it."

In Beth's approach to songwriting, "the song already exists in perfect form," and the trick is to not to get in the way while it is downloading itself through you, which is similar to what Willie Nelson is getting at when he says, "We get in our own way more than anybody else does." Still, writing *Nothing I Can Do About It Now* took some time. "The next three months really tortured me," Beth explains. "I was jogging in the little rat-maze thing in the 'Y' that goes around and around, and unfortunately — for myself — I got the title first. *Nothing I Can Do About It Now*. Which is the kiss of death for me. I never write the title first. I usually write the melody and then the words are — I usually kinda hear the vowels before the consonants — it's very, very subconscious, the way I write. It's almost like the song is already written and it's sort of appearing subliminally first. So, the way of writing where you come up with a title and then you decide what it's about, and you think about it, and you do it more intellectually, is a very alien way for me, personally, to write a song. I knew I was gonna be workin' myself crazy. And I did. It took me three months to write it. I sat down and I got the music pretty quickly. But it was one of the hardest songs to write that I have written. Because, first of all, the structure of it, and the fact that I had to rhyme 'now' with all those words . . . I tell you what, every time I got one I lit firecrackers with joy, because it's so hard to rhyme with now'. There's 'ough!' There's 'how'. My favorite one was since the cradle broke the 'bough', and to not have to work with 'o-w' and 'b-o-w'. I was trying to make a line work with 'take a bow'. And it was just all not working. And then all of a sudden I thought of the nursery rhyme. And there was the fact that I was writing for someone whom I looked up to so much that it was almost laughable that I would actually be in a position of writing something that he would record. I was so shocked and thrilled when he liked it and recorded it."

When I confessed that, before I checked out the credits, I assumed from the lyrics Willie had written the song, Beth responded, "People ask me, what's the greatest compliment that I've had as a writer — we're not even talking about Willie Nelson — and I say, 'When people have told me that they thought that Willie Nelson wrote that song.' Because, to me, that was the highest compliment that I could get. He *is* one of the great writers." When Beth next mentioned one of Willie's old songwriting buddies from the days spent in Tootsie's Orchid Lounge, she struck a chord that rang loud and clear. "One of my best friends is Harlan Howard," she said. "He is one of the great spiritual masters of this town, in my opinion, and he was first interested to write with me because of those songs. He said, 'Finally, somebody got Willie to sing on the damn downbeat!' He was so tickled when he found out, because he thought that Willie had written *Nothing I Can Do About It Now*, too."

Imbuing her lyrics with the essence of Willie Nelson was the culmination of years of listening to his music. "I sang all his songs in little clubs for years," Beth explained. "I'd sing *On The Road Again* . . . and I'd do a Willie imitation with my voice. So, for me, to get into character was not that hard because I had listened to his music so much. I sang *Nothing I Can Do About It Now* at the Bluebird just the other night, and, at the end I'll just go into Willie's voice. And then I'll do this thing where I have Willie say, 'Sing it Bob . . .' And I'll do Bob Dylan singin' Willie Nelson! And it just brings the house down, because people don't expect me to be so disrespectful, but I think Willie would think it was funny, you know — I do a *really* poor imitation of him, but for a white girl, it's not bad. I listened to all of his albums while eating barbeque, for years. I just soaked 'em up. So, it was just in my cells. And when all that came together in that song, I knew his life had blown up. I knew he was in love. And I knew that there was a lot of chaos around him. And all I could sense from that — and this isn't to say anything about what was going on in his life — but that old saying 'that you're either pregnant or you're not.' There's nothing you can do about it now. That's where that came from. It started off with 'it *is* what it is' — 'this is who I am, and I'm learnin' — you know, not a 'self-putting-down' kind of thing, and *not* a flip kind of thing."

Recording the song was no less exciting for Beth. "I finished the song, literally, an hour and a half before Fred Foster got on the plane to go to Austin to play the song for Willie," she recalls. "And I was scrambling to make this demo tape, which I did on this little 4-track recorder, and it came together, as funky as it was, and I met him in this parking lot — with my slippers on and my jammy-bottoms and my coat over my pyjamas because I hadn't slept the night before — and handed him the tape. And just felt, as a songwriter, the most euphoria I had ever felt. Because there wasn't even a question whether he was gonna cut it. In my mind, there was no way he was going to cut it, 'cause that was way too amazing." Fred Foster flew to Austin, and the next night Beth got a call. "It was Fred callin' me, and Willie got on the phone, and talked to me, and they said, 'We love the song, why don't you fly to Austin and come play guitar on it?'" She was "completely out of my mind with joy," and caught a red-eye flight out of Nashville. When she stepped off the plane, someone was there to pick her up. "I got picked up by a limo, and we drove to the 'cut and putt' golf course. I hadn't slept all night, I'm so excited. And Willie opens the door of the limo and I'm face-to-face with my hero. I am *not* believing this, and he said, 'Do you want to play some golf?' And we did that, and I hadn't even taken my luggage out of the limo. He's *so* laid back."

After they'd played their round, their golf cart was pulled up to the recording studio. "Being set up in the studio, five feet away from him, set up with my guitar, and actually playin' rhythm guitar on the record with him and his band," Beth recalls, was special, too. "They just put it down so fast, and, bam! It was over. But it was so exciting. I hung out with him for a couple of days. And a month later, when they did overdubs in Nashville, I came in and 'framed' the background vocals. And they did that ballad that I wrote, *If My World Didn't Have You*, and I sang on that, too."

Before A HORSE CALLED MUSIC was released, Beth got another call. This time it was Waylon on the line, except that she wasn't home at the time. Waylon and Willie were out golfing, so the story goes, and Willie had this boom box in his golf cart that he was using to play the final mixes for Waylon while they proceeded up and down the fairways. When Waylon heard *Nothing I Can Do About It Now*, he wanted Beth's phone number. "He was really taken with that song," she told me. "And he called me up from the golf course and left me a message on my machine, which I still have because it warms my heart. He says, 'Hey, this is Waylon Jennings. I want you to write me a damn song. Quit givin' all your damn songs to Willie Nelson.' So, I ended up becoming friends with Waylon, and I wrote a song for him, *Old Church Hens And Nursery Rhymes*, on an album called THE EAGLE. I decided I've got no business writing an outlaw song. He has this sort of rough but gentle vibe, so I wrote a song about sitting with a little child on your lap on a swing and he recorded it. I was really lucky that year."

Right away Willie wanted another song for his next album. This time Beth did not agonize for three months over the task at hand, although at first she had to trick herself into getting started. "I really wanted it to be a completely different thing," she told me, "but, you know, there is this sympatico between those two songs, *Nothing I Can Do About It Now* and *Ain't Necessarily So* because they were both written for Willie. What is interesting about *Ain't Necessarily So* is that the lyric is about being told you can't do something. I was telling myself, 'You can't do this again, you can't do this again,' for hours and hours. I wrote that song to myself, like, 'Who says you can't?' So, I said, 'You know what? I'm not going to try to write another Willie Nelson song, I'm going to write a children's song about, you know, You *can* break your eggs to count your chickens.' People say, 'Don't break your eggs! You can't count your chickens . . .' So, I went through these little examples of these things little old ladies would say to children. It's like 'don't be afraid to try something,' basically. I wasn't even going to write another Willie Nelson song, but once I got over the hump, I said, 'Well, hell — this would work for Willie! And again, I turned it in, thinking, who knows if lightning would strike twice.' But it did!"

Indeed, in the lyrics to her song *Ain't Necessarily So*, Beth Nielsen Chapman seemed to be articulating the gospel according to Willie, a song which became his final Top 20 radio hit of the old millennium, recorded in October 1989 and released just before Christmas on his BORN FOR TROUBLE album.

You can break your eggs to count your chickens
And you can break your neck to keep your ducks all in a row
But don't think every chance you take
Has to mean a new mistake
It ain't necessarily so

Now depending on the soil and the season
You can plant a seed and you can watch it grow
You can't have a guarantee
Cause everything that ought to be
Ain't necessarily so

I laugh when I can and I live with the rest
I've learned that holdin' on means lettin' go
I try to be a friend to the person on my left
They say you just can't be too careful who you know
But that ain't necessarily so

I'd like to have more faith in human logic
Based in all the rules on the proof that you can show
But I can take my guess back
That I based on all those facts
That ain't necessarily so

And every time I follow what I'm feelin
I end up in the same place my heart would have me go
There's one rule in life I trust
Cause everything outside your gut
Ain't necessarily so

— *Ain't Necessarily So* (Beth Nielsen Chapman)

This combination of barnyard images with a homespun philosophy in the sing-song manner of a children's song suited Willie to a tee. He was a man of the earth. He had committed himself to helping out the farmers. But he also knew he was not in control. He was just letting go of it all because "It ain't necessarily so." The chorus, when it came, seemed to soar above all possible earthly cares and woes, touching on the wisdom of ignoring advice that prompted caution and distrust, and, ultimately, following one's intuition. Which was the Willie way, and, no doubt one of the strengths that brought him through this trying period of his life, even though it was Beth Nielsen Chapman who had put his resolve into the lyrics of the song.

The production in the studio — bristling with mandolin wind, a river of guitars, pedal steel, and a driving electric sitar, with backing vocals from Nashville's first-call session singers Jana King, Lisa Silver, Lenaye Stanfield, Karen Taylor-Good, Debbie Bergen-White, and sweet, sweet harmonies from songwriter Chapman and Bergen-White — was pause to stop and wonder what different directions Willie Nelson's career might have taken in 1964 if he had stayed with Fred Foster at Monument, stayed a little longer.

Beth Nielsen Chapman is a gifted songwriter who got lucky. For Willie, it was just a little old-fashioned karma coming 'round. For Beth, it had been a matter of decoding the perfect song and getting it down right. "I teach songwriting," she noted, "and I talk a lot about there being a hole in the top of your head. And you download. And you can have a certain accessibility to what you can download, based, partially, on what you believe is possible. I know that sounds really corny, but, for me, that's been a guiding presence in my writing. And I do think we're not writing alone. People who are painting are not painting alone. I really do have a sense that there is a collective soul . . . that is what art is and breathes into people that are here. And there's a way that becomes tarnished or shut off or messed up by worrying about what's going to be on the charts. I really believe you have to keep that creative channel pretty pure. Sometimes it means you starve and you don't get recognized until after you're dead. But when it's really pure, it's undeniable, whether or not it is recognized in its time."

Even though he was recording songs written by other artists like Beth Nielsen Chapman, Willie was not concerned that his well had run dry. He still saw himself as a songwriter. Well," he told one interviewer, "a lot of people think my writing career is over, that I'll never write another song. But I do have one or two left in me." He was right.

4

THE I.R.S. TAPES

In the fall of 1990 the rest of the world learned what Willie Nelson had known for some time — the Internal Revenue Service had handed him a bill for a whopping $16.7 million, charging that he owed the money in back taxes, interest, and penalties. The agency seized most of his assets and auctioned them off. Some people were shocked by the announcement; others, feigning insider knowledge, would say, "It's a wonder they hadn't caught up to old Willie sooner."

As the controversial decision sparked public debate, people wanted to know all the details, and a syndicated news-wire story by David L. Beck filled in some of the blanks. "What happened," Beck explained, "is that at a time when he owed $2 million in taxes, he was advised to borrow not $2 million to pay those taxes but $12 million to put into a tax shelter." Apparently, the I.R.S. had ruled against those shelters and were after a whole raft of people, not just Willie Nelson. Also rattling around was the rumor that Willie Nelson was suing Price-Waterhouse, the accounting firm that had allegedly steered him in this direction. The claim, filed in Dallas Federal Court, was said to be for $45 million. A spokesperson from the accounting firm denied all liability and alleged that only tax and accounting services were performed, not financial advice.

Earlier in the year, before the I.R.S. ruling was made public, Willie Nelson appeared to be on a roll with the made-for-tv western *A Pair of Aces* being released by his Pedernales Film Company and Stanley M. Brooks' Once Upon A Time Films. Around the same time, the press had begun to refer to Willie Nelson as a real-estate and communications tycoon. "Between a couple of hundred road engagements and an occasional movie projected for this year," Eirik Knudsen reported in the January 10, 1990 issue of the *Boston Herald*, "the Texas real-estate tycoon plans to launch a cable operation based in Spicewood, Texas, known as the Cowboy Television Network (CTN) in late spring." "I got involved with CTN," Willie said, "because I had too much time on my hands — working just two hours a night in concerts, I had 22 hours to get in trouble and frequently did." He also said he aimed to "fill the need for good programming on television. I'm selfish, so I want to bring back old John Wayne westerns and shows like *Bonanza* and *Gunsmoke*."

The photograph of Willie accompanying the newspaper article shows him seated on the ground, a ball and chain shackled to his right leg, frowning. No doubt, this was a promo shot from the film shoot, but there was every likelihood that it was becoming more and more difficult to smile for the cameras as the impending I.R.S. decision weighed on his mind. It was also mentioned that Willie had recently fathered his sixth child, Lukas, with "girl-friend Annie D'Angelo, who also worked as a makeup artist on *A Pair Of Aces*." The couple were expecting their second child.

That summer, despite the financial debacle at the 1987 Fourth of July Picnic held at Carl's Corner and two years of no picnic at all, Willie Nelson and many others were back at it again, this time at Zilker Park in Austin where some 15,000 turned out on the hottest day of the year. With a temperature of 101 degrees the celebration was smaller than expected, but Willie told *Houston Chronicle* reporter Rick Mitchell that it was also "the smoothest picnic ever." But the spirit of the picnic had changed, Mitchell noted. "Police reported six arrests for public intoxication. About 50 people were treated for heat exhaustion. One occasionally detected the smell of marijuana smoke wafting through the air, but for the most part the crowd was well-behaved. The scene was a far cry from the thrilling days of yesteryear at Willie's picnics when guns seemed to outnumber guitars, illegal drugs were consumed openly, and the Decency Patrol kept an eye on public nudity. Apparently, all of Willie's rowdy friends have settled down." Willie appeared solo, with the Highwaymen, and with the Tejano band Little Joe y la Familia, featuring Little Joe Hernandez. Billy Joe Shaver and his son Eddie, who had taken the day off from his regular gig as lead guitarist in Dwight Yoakam's road band, marked the songwriter's return to Austin with a brief but rowdy set. No farmers sued Willie for upsetting their laying hens, no citizens groups mounted petitions.

When the I.R.S. ruling came down, Willie was back to square one. Plans for the Cowboy Television Network would be put on hold. With just his guitar he went into the studio and cut an intimate set of his lesser known songs and appealed to the record buying public to bail him out. He sold cassette tapes of these sessions by mail-order only. With production costs at a bare-bones minimum and no songwriting royalties to be paid to outside writers, this idea wasn't entirely off the wall. THE THE I.R.S. TAPES, WHO'LL BUY MY MEMORIES were later said to have sold a million cassettes. "I was just trying to test the I.R.S.'s sense of humor with the title," Willie told Robert Hilburn, who had wondered if a bit of bitterness had been involved. "And they thought it was a great idea — at least that's the feedback I got. They want us to keep promoting the album because the more albums we sell, the more money they get. The funny thing about the album is that I've never had an album promoted so well as this one. Everybody heard about it. So far, we've raised a little over one million dollars and now CBS is going to sell it in the stores, which should mean a lot more sales."

In the early months of 1991, as more and more details of Willie Nelson's tax problems leaked out, reporters noted that the I.R.S. had seized a 40-acre ranch in Dripping Springs; a Dallas bank that held a mortgage on the Pedernales Country Club and Recording Studio had sold it to Coach Darrell Royal; and properties in several other states were to go up for auction. Also noted was that agents handling these I.R.S. seizures were "surprised to learn that he wasn't nearly as rich as they thought he was." When *Los Angeles Times* music critic Robert Hilburn asked Willie about his reaction to the I.R.S. action, he responded, "Oh it was anger — for sure — much more than humiliation or feeling sorry for myself. That's why I decided to sue. I wasn't angry at the I.R.S., but the people who were supposed to have been advising me, and angry that I went along with their advice, even though I had a gut feeling that it was the wrong thing to do."

One aspect of the Willie Nelson tax case that the federal agency had not counted on was the number of people that would come to his immediate aid, buying stuff at the auctions and simply handing it back to him, sometimes right under their noses. "The response was overwhelming," Willie admitted to Hilburn. "I got phone calls and letters from people wanting to do this and that. People would just come up at shows and try and give me money. In fact, some farmers went down when they auctioned off my ranch, and they bought it and they are holding it for me, so that when my problems with the I.R.S. are over, I can get it back from them." A similar thing had taken place with the golf course and recording studio. "What happened is that the I.R.S. put the property up for auction and Darrell went in and bought it, but then the I.R.S. decided that he didn't pay enough and they sold it to another guy. But then another friend bought it from him, so it's in friendly hands and I'll eventually get it back. In fact, I'm already leasing it. The recording studio is open and we're using it."

As part of an ongoing agreement with the government agency, Willie Nelson soon found himself leasing a theater in Branson, Missouri, the country music tourist mecca where some four million fans per year paid homage to country legends like Mel Tillis, Loretta Lynn, Glen Campbell, Cristy Lane, Roy Clark, and Ray Stevens. In his book *The Town That Country Built*, Bruce Cook notes that a new souvenir item was for sale in the lobby of the Willie Nelson Ozark Theater in Branson: *The Willie Nelson Cooked Goose Cookbook & I.R.S. Financial Adviser*. Apparently, Willie had not lost his sense of humor, even though he might have lost his shirt. But a prolonged stint such as he was signed up for here, performing two shows a day in Branson, was likely to drive a gypsy guitarist like Willie Nelson bananas before long. Climbing aboard the *Honeysuckle Rose*, which was parked outside a motel next to the Willie Nelson Ozark Theater, Bruce Cook learned that Willie was not exactly wallowing in self-pity, after all. In the way that phases and stages, circles and cycles had been looping his life, Willie was not far from the Arkansas border where Quantrill's Raiders regularly rode north into neutral Mississippi to ransack cities, towns, and villages during the Civil War, and not much further from the mountain homestead where Daddy and Mamma Nelson had raised their son Ira before pulling up stakes and heading to Abbott.

This Silver Eagle bus, Cook noted, had been "built by the Florida Coach Company at a cost of just about half a million dollars. It has hand-carved woodwork and, as *he* puts it, 'a bedroom bigger than some of the joints I've played in.' That's it back there with the big six-by-eight American flag over the bed." Working on stage at Branson had not proven to be onerous. "It's a lot like working a big club, really," Willie told Cook. "One that doesn't sell alcohol. So, naturally, it's a little quieter, but that's alright, too. Fifteen hundred is a nice crowd. Not too big, not too little. You can go out and do it with your band, or you can go out and do it with your guitar. Course my band would be mad if I did." After some talk about Willie's show, the lines of autograph seekers that often stretched round the block, and how Willie would sign everything and talk with everybody in the lineups, the interview moved on to how Willie had come to be there for the prolonged booking. "Even though the theater carries his name," Bruce Cook explained, "he is not the owner. It is owned by promoter Jack Harrington. 'Actually,' Willie said, 'Jack and I are good friends, and I came here because I liked him and I liked the idea of being here. I've been here a few times before. We did outdoor venues and always had a good crowd. But I'm not much of a theater owner type of guy. I'd rather have someone else do that and me just come and play there. I still enjoy traveling and I miss that part of it, but I'll probably be back and do some next season. I thought I would just play it by ear. It's hard to say if this boom will last, but it's definitely here now.'"

When Bruce Cook mentioned the I.R.S. situation, noting to his readers that "it had seemed to me, as it had to a lot of other people, that he just might be working for Uncle Sam this summer in Branson," Willie was candid. "When you're looking at $17 million, and you're looking at a building that holds 1500 people, that's definitely a very big debt and a big problem. What it does do is provide a good living for the band, provides us a place to play, and we have an arrangement where I'm allowed to make up to, you know, x-amount of dollars a month, no matter whether it's Branson or where it is, and they get a percentage. They get half, and I get half, after expenses, and that's not really a bad deal." Willie Nelson was not depressed. He was just working things out. "I've had some serious problems," he told Bruce Cook, "and that's not one of them."

What also came out over the period of time before Willie Nelson settled with the I.R.S. was the number of people he'd been supporting. The number of people he'd built houses for. The number of people he'd bought cars for. He simply was not your typical self-serving tax-evader. He was not hoarding his wealth in off-shore accounts or Swiss banks. And when all was said and done, he settled for somewhere around half of the original figure mentioned and walked away a free man. Kinky Friedman would speculate in *Road Kill* that if Willie Nelson had made any enemies at all, the negativity must have come from his involvement in various political fundraisers, or from his support of benefits for people like accused (and now convicted) cop-killer Leonard Peltier, who many felt had merely been defending his home. Some law enforcement officers, Friedman speculated, might possibly have resented Willie supporting someone who had in their eyes killed one of their own. Then there was his meddling in the matter of the ongoing conspiracy between big business and big government to disenfranchise the American family farmer.

ON THE ROAD AGAIN

While Willie Nelson had been fending off the 'revenuers', both Sony Records and Rhino Records had come out with significant career retrospective packages — which was fine for a guy who was at the end of a career, but Willie kept recording new albums, collaborating with a wide variety of artists throughout the 1990s. The BORDERLINE album, released on Sony Records in 1993, featured two tracks with Paul Simon. During the months leading up to the release, Willie was enthusiastic about cutting *Graceland*, Paul Simon's personal favorite out of all his considerable song-writing accomplishments, with the unforgettable opening images of his trek to pay homage to Elvis already engraved upon our collective soul: "The Mississippi delta was shinin' like a National guitar. I am following the river down the highway through the cradle of the Civil War. Going to Graceland."

"It's a great song," Willie told the *Los Angeles Times*. "We cut it in New York, and Paul put together a band that included some musicians from Africa as well as some members of the Highwaymen band. Don Was is doing a lot of the tracks with me for the album. I do like working with all sorts of musicians. To me, I don't really feel there is that much difference between a rock musician and a classical musician and country. As long as there's an honesty there, the rest is just wrapping." Willie Nelson fans were also keen to hear Willie's cover of Paul Simon's '70s hit, *American Tune*. When BORDERLINE was released, the musicologists in the audience pointed out that this melody had been adapted from a composition by baroque composer J.S. Bach. Hence, Willie's reference to classical musicians. For the cowboy audience, Willie and Don Was resurrected the rodeo classic *Farther Down The Line*. Willie also covered himself with versions of *Valentine* and *She's Not For You* and an intriguing treatment of his short but poetic *Moving Is Still Moving To Me*. But the show-stopper on the set was *Heartland* with Bob Dylan joining Willie on the choruses, the world-premiere of their song-writing collaboration.

1993 turned out to be a banner year for Willie. He celebrated his 60th birthday in style with a television special, *The Big Six O — An All-star Birthday Celebration*. During a trip to Nashville, Willie met with his old pal

Charlie Dick, Patsy Cline's husband, who was collaborating with Hallway Productions on an authorized video biography of Willie, *Willie Nelson: My Life*, which assembled in video many of Willie's friends and colleagues over the years to tell stories and pay tribute. Willie was also called upon by Hollywood filmmakers to play cameo roles where he simply played himself. He would play himself in *Big Country*, a lawyer in *Dust To Dust*, and himself again in *Big Dreams and Broken Hearts: The Dottie West Story*. In the Danny Glover – Joe Pesci comedy *Gone Fishin'*, he would play fishing guru Billy 'Catch' Pooler, but people would say that's old Willie in that there movie. His cameo role as a 'historian smoker' in the pro-marijuana film *Half-Baked* is pure gospel according to Willie.

Learning that Willie Nelson was scheduled to shoot scenes for a sci-fi thriller in Nelson, British Columbia, my home town, in 1995, I was naturally intrigued, and when I heard through the grapevine that the film was to be called *Starlight* and involved country music and aliens, I was surprised. I had just completed a novel, which would soon be issued as an audio book through Penton Overseas in Los Angeles, featuring Canadian country singer and actress Beverley Elliott (*Unforgiven*, *Bordertown*) and narrator Steve Scherf with a full cast of actors and a soundtrack scored by ex-Reclines pianist Michael Creber. In my audio book, *Cheatin' & Hurtin' with the Plasmates from Altair IV*, the good aliens have landed because they love country music and want to attend all the concerts. The bad aliens have tunneled from Roswell to Nelson and are breeding an invasion army below the rocky mountain cordillera. Most of the action in this campy production takes place in Nelson, where Willie Nelson had just shot scenes for a movie in which an alien (Rae Dawn Chong) comes to earth to search for DNA that will save her planet. When I first caught wind of the production, I called director-producer Jonathon Kay, but I had missed out on the shoot. It was already a wrap. When *Starlight* was released in 1996, film critics tore it to shreds, but many of these critics chose to mention a scene featuring Willie Nelson as Uncle Liam zapping bad aliens with psychic energy blasts from his eyes. Lovers of the B-movie genre have already begun to search out VHS copies of this neglected gem. Rae Dawn Chong and Willie Nelson are worth the price of admission alone. Veteran Vancouver actor Jim Byrnes, a blues singer also known for his acting as a cast member of both *McGyver* and *Outlanders*, played father to a boy who discovers that he's really half-human and half-alien, the result of an earlier interracial bonding, and his DNA is the prize being sought by both sides. Hokey special effects and bad dialog, with overtures to ecological concerns smack dab in the middle of action sequences, are on a par with B-movie classics of yesteryear like the early Steve McQueen film *The Blob*, *I Married a Monster from Outer Space*, and *The Applegates*. The film had bombed but people remembered ole Willie.

Willie Nelson would play an outlaw, along with comrades in arms Travis Tritt, Kris Kristofferson, and Waylon Jennings, in *Outlaw Justice*, where the son and ex-partners of a gunslinger shot in cold blood seek revenge. But he would be back to playing himself in the 1998 tv special *The Kennedy Center Honors*. When the Red Headed Stranger learned that he was to be honored along with Andre Previn, tin-pan-alley songwriters John Kander and Fred Ebb, and Shirley Temple Black, he told the *Austin American Statesman*, "I was surprised. I'm really in there with a nice group of people." The Kennedy Center honors its recipients for lifetime achievement in the performing arts, and is believed by many to be the highest honor awarded to entertainers. In an official statement to the press, Chairman James A. Johnson called Willie "a restlessly creative soul," adding that Willie Nelson helped reinvent country music. "Throughout his career, he has not only entertained, but he has given us part of our heritage." Fielding questions via phone aboard the *Honeysuckle Rose*, Willie told the newspaper, "It's always a good show. I'm looking forward to going there." This honor made it official, although people had been saying it for nearly a decade: Willie Nelson had become an American Icon. Newspaper headlines across the nation would reiterate the phrase, "from outlaw to icon." A brief cameo in Mike Myers' *Austin Powers: The Spy Who Shagged Me* demonstrated just how recognizable an American icon Willie Nelson had become.

After another July 4th Picnic in Luckenbach, Willie Nelson & Family were on the road again, making their way to Woodstock '99 for a July 25th performance, via New York City, Washington, Hyannis, Massachusetts, and Westport, Connecticut, where they hooked up with Keith Richards. The day-to-day happenings of this summer tour were 'published' online by Willie's daughter, Lana. As producer of many award-winning Willie Nelson videos and author of the superbly assembled 1980 book *Willie Nelson: Family Album*, as well as a newsprint predecessor to the '*Pedernales Poo Poo*' website diary, Lana Nelson Fowler is the person best equipped to chronicle the on-the-road life of Willie Nelson & Family Band. Her postings are humorous and ironic, candid records of the backstage camaraderie, the concert highs and lows, and the endless roads these wandering gypsies traveled in the summer of 1999.

After driving 36 hours from Austin to New York City, Willie appeared on *The Charlie Rose Show*, did some National Public Radio interviews, taped an afternoon interview with Dan Rather for 60 *Minutes*, all before taking the stage in 110 degree weather. Just another day in the life of the Red Headed Stranger, who hung around till all hours of the night signing autographs and meeting with his fans. On July 18th, Willie took a side trip into the Arlington cemetery where funeral ceremonies for astronaut Pete Conrad were being held, and Willie sang *Amazing Grace* in honor of the third man to walk on the moon. Later that day in Hyannis, Massachusetts, as Coast Guard helicopters and other sea and sky rescue teams searched offshore for the bodies of John F. Kennedy Jr. and his family, the wandering gypsies recalled that they had been performing in Memphis the night that Elvis passed away.

On July 23rd Willie Nelson & Family Band performed a show in Westport, Connecticut, where Keith Richards climbed onto the bus with his wife and a few friends to visit his pal, Willie Nelson, and joined him onstage along with ex-Miles Davis sax man Bill Evans for some wild and wonderful music-making moments that night. Two days later, in the wake of a party attended by 200,000 the night before, the gypsies were setting up for their show at Woodstock '99 near Rome, New York. As the crew readied the stage, some 10,000 eager beavers took the front row seats, and, as Lana notes in her diary, "by the time Willie Nelson and Family took the stage, another 50,000 had meandered up. As Dad sang, they still came from as far as the eye could see, and they just kept coming. He gave the best show I've ever seen him do. Half way through the set, he had them all singing *Amazing Grace* with him, which was definitely the most powerful moment of the three day concert. As he sang, the stage quickly filled with musicians, producers, security guys (The Peace Patrol) and almost everyone else that had the proper yellow laminate passes with the chicken on the neck of the guitar. I overheard a Peace Patrol guy tell a guy in an MTV crew t-shirt, 'This is the first singer in two days that I could hear the words to his songs.'"

Willie did hang around for hours signing autographs and meeting and greeting, but the gypsies' buses had pulled out of the compound well before the fires started by vandals set the evening sky ablaze. Like the rest of us, Willie watched those odd acts of vandalism from a safe distance. "We were two states away," Lana reported, "whenever the fires began, and watched on television with the rest of the world as things got terribly out of control at Woodstock '99. 'I've heard of burning one down,' Dad said, 'but this isn't what they mean.'"

Next up on the Willie Nelson & Family tour was Music City U.S.A. "Nashville," Lana notes, "is usually guaranteed to evoke a flood of memories, positive and negative. I shared my years here with turmoil, bad marriages, births, deaths, life long friendships, Krystal Burgers and Shoney's strawberry pies. Sometimes, it's okay." The arrival of Hank Cochran, Brenda Lee, and Waylon Jennings on the bus was a good omen. Sean Colvin and Lyle Lovett & His Large Band opened for Willie Nelson & Family. Waylon joined Willie on stage to sing *Mammas Don't Let Your Babies Grow Up To Be Cowboys*, *Good Hearted Woman*, and Lana's favorite, *It's Not Supposed To Be That Way*. Lyle joined Willie for *Pancho and Lefty*.

After an August 1st Willie Nelson Picnic in Houston, the band headed 2200 miles north to the most spectacular gig of the summer. In Big Sky, Montana, a drenching downpour followed by a sudden rainbow had Willie's stage manager, Poodie Locke, convinced that conditions were safe enough for Willie Nelson and Family to take the stage. It was a humdinger of a rainbow, but when hail stones the size of golf balls began pelting down it became 'clear' that *The Storm Had Just Begun*. Poodie had settled into a meal in the mess tent when the sky began falling and the screaming started. He grabbed up his walkie-talkie and turned it on to hear sound-man Flaco yelling as he scrambled to save the canvas roof over the sound board and lighting technician Budrock screaming at a woman who was climbing his lighting tower. Flaco calling for towels to cover his sound board. Bee Spears had already unplugged his bass and headed for one of the buses that someone had warned him was sinking past its hubcaps in a sea of mud in the parking area. Poodie, trying to work the defective radio, was asking, "Hey, why is Bee leaving the stage?" But no one could hear him. Flaco was really screaming now, "Help! The sound board is shorting out. We need towels!" David was screaming, "Poodie get another radio!" The lightning was real close now, crackling and illuminating the dark evening, and Tom was yelling, "Someone's going to get electrocuted!" Flaco's board was screwed. "I've lost Bobbie's piano," he warned. "Nothing. Shit, there goes Bee's bass." Then Budrock amidst a snarl of expletives informed them, There goes the tower." And Willie Nelson was singing, "Bathing my memoried mind in the wetness of it's soul . . ."

Responding to the wonder of it all, or for some reason beyond reason, a pack of people had begun to rush the stage. "Get Willie out!" David screamed. "Where's security? Tom, grab Bobbie. Get her off the stage! Security!" Poodie, with a new radio in his hand, was saying, "Okay. Now I got a new radio. You copy? Like I said, dinner's awesome. You get any of that pie? Guys? Guys? Guys? Anybody read me?"

The tour may not have been that much fun every night, but there was no lack of excitement. A steady stream of high profile and low profile friends climbed on and off Willie's bus at every stop on the tour. James Caan and family would drop by to visit. Jesse Ventura would visit. In Little Rock, instant celebrity Paula Jones would stop by, preceded by a whirlwind of vortex energy also known as David Alan Coe, who seemed to believe the gypsies needed to be warned of her impending arrival. When she did appear on the arm of the mayor of Little Rock, the boys in the band were taken with her companion, someone they kept referring to as "Miss Pretty Swallow." According to Lana, Miss Jones ignored these rude men and hustled the Red Headed Stranger off for a tête à tête. Or whatever. Other days were less hustle and less bustle. Former fireballing relief pitcher Goose Gossage would put in several appearances at stops along the way. Willie would play dominoes with an old friend, and sit quietly studying a chessboard with his favorite opponent, Paul English, as they rolled through Old West towns with their museums and their parades and pageants. As they drove through the mountain passes of New Mexico and past the Museum of the Horse and the Billy the Kid Museum, the band bus had to be cooled and coaxed every mile along the way. The concert that night would be in Ruidoso, New Mexico, some 60 miles west of Roswell, a location that would lend a little excitement to the appearance of a bright white unidentified object in the sky immediately after Willie Nelson & Family concluded their show. Which prompted one of the techies who were tearing down the gear to step to an open microphone and announce: "Willie has left the planet. I repeat. Willie has left the planet."

As they drove off through the night, avid UFO-logist and bus driver, Gator, had the radio tuned to Art Bell, as was his habit. On a Denver station, the tired gypsies heard eye-witness reports of this mysterious sighting. Some callers were convinced they'd seen one of them real deal flying saucers. What did Gator think? Lana wanted to know. Gator thought he'd wait for the "official government coverup before making a decision either way." When there were no celebrities or friends or strange things going flash in the night, there were people waving banners that declared "When I Die I Want To Go To Willie Nelson's House."

The '99 Willie Nelson & Family tour would continue to have its moments. Hundreds upon hundreds of Harley Davidsons were lined up outside the concert site at Deadwood, in the Black Hills of South Dakota, where the gypsies were to entertain at the 59th Annual Sturgis Bikers Rally. Willie Nelson, star actor in the biker film *Hells Angels Forever*, was, as they say, in 'hog' heaven. While the bikers posed no threat to Willie's well-being, an ardent fan on a wayside golf course did — at least in the eyes of the law.

Whenever Willie could, he headed off with the boys on the band bus to the nearest golf course. On the fairway one day they encountered several police vehicles and a small posse of officers, their guns drawn, surrounding a distraught Willie Nelson fan. The fellow had spotted Willie, hastened back to his condo adjacent to the 8th hole, grabbed up his camera to get a shot of himself with the Red Headed Stranger, and in the process set off his own security alarms, which could still be heard ringing. Sometimes the gypsy golfers would return puffed up by tales of conquest, other times they just weren't talkin'. Golf is like that — the most frustrating game ever invented some days but other days when you hit that old sweet spot and your ball soars into the afternoon sun . . . Forget about the bad times. A day filled with hooks and slices is better than no golf at all.

At a truck stop somewhere in the Heartland, while the buses were grazing and the band and crew were ordering trucker's breakfasts, Willie fielded chat-room questions. Sometimes some of the questions gave him opportunity to wax poetic or slip in a joke or two. He never has been able to resist a pun-making opportunity. When asked who his all-time favorite duet partner was, he said, "Oh, I don't know, but Waylon was the prettiest." Another time, when asked if there should be more women guitar players, he said, "I think there should be more women, period." And for something entirely different, the Red Headed Stranger took on an alternate personality, 'Doctor Booger Nelson', to tape interviews with a roving reporter from the Pedernales Poo Poo website, a.k.a. his daughter Lana's daily internet diary. Doctor Booger Nelson had lots to say, some of it wild and wonderful and some too colorful to print, but his bottom line medical advice was: "If it hurts, don't do it." This advice from a guy who liberally doused his breakfast eggs with 'hiney-hurtin' hot sauce flashed some readers of the daily diary to parallel universes where the Red Headed Stranger was still known as Booger Red.

Heading west toward wide open spaces, with the full heat of the summer upon them now, the band bus, which had logged more than one million miles, was experiencing difficulties. Perhaps it was merely saying it wanted to be put out to pasture, but breaking down every second day was not the most convenient form of communication. In the early days when Willie Nelson got his first bus, the boys in the band had often had to push it to get it started and lived in fear of it not stopping when the brakes failed. Now, they were stopping on mountain grades and pouring gallons of Evian water into its steaming snout. As they pulled through Washington, Idaho, and across Nevada toward Las Vegas, band members and roadies aboard the buses and even the merchandise truck that held the completely collapsible portable town of Scooterville, all realized just how much they were missing L.G. Larry Gorham, longime security man for Willie Nelson, had retired in July, and Tunin' Tom had come on board, but for a while after L.G. left things just were not the same for the gypsies. Oh, yeah, by 2001, L.G. was once again back in the fold. Once a gypsy, always a gypsy.

On Labor Day Willie & Band were in Lawton, Oklahoma, where an ABC-TV affiliate would beam live reports to the mothership. Dwight Yoakam and Trisha Yearwood were on hand that night to help out entertaining at the Willie Nelson Picnic at Fort Still Military Base. They were six days away from Farm Aid '99 and counting. Dwight and his band dropped by the bus to let Willie know that he had begun to spread the word in interviews, telling everybody that Willie Nelson was the "hillbilly Dalai Lama." Not a perfect fit, but neither were Dwight's jeans. Dwight and Willie were kindred spirits, keeping their music honest, outside of Nashville, and getting into the movies and all. By the time they got to the Farm Aid site, the gypsies had pretty well seen it all — *The Promiseland* of broken dreams. CMT was broadcasting the shows, money was being raised, and people were rallying to the cause, but every week 500 family farms were being erased from the map. Family farm by family farm, the Heartland was losing its heart. No doubt, if he could, Willie Nelson would trade all of the awards he has received over the years in a New York minute, as they say, for a resolution to the family farm crisis.

TWISTED DISCOGRAPHY

And the awards kept coming. With lifetime achievement awards from TNN and the Academy of Country Music, as well as his induction into the Country Music Hall of Fame and the Kennedy Center honor already behind him, Willie next received a lifetime Grammy Award during the February 22, 2000 awards show, along with fellow performers Harry Belafonte, John Lee Hooker, and the late Woody Guthrie and Mitch Miller. During his acceptance speech, he recalled the time he'd been busted for possession of marijuana while sleeping at the side of a highway, and had to pull some strings to get himself released the next morning in order to be on time for his recording session with Frank Sinatra. "Lifetime achievements," he told the audience, "are done day to day." National Academy of Recording Arts & Sciences president Mike Greene cited Willie's "generosity of spirit, both as an artist and as a humanitarian."

While the accolades piled up, releases of Willie Nelson records continued at a steady pace, including several duets with Patsy Cline. "Some tracks that I did really quite a while back are finally seeing the light of day," Willie told *Country Music Live.com*. "Two or three tracks. *Last Railway To Heaven* is one of them." Willie was confident that Patsy would have approved of his 'dueting' her. "I knew Patsy, and I knew she wouldn't care. So that didn't bother me that much because I have never really had an opportunity to sing with her when she was alive even though she did *Crazy*, and I had worked a couple of shows with her when I played bass with Ray Price. We did some shows with Patsy and so I knew her and traveled the same tour with her. But I never sung with her." Willie would also mention other intriguing tracks. "I did some other things I hope will come out someday. I did a song with Aerosmith, and I did a song with U2 that Bono had written. Those are still laying around back there somewhere."

Over the years, there have been a goodly number of outright bootleg editions of Willie Nelson records, in addition to the official releases from D Records, Liberty, Monument, RCA, Atlantic, United Artists, Lone Star,

Columbia Records, and various subsidiary labels operated by the major labels like MCA Songbird, Pickwick, RCA Camden, RCA Realistic, RCA Pair, CBS Back-Trac, and others. To further complicate the task of putting together a comprehensive discography, there are dozens of demos that Willie and Hank Cochran made for Pamper Music in the early 1960s. When Hal Smith and Ray Price sold Pamper Music to Tree International, entrepreneurs seeking to clean up on Willie's sudden success as an outlaw released many of these demos on Texas labels like Double Barrel and Shotgun. Plantation issued a number of Willie Nelson records, including THE LONGHORN JAMBOREE PRESENTS WILLIE NELSON AND HIS FRIENDs in 1976 and WILLIE NELSON & DAVID (Allen Coe) in 1980. The more exotic the label names, the more blurred the lineage becomes, yet his music can be found on LPs issued in the '70s and '80s on Candlelite, Aura, Exact, Takoma, Orbit, Delta, OTD, Potomac, Allegiance, Romulus, and others. Rare items include promo records for films like *The Electric Horseman*. In the 1990s when Willie and Columbia/Sony parted ways, another batch of compilations and collections saw the light of day in the CD format. One such collection, WILLIE NELSON: THE CLASSIC, UNRELEASED COLLECTION, issued by Rhino Records, marketed exclusively through the Home Shopping Channel, and selected by Willie himself, ranged from his Willie Nelson Records debut in 1957 to a never-before-released 1980s Hank Williams tribute album, from the Pamper Sessions to out-takes and not-released cuts from his Atlantic albums, including a western swing set where Willie is backed by the Hag's Strangers.

Willie had also been issuing records on independent labels like Justice Records, Step One, and Luck Records because his major labels had not always been interested in releasing as many records as Willie wanted to make. At this stage in his career, simply releasing his recordings himself seemed to bother no one any longer. While the Napster MP3 controversy had all sorts of people all steamed up, Willie would maintain his cool: Willie knew as well as Merle Haggard that an artist didn't always get paid for records that were put out, not even by his official record company, so what was so odd about a new generation of kids sharing a few of his tracks around on the internet . . . at least someone was listening. Oddly, most of the opposition to the MP3 Napster site was coming from corporate record labels. Sure there were one or two rich superstars petulantly whining, but other artists were giving away preview cuts of their upcoming albums, up to 100,000 give-aways in some cases, although their labels would reign them in and force them to cease and desist. When an interviewer from *txcountry.com* asked Willie on board the *Honeysuckle Rose* what he thought about the MP3 controversy,

Willie said, "I've solved all that. I've started bootlegging my own records." Which broke up everyone on the bus all over again. "I got 'em right here," he said. "I'm not kidding. I've got them right here. It's a live show that we did several months ago in Vegas at The Orleans, but as the title says, IT COULD HAVE BEEN TONIGHT." Over the years, Willie had developed an appropriate response for people who came up to him and said, "You probably don't remember me, but we met a few years ago." Willie would reply, "No, to be honest, I don't. But I thank you for remembering me." It was good to be remembered, especially for your shows and your songs, even if someone downloaded that song as an MP3 file from the internet.

The release of ME AND THE DRUMMER, by Willie Nelson & the Offenders, provided the world with a glimpse at what Willie could accomplish if he put his mind to something. The recordings themselves, a result of Johnny Bush wandering into the Pedernales recording studio to record some tracks and then wandering over to Willie's office and asking him if he would care to lend a hand, represented a return to the straight-up traditional country music he and Bush had made in the 1950s and '60s together, when, for a while, they had called themselves the Offenders. In addition to the music tracks, the CD-Extra aspects of the release offered state of the art digital creativity. The people working with Willie at Luck Records did it right when they added these features to ME AND THE DRUMMER. When you insert the CD into your computer, the funs begins. From a colorful title page where a cartoon Willie sits seated playing his guitar, you can click on the pig to see Farm Aid film clips featuring interviews with Willie and Neil Young's passionate plea for help for the family farmer. Click on the Armadillo icon and you are treated to a ringside seat at Willie's 60th birthday bash. Click on the cow and you are viewing the Willie Nelson Family Album. Clicking on the stars-and-stripes-rocket get's you choice moments and interviews from Willie's July 4th Picnics. Click on Willie and you get Willie. It's interactive. It's fun.

Among the most endearing of the many phone machine birthday wishes from the April 1994, 60th Birthday party clips is Lana's message: "Daddy, I just wanted you to know that you're the best father that anybody could have ordered up. I love you. Happy 60th birthday." Another video clip has Terry Lickona stating, "the truth is, there would be no *Austin City Limits* if it were not for Willie Nelson." In Austin to help Willie celebrate during the taping of the tv Special were Bob Dylan, Ray Charles, Asleep at the Wheel, Waylon Jennings, Mary Chapin Carpenter, Gary Busey and many other well-wishers. Kinky Friedman would quip, "I wish you a long and a happy nose."

Just like Willie's music, his friendships crossed all boundaries.

Forty years down the road from the day that Willie Nelson wrote *Rainy Day Blues* and a mere decade and a half after he gave birth to *Forgiving You Was Easy*, the songs on ME AND THE DRUMMER seem wrapped in a timeless ease on the CD, as if they were written at the same time in the same place, such is the continuity in Willie's music. As Mickey Raphael has said, "he hasn't changed a thing." Characteristic of his best songs, the opening lines tell a whole story in very few words: "Forgiving you was easy, but forgetting seems to take the longest time." *Rainy Day Blues* is a 12-bar blues progression, but the way Willie sings it will always be a country blues.

Well, it's cloudy in the morning
Gonna be raining in the afternoon
I said it's cloudy in the morning
Gonna be raining in the afternoon
And if you don't like this rainy weather
You better pack your bags and move

— *Rainy Day Blues* (Willie Nelson)

When Willie turned 63, he became the first country artist ever signed by Island Records, a label that encouraged him to continue his musical explorations, extending his country approach to blues and reggae. SPIRIT was Willie Nelson's debut release on Island Records, but it was not the pilot project pitched to Island by his producer, Don Was. That project had been a reggae album, UNDO THE RIGHT, shelved it seems by a changing of the guard in the label boardroom. But with the release of the gently acoustic set SPIRIT, taken from sessions that no doubt came from Willie's relaxed lifestyle of golfing till dark then playing till dawn, was fortuitous. This same approach had already yielded the very pleasant album HEALING HANDS OF TIME in 1994, an independent release on the Justice Records label. Sitting down with Bobbie on piano, Jody Payne on rhythm guitar, and Johnny Gimble on fiddle, stripping the instrumentation to basics, left a lot of room for Willie's soulful vocalizing. And it had inspired him to write new material, although the operative word was 'casual'. Essence of living room music. "I don't write as many songs as I used to," Willie told an interviewer from *Rolling Stone.com*. "But the new album, SPIRIT, is all original stuff." One record reviewer at *jellyroll.com* instantly fell in love with SPIRIT, seeing at once its Americana values and its reiteration of Willie's concept album heritage. "This homespun album sounds like it could have been recorded before country got separated from western, before there was an Opry, even before Jimmy Rodgers rode a train . . . . The songs, all by Willie, tell of loves lost and found, bittersweet memory and the solace of prayer. Taken together, they create a sense of resignation turning to cautious optimism, akin to the relief autumn can bring after a tumultuous summer. This album is not perhaps quite as openly thematic as RED HEADED STRANGER, but it is strongly affecting. Each listening has strengthened the album's emotional depth for me."

SPIRIT was a return to Willie's concept albums of the 1970s. In 1994, Johnny Cash had gone back to basics with his AMERICAN RECORDINGS album, peeling away the radio gloss and delivering good songs in a full rich voice. With SPIRIT, Willie Nelson seemed to be doing the same. As a reviewer at the *Rolling Stone.com* website, observed, "Nelson brings his own bunkhouse-Romeo charm to the concept. These are songs of amour and wonder rendered with sumptuous ease. The album is so hushed in tone and gentle in temperament that at times it seems weightless, lacking in emotional gravity. But Nelson's singing — with its craggy humanity and ruminative ache — remains a heavy wonder in itself, and the exquisite fiddling of old Bob Wills sidekick, Johnny Gimble, is always something to behold."

What was up with the reggae album? "Don Was, the producer," Willie told *Rolling Stone.com*, "he and I have done a couple of things together. He wanted to do something else, and I'm always willing to do whatever Don wants to do. He is, in my mind, the best producer around these days. He thought a reggae album would be good with me singing my songs with a reggae beat. I would never have thought of it. Not that I wasn't a reggae fan; I just didn't realize that it might work. He was sharp enough to hear it. So, we went into the studio and cut a song called *Undo The Right*, and it turned out so good we used all reggae musicians in Los Angeles, with some exceptions for steel guitar and harmonica. And then we flew to Jamaica to see Chris Blackwell of Island Records, because Don thought he might be interested in it. While we were down there, we played him both UNDO THE RIGHT and SPIRIT and he took both of them." The link between reggae and country music had been established long ago, Willie discovered. "Some of the musicians in L.A. were from Jamaica," he explained. "One guy played drums with Peter Tosh, and they were telling me that they used to listen to late-night radio in Kingston and other places. And they could pick up a couple stations from Miami, Atlanta, New Orleans . . . playing country music. Most of the rhythms in country music were just a guitar and maybe a banjo and a vocal, maybe a fiddle. So, they started putting their own rhythms to country songs.

That's how a lot of reggae music got started."

This ground-swell of enthusiasm for Willie's new music was not merely felt by reviewers. In fact, a whole generation of alternative rockers had heard the Willie message loud and clear and banded together to record a "non-tribute album" they called TWISTED WILLIE. Meanwhile, Texans were wondering what was up with the new bumper stickers they were seeing everywhere they looked. What the heck was "Titty Bingo?" While artists like Jello Biafra, the Reverend Horton Heat, and the Best Kissers In The World were dishing out their tribute versions of Willie Nelson songs, the "Titty Bingo" bumper sticker had become hugely popular in the Lone Star state. Everybody who didn't have one, wanted one. Titty Bingo, they discovered was a band they could catch if they went to Antone's and other Austin clubs where guitarist-vocalist Dakr Jamail, lead guitarist Derek O'Brien, bass player Steve Bailey, drummer Freddy Fletcher, and Freddy's mom, Bobbie Nelson, were said to be a hot item. Willie Nelson's favorite band, it gradually leaked out. Of course, ole Willie might just drop by to jam with Titty Bingo on any given night. Bobbie has said that when she and Willie were children, he was her little brother, but that over the years he has become her 'big brother'. Photos taken of Bobbie during the late 1990s show her to be as youthful as Willie, a beautiful woman and musician whose face shows the benefit of smiling rather than frowning throughout one's lifetime.

TWISTED WILLIE also turned out to be a multi-generational enterprise with people like Breeders' lead guitarist Kelley Deal singing *Angel Flying Too Close To The Ground*, backed by a rhythm section made up of a Kenmore 12-stitch sewing machine, Jesse Roff on muted guitar, and Kris Kristofferson on harmonica and vocals. Jesse Dayton, who had recorded his debut album at Pedernales, delivered nostalgia with an edge on *Sad Songs And Waltzes*. The melodic and maniacal Steel Pole Bath Tub delivered a totally twisted version of *The Ghost* that seemed to mystify all reviewers. Grunge survivors Gas Huffner tackled *I Gotta Get Drunk*. When Bobbie and Willie sat in with the Reverend Horton Heat, the reigning king of psychobilly, on a recording of *Hello Walls*, Willie was inspired to refer to the Reverend as the "King of Texas." Ex-Buddy Holly sideman Waylon Jennings contributed *I Never Cared For You*. Ex-Dead Kennedys leader Jello Biafra recorded *Still Is Still Moving To Me*, and described it as "a good abstract statement about being independent, intelligent, and observant among a sea of people who, if things seem still, will just stay still and fall asleep." The Best Kissers In The World — whose Sub Pop debut *She Won't Get Under Me Until I Get Over You* had led to them being referred to as

"Black Sabbath punishing the Box Tops" — enlisted Mickey Raphael's harmonica playing for their raunchy rendition of Willie's *Pick Up The Tempo*. There were others who raised a ruckus on the CD whose names were even more familiar. Johnny Cash, for example, jamming with ex-Nirvana bassist Krist Novosalic, Alice In Chains' drummer Sean Kinney, Soundgarden's lead guitarist Kim Thayil, and son John Carter Cash on 12-string. There were contributions from hard rocking Tenderloin, the Presidents of the United States, and the Supersuckers. "I grew up on Willie Nelson," said Alice In Chains guitarist Jerry Cantrell, "to even meet an Outlaw, let alone record a song of Willie's, was a thrill."

TWISTED WILLIE producer Jo Nick Patoski recalled the days when Willie's kickers and freaks first got together, writing in his liner notes, "There's still plenty of debate as to when Willie united these two previously separate cultures. For me, it was the gig his band played in the garage of McMorris Ford on Sixth Street in downtown Austin. The trappings suggested a classic country music function. Willie and band were picking and grinning atop a flatbed trailer to entice listeners to check out the new '74 models. Appropriately for a car lot gig, Nelson gave the audience who'd come to hear the free show a set list of pure country music tunes, then, in the middle of *Stay All Night Stay A Little Longer*, all of Willie's pickers started looking at each other real funny and everything turned cosmic, as the musicians locked into a groove that borrowed the best of the Grand Ole Opry and the essence of San Francisco's Fillmore to make something new and completely different. Needless to say, no one looked much at cars that night. Willie worked the same kind of spell a year later at the Northline drive-in movie theater in Houston, where he debuted a new album called RED HEADED STRANGER, which changed the course of the Western World. Today, Austin is recognized internationally as a music town where people actually make music for the sheer pleasure and artistry of it all, rather than a career. On any given night, country, rock, blues, hillbilly, jazz — you name it — can be heard in dozens of clubs as performed by hundreds of bands. And it's all because of Willie not giving a shit about what you call it, as long as you just go out and play music for all it's worth. Willie has taught all of us to trust your own instincts, and play the hell out of whatever kind of music you happen to play." Further along, Nick Patoski acknowledged his friend Danny Bland as the guy who came up with the idea for TWISTED WILLIE. The two were apprehensive about creating a traditional tribute album — after all, Willie Nelson was still very much among the living. "But once we decided to twist the songs to fit the bands," Patoski relates, "TWISTED WILLIE was born."

While SPIRIT got major coverage in the press, some reviewers noted that the albums leading up to it, MOONLIGHT BECOMES YOU, which retraced his *Stardust* era, and JUST ONE LOVE, a hard return to straight-ahead Texas style honky tonk, were two of his best. There were also his records with the Highwaymen. While Willie was to be found on Liberty Records and Justice Records before signing with Island, he hadn't changed anything. Sony had also released his Christmas album PANCHO, LEFTY & RUDOLPH on CD during this transition period, another landmark in the tradition of the records Gene Autry once made about Rudolph and other Yuletide themes. The 1990s were one of Willie Nelson's most creative periods.

On July 4, 1997, Willie Nelson and many others held their picnic in Luckenback, Texas. "Once more, they came peacefully trudging down dusty Hill Country roads," Shirley Jinkins reported in the *Fort Worth Star-Telegram*. "The buckskin-fringed and tie-dyed veterans of a quarter century of Willie Nelson happenings. Believe it or not, things have mellowed some since the Dripping Springs Reunion of 1972. A lot of people have been drawn by the nearby Jerry Jeff Walker-Robert Earl Keen bash happening in nearby Kerrville." With some pals taking up the slack, the crowd in Luckenbach would swell over the 10,000 mark but remain comfortably sized. Leon Russell had never missed a picnic. Jimmy Dale Gilmore was making his debut. And Ray Wylie Hubbard recited the Willyism he felt dearest to his heart and reason he always showed up: "Love of country, love of beer, love of Willie." Steve Fromholz remembered that at that first gathering of the tribes he hadn't brought his guitar. "I didn't have anything with me," he told Jinkins, "so I played Tex Ritter's guitar. It was a piece of shit, but it was Tex Ritter's guitar!" Geezenslaw Brother Fromholz remembered the wilder days and delivered a typical Fourth of July Picnic one-liner. "Last year," he told Jinkins, making sure he had her full attention, "a girl lifted up her shirt, like they always do at the picnics . . . and she was wearing a brassiere." Jinkins also cataloged some of the healthier foods and beverages now available on site, among them Jalepeno Sam Lewis' heart of palm, slices of Mexican mango, and his trademark jalepeno guacamole. The pick of the concessions was the 'Fresh Peach Freezes'. Jinkins ended her report with a quote from *Willie: An Autobiography*. "Willie said, 'the Dripping Springs Reunion had the seed of a sort of country Woodstock, and got me wondering if I could do better.' Yep. He did. And does."

TEATRO, recorded in four days in a converted Mexican movie theater in Oxnard, California, saw Willie Nelson working with Daniel Lanois, whose quirky gothic production of Emmylou Harris' 1995 album WRECKING BALL had helped the former Queen of Country Rock and ex-Hot Band leader find her sea legs in the post-Top 40 country era during which both she and Willie Nelson had been deleted from the charts. Working with Lanois had kindled a lasting friendship and in the process put Emmylou at the leading edge of what was now being called alt-country. Seeing as she and Willie Nelson were also pals, Emmylou Harris joined in on the sessions in California. "Emmylou's an angel," Willie told Nick Krewen. "I'm willing to sing with her any place, any time." As he had with Don Was, Willie now put his fate in the hands of Daniel Lanois. The man had won Grammys for his work with Dylan and U2, so it made sense to trust him. What did the Canadian producer bring to the sessions that made the difference? "His phone book," Willie told Krewen."He knows all the good pickers and players, and he knows what it takes to make a great album. I rarely allow myself to be placed wholeheartedly in a producer's hands, but I was willing to do it with him because I like his stuff." Well, almost. Willie *had* brought along his piano-playing sister Bobbie Nelson and harmonica player Mickey Raphael, just for good measure.

The set list included *Darkness On The Face Of The Earth* from Willie's Liberty Records days, a song that had sat neglected for some 37 years as an album track, as well as better known Nelson songs like *I Never Cared For You.* "I'm glad he liked all these songs," Willie told interviewers. "I've always thought that if it was a good song back then, it's a good song now. Most of the ones we chose were pretty obscure, so I don't think a lot of people had heard them." He was right. And no one had heard them performed like this, with Emmylou singing along, an angelic soul-shadow perched like a bird on a wire alongside Willie's vocal. As Rick Mitchell observed in the *Houston Chronicle*, "she doesn't so much attempt to replicate Nelson's idiosyncratic phrasing as place her vocal lines next to his and hope all's well that ends well. The loose vocals lend a casual living-room feeling to the arrangements, enhanced by Bobbie Nelson's gospel piano and Mickey Raphael's homespun harmonica."

And this was just fine with Willie. "Recording TEATRO in an old movie theater," Willie told Krewen, "felt like I was sitting at home in my living room. It was a nice atmosphere. In most studios, you usually have the drums in one corner and the guitars in a separate room, and you hear everything through earphones. I don't really like to do it that way, and I'm glad Daniel didn't like it either. We were all in the same room. It was like jamming." Rick Mitchell noted that Nelson's three new songs (not counting the closing instrumental, *Annie*) indicate his survivor's perspective. "While he once stumbled through the darkness of his failed relationships, he now pledges undying devotion in *Everywhere I Go* and I'*ve Loved You All Over The World.* Even when he's surveying recent wreckage on *Pick Up The Pieces*, his primary concern is for others who might learn from his mistakes." Per usual, there was a story to be told that gave focus to this latest Willie experience. "We'd watch old movies during the playback," Willie explained to Nick Krewen. "Daniel had some old movies that were left behind from the days the studio was a theater. So, we'd play these silent movies while we were listening to the playback of the music. It was certainly different." The inclusion of two covers of Django Reinhardt instrumentals as well as the instrumental tribute to his current wife, Annie, would anticipate the recording of a full set of instrumentals the following year.

NIGHT AND DAY, Willie's first ever instrumental album, was released in the summer of 1999. Like STARDUST, the record featured a smorgasbord of musical styles ranging from classic Django Reinhart compositions to covers of popular standards like *September In The Rain*, *Honeysuckle Rose*, and *All Things You Are*. "I always loved these songs," Willie told *Country Weekly*. "When I was playing every night in Texas, you had to play these tunes. The folks wanted to hear them. Songs like *Over The Waves*, we played all the time. I thought at this point in my life this would be the right thing for me to try these songs again. I like instrumental music because you can put it on and go about your business, driving down the road, without the distraction of a story to follow. You can make up your own stories."

Django Reinhardt, Willie's first guitar hero, receives heartfelt acoustic treatment on *Nuages* (Snows) and *Vous et Moi* (You and I). "I think Django was the greatest," Willie told Richard Haydan. "I love the music and really tried to do him justice." Longtime friend Johnny Gimble, who had gone on from Bob Wills' bands to play fiddle for Marty Robbins, Merle Haggard, Lefty Frizzell, and just about everybody else, was reunited once again with Willie for the title track *Night and Day*. Willie called Johnny "the greatest fiddle player, ever." Per usual, Willie's Martin N-20 guitar, with a hole in it from playing it so long and so hard with a pick instead of finger-style, was a front and center attraction.

In 1995 Willie spoke at length about that guitar to *Grammy* magazine interviewer Michael Hall. How had he come to own it? "Accident, really," Willie said. "The Baldwin guitar people gave me an amp and a guitar, and I accidentally broke the guitar. So, I sent it to Nashville, and Shot Jackson, who had a music studio there at that time, took the pick-up out of my guitar and put it in this Martin. It was on the shelf. He just picked it off the shelf and thought, maybe this . . . I bought it over the telephone. I think I paid

$750 or something. It was a hell of a buy, the combination of that guitar and that Baldwin amplifier stereo pick up, which is like a three-chord stereo pick up. Baldwin had a bunch of 'em back in the beginning. They're hard to find, now. A lot of people who have Baldwin guitars and Baldwin amps will drop one off to me every now and then, if they find one in a garage or a basement. They save it for me, because I'll take pieces out of it and put it in my old amp." What was broken *can* be fixed. What was auctioned can be returned. With a little old fashioned karma coming round now and then — and with a little help from your friends.

Willie Nelson continued to be featured in tributes and television specials throughout the 1990s. When Johnny Cash's manager Lou Robin called Cash and pitched a VH-1 Special, Cash was not sure he wanted to get involved. "All VH-1 wants," Robin insisted, "is two guitars, two stools, and you and Willie." Cash still wasn't sure but soon found himself seated beside his friend Willie Nelson with a show to be done. "The audience is three feet away," he recalls. "We pick, yet we know not what we pick. No planned program. Swapping songs from out the back of our heads. Just like a guitar pull at my house. He looks at me and sees that I am watching him. Now, he's watching me. I think he knows I made a wrong chord. He gets over it. We get into a song that feels good. Willie and me. I watch Willie's hands as he takes a guitar lead. He plows into a note and, at the same time, there is a slight grimace on his face, as if it might hurt just a little bit. As he pulls the note off, he grits his teeth. I've seen hands like that in the cotton fields. Rough. Gnarly. Dextrous. Determined. Precise. Concise. Fascinating. That said, how about greed. Lust. Anger. Sloth. Gluttony. Envy. Pride. The seven deadly sins. But none of them committed here tonight, except maybe envy on my part."

To be envied by the guy who wrote *Tennessee Flat Top Box* seems an ultimate tribute. But just how good a guitar player is Willie Nelson? Well, Grady Martin, who is hands down one of the all-time best guitarists, once said, "he's got a terrible problem with his golf swing and he's gonna have to live with it for the rest of his life cause he can't take no instruction." Carlos Santana has said, "Willie Nelson's impact on American music is indelible. He stands at the crossroads of all the sounds and colors of this country. What he reflects is true soul and sincerity. He's also a pretty mean guitar player." Chips Moman has noted, "when I first recorded Willie, I thought he was the weirdest dude I ever worked with . . . and I was right." Willie himself waxes humble and tells interviewers he knows his limitations and cites Django Reinhardt and Grady Martin as the greatest. "My golf game is up and down,"

Willie says, "you know, some days it's not that bad and some days it's not that good." Larry Trader, Pedernales Country Club golf pro, and Willie's longtime golfing partner, suggests that golf is therapy for Willie Nelson. "He's happy telling jokes and laughing while he's playing." Playing a round of golf at Pedernales before heading his golf cart toward the recording studio, Willie may be grouped with Trader, Morgan Fairchild, Dennis Hopper, Coach Royal, Kris Kristofferson and many others. He is not limited to mere foursomes. The rules, you see, are his own, and it's not that different with his guitar playing. He has a way of snagging onto something, bearing down on it, riffing on the bass strings up toward the nylon range, and cascading willy nilly back down. He might slice it a bit right or hook it into the rough, now and then, but finding his way back to the melody and landing on the beat may just be the adventure of a lifetime. Which is the stuff that inspired solos are made of.

PRESIDENT WILLIE

Over the years, Willie Nelson has become increasingly involved with the politics of the nation, especially the state of the American family farm. Willie has seldom sided with the government, and even though he has become a favorite of presidents, since 1980 he has supported presidential candidates, like Ross Perot in 1992, who have not won the election. Who looked good in the 2000 presidential race? interviewers from txcountry.com asked him during the campaign. "I'm waiting . . . I'm waiting for the candidates to start talking about the family farmers. I haven't heard two words put together by any of these guys and that's what I'm waiting for. I've talked to Ralph Nader. He's also running for president. I just want to hear what they all have to say about the family farmer. And if they're really interested in getting my vote, they're going to have to say those two words together a lot."

In an interview with *Ag Journal*, Willie was blunt when asked a series of questions about Farm Aid 2000. "We are sick and tired of Farm Aid," he said. "There should not have been a need for the first one, much less to still be doing it years later. It's time we took control of the food that we eat and tell the government what we want. We are still losing 500 farmers every week. The loss of farmers means the loss of other rural businesses and eventually everyone leaves the community and moves to the next-largest town. The reason for Farm Aid was not to make millions of dollars, the reason for Farm Aid was to raise the awareness of the world and the American people, especially of what is going on in the farmland and how it affects them. Over the years Farm Aid has worked with a lot of organizations throughout the states to help farmers trying to stay in business. The money that we have taken in has gone directly to these organizations. This farm bill runs out in a few years and it's time to start putting together the new one. It has to be one which allows the farmer to get his production and labor back to cost."

In an open letter, Willie invited all of the presidential candidates to stand up for the family farmer, "not necessarily for votes but because it's the right thing to do." Willie's vivid picture of his childhood days down on the farm was passionately phrased. "Where I grew up in the town of Abbott, Texas, my backyard was six miles of beautiful farms and ranches all the way to the town of West. My playground was 20 square miles of cotton fields, corn fields, hay fields, grain fields, and home to everything from jack rabbits, deer, squirrels, birds, snakes, scorpions, cattle, horses, chickens, and hogs, right down to the small vegetable garden at my back door. I explored the whole 20 square miles on foot, on horseback, bicycles, and pickup trucks. I had the best of everything. I worked on farms to earn money. My sister Bobbie and I worked summers in the field to help pay for our school expenses, clothes, etc. The farmers were prospering, and we were, too." There were other issues, the President of Farm Aid, Willie Nelson, argued. He called for "closing apparent loopholes in the rules that could still allow genetically modified organisms, sewage sludge, and irradiation to be considered organic, even though hundreds of thousands of consumers told the USDA two years ago they wanted these production elements prohibited from organic farming."

With drought in the eastern seaboard states, floods cutting pastures and fields to shreds from the Red River Valley to the Mississippi delta nearly every second year, and wild-cat fires and mud slides tearing up California, Oregon, and Montana as El Nino conditions recurred with merciless insistence, farmers were hard-hit. As if corporate connivance was not enough opposition, mother nature seemed to have become severely challenged by global warming, threatening ever worsening conditions and crop failures throughout the heartland, and from sea to shining sea. As the *Honeysuckle Rose* crossed the Montana state line for an August 26 show at Fort Missoula, the musicians could smell the smoke of the forest fires burning. "A dark blue haze covered the horizon to the left," Lana Nelson notes in her website diary, "and of course the horizon is exactly where we needed to be. I can't tell you what it smells like to have six million acres on fire at the same time. A sick feeling came over us as we realized the seriousness of the problem. Our hotel was like Fire Fighter Central." During the show, conditions got worse and firefighters who'd been given hundreds of free tickets were obliged to head back to work. As the three buses headed on through the haze, all around them people's farms and homes were burning. Ranch land and forests were burning. In Red Lodge another fire broke out during their set and a nasty plume of smoke drifted toward the stage.

At 8:45 on the morning of September 17, after hauling ass all night long from a gig in South Carolina, the *Honeysuckle Rose* pulled into the backstage compound in Bristow, Virginia. Willie was just waking. Minutes later, he faced CNN camera crews and spoke to the nation about Farm Aid 2000. A town meeting followed with presidential candidates Ralph Nader and Pat Buchanan and members of Congress on hand to meet with a delegation of farmers, including Neil Young and Arlo Guthrie. "Issues were discussed and questions were asked," Lana Nelson reported. "Why does the farmer only get 5 cents for a loaf of bread when it costs $2 in a grocery store? Who lets this happen? Why doesn't someone help? Was it a systematic, controlled removal of 5 million family farmers? Will our food now be grown by 3 corporations who don't care about the land, or you, or even the food? They are a corporation. A corporation is an agreement on paper. It has no thoughts or feelings, only a bottom line. You helped Chrysler, why not help the Family Farmer? You punished Microsoft, how can you turn your head here? Whoever controls the land, controls the country. Whoever controls the food, controls you. Individuals or corporations, you decide. Pass a new Farm Bill in Congress that will put the Family Farmer back on their feet, and back on the land."

During an interview in *Flagpole Magazine Online*, Willie would lay the blame for the predicament of not only the family farmer but also country music on corporate America. When asked, "Why are the farmers getting such a raw deal?" Willie answered. "Because there's a big drive to take the small farmer out completely and replace him with factory farms, big corporate farming. That's not a new idea, it's been going on ever since the war. Back in World War II we were really geared up. We were strong. We had eight million farmers out in the land. All of our raw producers were really doing good. Everything was going fine back during the war and we were winning the war. We were guaranteeing our raw producers 100 percent of their production costs and labor. When we quit doing that, after the war, we were doing it intentionally so we could take a lot of these farmers off the land and move them into the city where they would be cheap labor building cars and all that. Every time you take five farmers out of the country, you lose one small business. In the last 40 years we've lost from eight million farmers down to less than two million. It's a concentrated effort by big corporations to take out the small farmer."

When Willie was asked, "Why doesn't Nashville seem interested in anything but cookie-cutter stuff," his answer would be the same. "It's corporate music," he said, "lawyers and accountants running the music business. The music business has nothing to do with the music, so that's where the problems are. Used to be, musicians were very active in the companies themselves and had a lot to do with their running. Bing Crosby started Decca Records, you know. Chet Atkins at RCA. Now, they have lawyers and accountants instead of artists, and that's why the music sucks so bad."

And when asked whether the lack of opposition to this trend was due to social apathy, Willie provided a thought-provoking answer. "I really think," he said, "it's a lack of heroes. It's a lack of somebody they can really believe in. They've been lied to by their own government. They've been lied to by their own presidents, vice-presidents, senators, congressmen, mayors, and schoolteachers. I think it's a matter of we're all looking for somebody to tell us the truth." While some of Willie's fans proposed that he run for president himself — and Lana Nelson even posted a mocked up 'Willie for President' campaign at the *Willie Nelson.com* website with Willie posing in front of before-and-after-shots of the dilapidated Willie Nelson Pool Hall in Austin, a real cutie of a pool shark, this guy — he declined. Had he not already done everything he could do for his country?

As the President of Farm Aid and a hero to the remaining 1.9 million family farmers, Willie had become a political spokesman for a movement that sought to reverse the economic course of more than 50 years of a corporate effort that had reduced the number of family farms in America from 8 million down to less than 2 million. Willie had become a hero, the trouble making kind, like Martin Luther King Jr, Joan of Arc, and Jesus Christ, the kind of hero Willie sang about years ago in the lyrics to *The Trouble Maker*, the title song from his third album recorded for Atlantic but released on Columbia Records.

I could tell the first time that I saw him
He was nothing but the troublemaking kind
His hair was much too long
And his motley group of friends
Had nothing but rebellion on their minds
He's rejected the establishment completely
And I know for sure he's never held a job
He just goes from town to town
Stirring up the young ones
Till they're nothing but a disrespectful mob

— *The Trouble Maker* (Bruce Belland, David Somerville)

This 'troublemaker' is arrested, found guilty, and sentenced to die on the cross at Calvary, a reminder that if Jesus were alive today, he might very likely receive the same treatment he received 2000 years ago. The opportunity to record a gospel album at the time had afforded Willie the forum in which to address the self-righteous in the audience, people who used Jesus to gain their own ends but might not necessarily recognize Him if He showed up in their living room. Jesus came here to remind people of God's Divine Law. Willie has reminded us of that divine law, 'the law of love'. "What puts the law of love into proper operation is the Golden Rule," Willie has stated in his autobiography, "*do unto others as you would have them do unto you* . . . . Most people don't believe in this law, to the whole world's regret. The leaders of world governments, concerned only with holding on to their power, ignore the law of love, and are overthrown as a direct result, and cause wars of terrible destruction. We are only one bad decision away from destroying our whole planet. We live with famine and disease and violence, and terrible corruption in our financial institutions — and we claim not to know why these things are happening. I know why they are happening, and so do you if you're not too cynical to admit it. We are not obeying the divine law. It is as simple as that."

While in days gone by Paul English with his six-shooters or L.G. would protect Willie, this day at Farm Aid 2000 the secret service accompanied Willie Nelson and Tipper Gore into the compound. While Tipper was there to support the farmers and to play bongos alongside Billy and Paul English, Willie Nelson's drummers, she was, nevertheless, the wife of a Vice-President. With politics done with for the moment, farmers and musicians strolled to and fro in the compound. Some moved to the catering tables where organic juices, fruits, and vegetables had been donated by the locals. There would be no river of beer and whiskey this day. Keyboard player Greg Hubbard, a veteran member of Sawyer Brown, pointed to the example of his band-mate Mark Miller and his brother sending some hay from a surplus crop to farmers in Texas. "That's one of the coolest things in the farming and ranching industries," Greg told reporters, "that sense of helping each other out. That's something that gets lost in the shuffle of all this. These people are not only trying to help themselves, but they're willing to pull for somebody else, too. You don't see a that a lot in the business world. If you ever see Willie talk about these matters, you can see he has a very real passion. For all of his laid-back style, he is so incredibly knowledgeable about farm bills. It's not a once-a-year-thing for him."

Willie was seen everywhere, dashing from media event to media event and taking to the stage to address the audience and sit in with several of the scheduled performers. Viewers of the CMT telecast saw and heard some bad-ass blues from the North Mississippi Allstars, a mellow set from Arlo Guthrie, then Travis Tritt, Pat Green, and the ever energetic Sawyer Brown, before Alan Jackson thrilled one and all with his performance. Crosby,

Stills, Nash & Young were as together as they'd been at Woodstock all those many years ago. Barenaked Ladies were hot. John Mellencamp was rootsy as ever. Neil Young came back for a set with Crazy Horse and wrung every bit of emotion out of his guitar that a guitar can possibly give. When Willie Nelson went on with his Family Band, he appeared exhausted. It was a wonder he had an ounce of energy left, but he did, and he thrilled everyone all over again before being joined by all of the performers for the finale. A message had been sent, along with a tide of goodwill music: Family farmers need our help.

Over the years Farm Aid had also helped launch the career of many acts. "We were lucky to have gotten on Farm Aid at all," Trent Summar recalls. "It was pretty much booked up. Maybe, because we opened up a couple of shows for Willie on the way up, was what might have kinda gotten us in the door. I ended up co-hosting it with a couple of people. I was on for eight hours. It was quite an honor. I really believe in what they are doing. I grew up on some small farms and raised pigs and cows and horses. I was a member of Future Farmers of America. I believe in the simple life, but now those farms are going away. I believe that you should have a choice whether you eat meat and vegetables that are mass produced and genetically engineered or grown on a family farm." Being a Farm Aid rookie, Summar remembers that he and his band arrived early. "I really didn't know what to expect, but from the minute we hit the gate there was someone there leading us through it. It was so well run that it was unbelievable. Good food, good people, and the energy was amazing; everybody was there to help." *Playboy* would call Summar's VFR Records debut "the most impressive rock record to come out of Nashville, ever!" No doubt, his performance and presence at Farm Aid 2000 was a factor in the success he was achieving with his music in the months that followed. From 1985 to the present day, Farm Aid has served as a springboard for new acts to break onto the national scene. In '85 John Fogerty made his solo debut, showcasing material from CENTERFIELD and propelling the album up the *Billboard* Hot 200 album chart to number one. That same year a little known group who called themselves Bon Jovi played Farm Aid and went on to sell more than 11 million copies of their sophomore album in 1986. As Greg Hubbard points out, "People just want to hear what it is that you do, to put your passion for your music out there for the cause. That makes for great performances."

Willie has spoken out on two other political issues of the day — the legalization of marijuana and native rights. When a reporter from *Details* magazine asked about the laws against the use of his "favorite green thing,"

Willie laid it on the line. "I don't want to call it a drug . . . an herb is not a drug. It's good for stress, which is the biggest killer on the planet." As he added in *Flagpole Magazine Online*, "I think more and more people are realizing what a dumb law it was to begin with. More and more states are trying to come around. Of course, the federal government is not only ignorant about it, but the ones that are smart are smart because they don't want the hemp industry to come in and start trying to interfere with your paper industry, your medicine industry, and all the different things that can be done with hemp. I know that, in the Clinton administration, over four million people have been arrested. So, in that respect, it's as bad as it ever was or worse. When I say it's better, there are more people who are aware but there's still so many political things against it, and they violate a lot of people's personal rights, individual rights. I can't think negative. I have to believe there's a light at the end of the tunnel and all the work that everybody has done from the past up until now, all the positive things, will sow positive results. I'm not sure whether we've hit the bottom yet or where we're at in the whole process. I think we all have to be pretty much aware of where we are right now and keep things as peaceful as we can. That's about all we can do."

For many years, the only poster displayed in Willie Nelson's bus depicted Lakota Chief Frank Fool's Crow, chief and medicine man to the Lakota First Nation. On a red granite mountain some 17 miles distant from Mount Rushmore, the Lakota are carving a monument to their ancestral chief Crazy Horse, which, when fully completed, will dwarf the nearby stone-gray dead presidents on Mount Rushmore by tenfold. The stone head of Crazy Horse alone is as tall as the Washington Monument, nearly twice as tall as the Rushmore heads. The feather being placed atop Crazy Horse will be 50 feet in height. This stone native son will tower over what came both before and what will come after him. Mounted on a stallion, Crazy Horse will stand as testimony to a lost heritage, swept away by ethnic cleansing, kept present here on earth by his people who would not let him be forgotten, as a reminder of that lost heritage and their hero. Born in the Black Hills sacred to the Lakota tribe, Crazy Horse was a leader of his people in the gold rush days when big business and the U.S. Cavalry rushed in where mere prospectors feared to tread, intent on consigning the remaining First Nations people to reservations that were seldom appropriate to their survival but were convenient to the aspirations of settlers, ranchers, and mining companies. Crazy Horse led his warriors to victory at the Battle of the Rosebud in June 1876 before humiliating Custer's cavalry at the Little Bighorn eight days later. He was ignominiously bayonetted by a military guard after surrendering the following year. Lakota chiefs, after watching Belgian sculptor Gutzon Borglum and his laborers carving out the images of Presidents Washington, Jefferson, Roosevelt, and Lincoln on Mount Rushmore for a decade, decided a native American hero needed similar elevation, and, in 1948, commissioned rival European sculptor Korczak Ziolkowski to begin blasting and chipping away at the rock face. Fifty-three years later, his descendents are completing the task.

The words on the poster of Chief Frank Fool's Crow aboard Willie's *Honeysuckle Rose* are the words to the Four Winds Prayer, once recited by the chief from the stage during one of Willie Nelson's concerts. This prayer is addressed to "Grandfather God" and asks for mercy from the outsiders encroaching on Lakota land. While Nashville chose to call Willie Nelson an 'outlaw', they might have pondered the Cowboys and Indians mythology a little deeper and looked to his Cherokee ancestry and his time spent as a member of Ray Price's band, the Cherokee Cowboys. Willie Nelson is an entertainer, a healer, and a shaman, not a bank robber, who reminds us that music is a live and living wonder, not merely a two-and-a-half minute plastic record or a contract on a piece of paper. Writing a song means tapping in to the collective soul, not plotting lyrics and melodies to correspond to marketing surveys in order to make the maximum amount of money. Nashville, Hollywood, and even Washington have all sought to be included in Willie Nelson's legend by handing him trophies and awards. Sometimes, however, trophies are not enough. If people sincerely want to acknowledge Willie Nelson and pay tribute, the very best way would be to listen to what he is saying — about the family farmer, about the food we eat, about the law of love.

"His social conscience," *Music Hound* critic Bob Cannon notes, "and mastery of all forms of country music have made him one of the genre's true giants. If they ever carve a country music version of Mount Rushmore, they'll have to include Willie Nelson." No one has begun to carve Willie Nelson's profile into the hills west of Austin, nor would he advise them to begin blasting and chipping away. But whatever we make of ourselves in the coming years, we can't say we have not had one hero in our generation, one person who stood up for many others.

Cynics abound in the material world, but in the early years of the Willennium, Willie Nelson's fans still wear t-shirts that read: "Where there's a Willie, there's a way." Only the other day, someone who had just returned from Nashville gave me such a t-shirt. She said, "I heard you're writin' about

Willie, so I thought you might like this." I wore it every day for a week, just to break it in. Joni Mitchell once wrote, "We are stardust, we are golden. And we've got to get ourselves back to the garden." Willie Nelson, more than most of us, is working on it.

On October 10, 2000, Willie Nelson and many others arrived in Austin for a taping of the 25th Anniversary show of *Austin City Limits*. The gang from his online chat room, who called themselves WOLF, which stood for Willie's On Line Friends, were on hand to greet their idol, crowding onto the bus. They had reason to celebrate. This show would mark his 15th appearance on the little show that could. Leon Russell had been along for the ride in February, for his 14th show, but for this show Jimmie Vaughan, Francine Reed, and the blues band featured on MILK COW BLUES would take the stage with the strange red headed blues dude. The show and the music had not changed all that much — excellence was still the bottom line — but the fake Austin City skyline, which had mystified fans, many of whom believed the show was shot outdoors and even phoned in to find out if the weather would be favorable, had not kept up with the times. The land surrounding the state capital had become prime real estate during the silicon revolution in the 1990s, and industrial sprawl and the cement and glass towers formerly more familiarly etched on the skylines of Dallas and Houston had changed the Austin skyline. As Lana Nelson would note in her digital diary, "It sure as poo doesn't seem like 25 years since the first *Austin City Limits* taping. So much has obviously changed over time, but nothing has changed as much as the actual city limits of Austin. Janis, you wouldn't recognize it."

THE PARTY'S OVER

As he took his music to the world, Willie Nelson became many things to many people, and although he may spend 200 days of the year on his bus, Willie is always heading home to Texas. "I can be on the bus sound asleep in the middle of the night," he recently confided to *Country Weekly* reporter Larry Holden, "and I know when we cross into Texas. I wake up with the incredibly good feeling of 'Well, we're back.' Then, when the bus pulls onto the road leading up to my Austin ranch, a peace floods over me. My house there, like the ones I have in Hawaii and Abbott, are my hospital zones. That's where I go to heal and get ready for life's next battle."

I am a roving cowboy
Riding all alone
And for such a roving cowboy
I've sure made myself at home

I love your sunlight
I love your flowers
I love your oceans rolling in
And for such a roving cowboy
I've sure found myself a friend

I am a cowboy
I am a sailor
I have drifted far and wide
I have crossed the seven oceans
I have crossed the Great Divide

But if you're ever looking for me
Let me tell you where I'll be
I'll be somewhere soaking up sunshine
In my island in the sea

— *Island In The Sea* (Willie Nelson)

At age 68, Willie Nelson celebrates a full decade of marriage with Ann Marie D'Angelo. This fourth marriage is a good one, which, Willie informed Larry Holden, is probably due to "the fact that I'm gone a lot. We're always glad to see each other. I always hate to leave, and that helps. We have two great boys, Lukas, 11, and Micah, 10, we're raising, and they keep me comin' back home." His whole family is gathered 'round these days, lending a hand when they can, doing their own thing, too. In the 1980s, when her husband, Tony, was killed in a collision with a carload of drunk teenagers, Susie Nelson found her strength and her voice. She assumed the duties of managing the Jo Bangles Band Tony had been working with and applied her knowledge of the music business. Not long after assuming her management role, Susie fired the singer for failure to think positive — more specifically, for being rude to a sound tech at Billy Bob's in Fort Worth — and started her singing career then and there simply because there was no one else to go on that night. As she recalls for her book *Heartworn Memories*, "we were just a warmup act and we didn't have a lot of time. Between instrumentals and the two or three songs I did, we got through alright. We may not have turned any heads, and we sure didn't have any record label company executives offering us contracts, but we opened on time and did our job to the best of our ability. We acted like professionals." A few weeks later, in the backstage area at one of her father's outdoor events, Susie climbed on board the *Honeysuckle Rose* and told Willie that she wanted to sing on the show. "Do you know any songs?" Willie quipped, which, once again, broke up everyone on the bus, including Susie Nelson. Determined to explore this avenue, Susie looked up her mother number two, Shirley Nelson, and together they recorded an album together.

Paula Nelson (she's dropped the Carlene) has an album out on Luck Records, while Micah Nelson contributed illustrations to the artwork for Willie's MILK COW BLUES and Lukas Nelson wrote the liner notes. Lana Nelson Fowler and Rachel Fowler oversee Willie's website, where there is a 'Willmart' for people who want to buy all things Willie and a daily diary posted from the *Honeysuckle Rose* on the road. Lana made many of Willie's first videos, including the one for *Pancho And Lefty* which won an award during the infancy of CMT. She is often by her father's side. Jody Payne has an album out on Luck Records. Ditto for Mickey Raphael. As they say, when you're in Luck, you're in luck, and, as the Willennium unfolds, the ole five and dimers are still singing. Billy Joe Shaver brought several of them together for a reprise of the HONKY TONK HEROES album not long ago — Willie and Waylon and Kris and Billy Joe — all of them recording at the Pedernales studio. His son Eddie Shaver produced this record and played lead guitar, which turned out to be a blessing because Eddie has passed away.

In Kinky Friedman's *Road Kill*, the fictional Kinky describes people who have passed away as having "stepped on a rainbow." That's a poetic way to look at death, passing on to our next reincarnation or recurrence or whatever our creator has in mind for us. But Willie, the wandering gypsy, is not quite ready to step on a rainbow, not just yet. And when he does, he may take many others along with him, just for the ride, though the fictional Willie insists that death does not exist. Maybe we're all just dreaming Willie. Or Willie is simply dreaming us. As Waylon Jennings has said, "I think people like Willie are forever, you know. He's crossed all the boundaries in music. He's bigger than music, that's what the whole thing is."

Turn out the lights, the party's over
They say that all good things must end
Let's call it a night, the party's over
And tomorrow starts the same old thing again

— *The Party's Over* (Willie Nelson)

REFERENCES

Books

Alden, Grant & Peter Blackstock. *No Depression*. Nashville, TN: Dowling Press, 1998.

Allen, Bob. *Waylon & Willie*. New York, NY: Quick Fox, A Division of Music Sales Inc., 1979.

Bane, Michael. *The Outlaws Revolution In Country Music*. New York, NY: KBO Publishers, 1978.

Cayce, Hugh Lynn. *Edgar Cayce on Atlantis: His Authentic Accounts of Past Lives on the Fabled Lost Continent Can Help You Attain A State Of Heightened Awareness and Self-Improvement*. New York, NY: Warner Books, 1968.

Cook, Bruce. *The Town That Country Built*. New York, NY: Avon Books, 1993.

Cornfield, Robert & Marshall Falwell Jr. *Just Country: Country People, Stories, Music*. Foreword by Minnie Pearl. New York, NY: McGraw-Hill, n.d.

Davis, John T. *Austin City Limits 25 Years of American Music*. Preface by Bill Arhos. New York, NY: Billboard Books, 2000.

Dellar, Fred, Alan Cackett, Roy Thompson. Foreword: Ricky Skaggs. *The Harmony Illustrated Encyclopedia of Country Music*. New York, NY: Harmony Books, 1986.

Ellison, Curtis W. Country Music Culture: *From Hard Times to Heaven*. Jackson, MS: University Press of Mississippi, 1995.

Emery, Ralph (with Tom Carter). *Memories*. New York, NY: Pocket Books, 1991.

Emery, Ralph. (with Patsi Bale Cox). *The View From Nashville*. New York, NY: William H. Morrow & Co., 1998.

Friedman, Kinky. *Road Kill*. New York, NY: Simon & Schuster, 1997.

Geldof, Bob (with Paul Vallely). "Is That It" London Viking Penguin, 1986.

Haggard, Merle (with Peggy Russell). *Sing Me Back Home*. New York, NY: Pocket Books, 1981.

Hall, Tom T. *The Storyteller's Nashville*. New York, NY: Doubleday, 1979.

Jennings, Waylon (with Lenny Kaye). *Waylon: An Autobiography*. New York, NY: Warner Books, 1996.

Joplin, Laura. *Love Janis*. New York, NY: Viking Penguin Books, 1992.

Leary, Timothy. *Flashbacks: A Personal And Cultural History Of An Era*. New York, NY: A Tarcher-Perigree Book, The Putnam Publishing Group, 1983.

Mansfield, Brian, & Gary Groff, editors. *Music Hound Country: The Essential Album Guide*. Detroit, MI: Visible Ink Press, 1997.

Melhuish, Martin. *Oh What a Feeling: A Vital History of Canadian Music.* Kingston, ON, Quarry Press, 1996.

Nelson Fowler, Lana. *Willie Nelson Family Album.* Amarillo, TX: H.M. Poirot & Company, 1980.

Nelson, Susie. *Heartworn Memories: A Daughter's Personal Biography of Willie Nelson.* Austin, TX: Eakin Press, 1987.

Nelson, Willie (with Bud Shrake). *Willie: An Autobiography.* New York, NY: Pocket Books, 1988.

Nash, Alanna. *Behind Closed Doors: Talking with the Legends of Country Music.* New York, NY: Alfred A. Knopf, 1988.

Nickerson, Marina (with Cynthia Farah, photos). *Country Music: A Look at the Men Who've Made It.* El Paso, TX: C.M. Publishing, 1981.

Oermann, Robert K. *America's Music: The Roots of Country.* Atlanta, GA: Turner Publishing, n.d.

Ouspensky, P.D. *A New Model Of The Universe.* New York, NY, Alfred A. Knopf, 1931; Vintage Books edition, 1971.

Reagan Wilson, Charles & William Ferris. *Encyclopedia Of Southern Culture.* New York, NY: Anchor Books, Bantam Doubleday Dell Publishing Group, 1991.

Riese, Randall. *Nashville Babylon.* New York, NY: Congden & Weed, 1988.

Rogers, Will (ed. Donald Day). *The Autobiography of Will Rogers.* New York, NY: Lancer Books, 1971.

Talbot, Michael. *Mysticism & The New Physics.* New York, NY: Bantam Books, 1981.

Scott, Randy. *Country Music Revealed: True Stories of Boozin', Cheatin', Stealin', Tax-Dodgin', and D-I-V-O-R-C-E.* New York, NY: Metro Books, 1995.

Tichi, Cecilia (editor). *Reading Country Music: Steel Guitars, Opry Stars, and Honky Tonk Bars.* Durham, NC: Duke University Press, 1998.

Whitburn, Joel. *The Billboard Book of Top 40 Albums.* New York, NY: Billboard Books, 1995.

Whitburn, Joel. *The Billboard Book of Top 40 Country Albums.* New York, NY: Billboard Books, 1996.

Whitburn, Joel. *The Billboard Book of Top 40 Country Hits.* New York, NY: Billboard Books, 1996.

Whitburn, Joel. *The Billboard Book of Top 40 Hits.* New York, NY: Billboard Books, 1996.

Williamson, J.W. *Hillbillyland: What the Movies Did to the Mountains and What the Mountains Did to the Movies.* Chapel Hill, NC: University of North Carolina Press, 1995.

Wills, Rosetta. *The King of Western Swing: Bob Wills Remembered.* New York, NY: Billboard Books, 1998.

Newspaper & Magazine Articles

Aguilante, Dan. "Fans Still Crazy for Outlaw Willie." *New York Post*, March 13, 1998.

Albrecht, James. "It's High Time: Willie Gathers His Disciples." *Country Style*, October 1978.

Alexander, Mike. "Funky Willie." *Dallas Times Herald*, June 2, 1972.

Alexander, Mike. "Into The Land Of Rock." *Dallas Times Herald*, October 12, 1972.

Alexander, Mike. "Willie Nelson Throws A Little July 4th Picnic." *Dallas Times Herald*, July 17, 1973.

Allen, Bob. "Willie Nelson: On the Road with the Grand Guru of Country Music." *Country Style*, September 1980.

Anders, John. "Kilroy Was, Willie Wasn't." *Dallas Morning News*, March 13, 1976.

Anonymous. "Armadillo Country Music Review." *Wichita Falls Record*, September 14, 1972.

Anonymous. "Willie at Kerrville Festival." *Dallas Times Herald*, May 20, 1973.

Anonymous. "Willie Nelson." *Plain Talk (Newport TN)*, March 25, 1974.

Anonymous. "Lazy Writer Keeps Turning Out The Hits." *Waco Tribune Herald*, March 17, 1974.

Anonymous. "Hillbilly Heaven In Aggieland." *Texas Monthly*, June 1974.

Anonymous, "Willie & Jimmy." *People*, July 5, 1978.

Anonymous. "President, Wife, Go To Concert." *Durham Morning Herald*, July 22, 1978.

Anonymous. "Two Top Secret Fans Cheer Country Music." *L.A. Times*, July 23 1978.

Anonymous. "County Bills Willie $3400 For July 4th Concert Expenses." *Austin American-Statesman*, July 24, 1979.

Anonymous. "Willie's making a movie here." *San Antonio News*, October 5, 1979.

Anonymous. "Martial Arts Meets Wild West in Willie Nelson's New Movie Diamonds in the Rough." *Fort Lauderdale Sun-Sentinel*, August 4, 1997.

Anonymous. "Willie Nelson, Method Actor." *Fort Lauderdale Sun-Sentinel*, September 26, 1997.

Anonymous. "Willie Nelson Founds New Music Channel." *Vancouver Columbian*, February 12, 1998.

Anonymous. "Singers Oppose Irradiation Of Organic Food." *Atlanta Constitution*, April 23, 1998.

Anonymous. "Willie Nelson Turns 65." *Dallas Morning News*, March 23, 1998.

Anonymous. "Record Review: Teatro." *New York Times*, August 16, 1998.

Aregood, Rich. "It Is Now Certified Hip To Be a Willie Nelson Fan." *Philadelphia Daily News*, April 28, 1978.

Arrington, Carrie. "Nelson's 'Stardust' Splendid." *New York Post*, May 5, 1978.

Axthelm, Pete. "Willie Nelson: King of Country Music." *Newsweek*, August 14, 1978.

Bane, Michael. "Nelson Found Young People Who Liked His Music." *Look*, August 30, 1979.

Buchalter, Gail. "Willie Nelson Becomes A Star." *Baltimore News American*, April 1, 1979.

Butts, Gene. "King of Red Neck Rock." *Birmingham News*, May 14, 1976.

Cain, Linda. "Willie Nelson Gets the Acting Bug." *Country Style*, March 1980.

Carr, Patrick. "Willie, Waylon, Way Out." *Baltimore News American*, February 10, 1974.

Carter, Tom. "The Right Track." *Tulsa Daily Herald*, July 6, 1975.

Cooper, Texas Jim. "True Tall Texas Tales: Willie Nelson." *Suburban News*, October 27, 1966.

Coppage, Noel. "Tom T. Wants to Reform Outlaws." *Stereo Review*, May 1978.

Cott, Jonathan. "Deepak Chopra: God, Man and the Media." *Rolling Stone*, September 28, 2000.

Cox, Patsi. "Whatever Happened To Barbarosa" *Rocky Mountain Country*. Premiere Edition.

Croft, Jack. "He Personifies the Outlaw Movement." *Delaware State News*, January 23, 1977.

Dangaard, Colin. "Meteoric Rise to the Top No Surprise to Hard-living Outlaw Willy Nelson." *Baltimore News American*, November 17, 1978.

Dangaard, Colin. "His Ex-Wife Sewed Him into Bed and Beat Him." *San Francisco Chronicle*, November 18, 1978.

Dart, Bob. "Willie Nelson Named for Kennedy Honors." *Austin American-Statesman*, August 21, 1998.

Davis, John T. "Willie's Hat Trick: With 3 New Albums Austin's Favorite Native Son Ups Ante on Transcendent Career." *Austin American-Statesman*, August 27, 1998.

DeVault, Russ. "Rules, Schmules: Course Is on a Par with Wild Willie." *Atlanta Constitution*, March 30, 1997.

DeYoung, Bill. "Funny How Time Slips Away." *Goldmine*, January 6, 1995.

Dove, Ian. "Nelson Puts Heart in Country Music." *New York Times*, May 18, 1973.

Duke, Beth. "Movie Premiere to Aid Scholarship Fund." *Amarillo Daily News*, July 6, 1980.

Eipper, Laura. "Willie Nelson Makes White House Debut." *Tennessean*, August 13, 1978.

Englade, Kenneth. "How You, Redneck." *San Antonio Light*, August 29, 1976.

Flippo, Chet. "Picnickers Shown A Rocky Time." *Wichita Beacon*, August 2, 1974; originally published in *Country Music*.

Flippo, Chet. "Matthew, Mark, Luke, and Willie." *Texas Monthly*, November 1975.

Gold, Kerry. "Nashville's Burning." *Vancouver Sun*, October 7, 2000.

Goldman, Stuart. "Country Goes Hollywood." *Van Nuys Valley News*, July 1980.

Graham, Brad L. "Willie Nelson Keeps Toes Tapping." *St. Louis Post-Dispatch*, February 27, 1998.

Haas, Jane Glenn. "Nelson's Still On The Road Again at Nearly 65." *Orange County Register*, January 26, 1998.

Halbersberg, Elianne. "Picture Perfect with Roy Orbison & Willie Nelson." *Country Song Roundup*, January 2000.

Hall, Michael. "Funny How Time Slips Away." *Grammy Magazine*, Summer 1995.

Hance, Bill. "Willie Has Triumphant Return." *Nashville Banner*, October 24, 1975.

Hance, Bill. "Nashville's Early Beard Gets The Stage." *Garden City Newsday*, May 7, 1976.

Harvey, Lynn. "Willie's Third Fourth." *The Tennessean*, July 13, 1975.

Hayden, Richard. "Willie's Guitar Stars On Instrumental Album." *Country Weekly*, July 6, 1999.

Hellmich, Nancy, Jeffrey Peisch & David Zimmerman. "Stars Relax, Reflect Backstage. *USA Today*, September 23, 1985.

Hendricks, Bill. "Willie & the Commissioner." *Country Style*, July 1978.

Henson, Rick. "Behind the Scenes: *Honeysuckle Rose*." *Country Style*, May 1980.

Hershorn, Connie. "For A Song." *People Weekly*, May 3, 1976.

Hilburn, Robert. "New Album Breakthrough." *Long Island Press*, March 24, 1974.

Hilburn, Robert. "Musical Gold Mine." *Nashville Banner*, July 27, 1976; first appeared in *Los Angeles Times*.

Hilburn, Robert. "High Marks For Waylon & Willie." *Los Angeles Times*, January 24, 1978.

Hilburn, Robert. "Willie: After the IRS and on the road to 60." *Los Angeles Times*, August 20, 1992.

Holden, Larry. "Road Warrior." *Country Weekly*, June 13, 2000.

Hume, Martha. "Waylon & Willie Headed for Monster Hit." *US Weekly*, March 7 1978.

Hume, Martha. "Forget the Beatles: It's Williemania for the '80s." *US Weekly*, February 5, 1980.

Hunt, Dennis. "Setting Dramatic Stage for Nelson's Teatro." *USA Today*, September 11, 1998.

Hurst, Jack. "Outlaw Nelson Bears No Grudge against Nashville." *Chicago Tribune*, March 15, 1978.

Hurst, Jack. "Willie Nelson: Guru Sings with intensity." *Chicago Tribune Newservice Story: Philadelphia Inquirer*, April 16, 1978.

Jinkins, Shirley. "Country, Beer and ol' Willie; a Texas Saga." *Fort Worth Star Telegram*, July 5, 1997.

Jolidan, Lawrence. "A Chance to Get Burned." *Dallas Times-Herald*, July 5, 1977.

Joyce, Mike. "At Willie Nelson's Show: A Survey of a Fine Career." *Washington Post*, July 24, 1998.

Kanzler, George Jr. "Country Idiom Well-Served by Willie Nelson." *Newark Star-Ledger*, June 9, 1974.

Knutzen, Eirik. "Willie Won't Sit Back on His Laurels." *Boston Herald*, January 10, 1990.

Krewen, Nick. "Silent Movies, Loud music: Willie Nelson's Teatro." *Country Weekly*.

Lewis, Randy. "Red Headed Stranger Goes Blues." *Tennessean*, September 28, 2000.

McAllister, Bill. "Darrell, You and a Good Album All Helping Rediscover Willie Nelson." *Fort Worth Star-Telegram*, August 4, 1973.

McAllister, Bill. "Nelson Coming Home to Abbott for Concert." *Fort Worth Star-Telegram*, November 3, 1973.

McCabe, Peter. "Hard Living Is Trademark of This Musical Clique." *Miami Herald*, November 17, 1973.

McNally, Joe. "Interview: Willie Rides the Outlaw Wave." *Milwaukee Journal*, August 13, 1979.

Miller, Townsend. "Trekking up to Abbott with Willie." *Austin American-Statesman*, November 3, 1973.

Mitchell, Rick. "Willie Goes to Town with Picnic." *Houston Chronicle*, July 6, 1990.

Mitchell, Rick. "Willie Nelson Covers Himself: Teatro Revisits Lyrical Originals. *Houston Chronicle*, August 30, 1998.

Mitchell, Sean. "A Visit with Willie Nelson's Momma and Poppa." *Dallas Times Herald*, September 5, 1976.

Mr. Bonzai. "Willie Nelson: Deep In the Heart." *Mix Magazine*, November 1992.

Mulholland, Dave. "Composer Needs His Own Band to Shine." *Ottawa Citizen*, June 2, 1980.

Nania, Gina. "Crazy Horse Rides Again." *Vancouver Province*, September 24, 2000.

Nielsen Chapman, Beth. "Beneath The Surface: Subconscious Writing." *Performing Songwriter Magazine*, January 2001.

Newcomer, Wendy. "Waylon Recalls First #1." *Country Weekly*, April 27, 1999.

Newcomer, Wendy. "Cyber Country Willie Wonkin'." *Country Weekly*, July 11, 2000.

Oates, Greg. "Lives and Times of Willie Nelson and Emmylou Harris." *Fort Lauderdale Sun-Sentinel*, May 11, 1979.

Olderman, Murray. "Unspoiled Willie Nelson Calls His Songs His Philosophy." *Plymouth Pilot News*, January 30, 1979.

Patterson, Rob. "The Last Hurrah For Willie Nelson's Picnic." *Chatanooga News Free Press*, January 25, 1980.

Perry, Milt. "Emmylou, Merle & Willie Had 'em Stompin' for More at Anaheim Show." *Van Nuys Valley News*, October 28, 1980.

Pinkster, Beth. "Script Is Mamets', But They Don't Maim It. Country Star Shines in Stellar 'Wag' Cast." *Dallas Morning News*, January 3, 1998.

Pond, Neil. "Willie Nelson's Casting Call: Fresh Off the Set of New Movie, He Spearheads Concert for America's Farmers, Christens his Hall of Fame Exhibit & Continues to Churn Out Duets with Everybody." *Country Style*, October 1985.

Pond, Neil. "Country Stars Rockers to Aid Farmers." *Music City News*, November 1985.

Powers, Guy. "Sleuth Goes On The Road to Help Willie Nelson." *Detroit Free Press*, September 10, 1997.

Puterbaugh, Parke. "Review: Milk Cow Blues." *Rolling Stone*, September 28, 2000.

Rector, Lee. "Willie's Picnic Back Home in Austin." *Music City News*, August 1979.

Reinert, Al. "An American Original." *San Francisco Chronicle*, March 30, 1978.

Roberts, Doug. "Willie Nelson Performing Talents Up, Writing Talents Down." *Quincy Patriot Ledger*, July 27, 1978.

Rockwell, John. "Willie Nelson on Stardom Trail." *New York Times*, August 8 1975.

Rockwell, John. "Willie: Hippie Cowboy" *New York Times News Service*, 1976.

Roland, Tom. "Willie Receives Lifetime Grammy." *Tennessean*, February 23, 2000.

Ross, Bob. "Concert the Epitome of Class." *St. Petersberg Times*, May 18, 1978.

Sattersfield, Kathy. "Willie & Kris." *El Paso Times*, January 29, 1980.

Sherman, Jay. "Nelson Album Hits Internet Road." *BPI Newswire*, April 16, 1998.

Staten, Vince. "Outlaw Sheds Twang." *Dayton Daily News*, May 20, 1976.

Schulian, John. "Sad-Eyed Willie Nelson Writes C&W's Answer to Sgt. Pepper." *Baltimore Evening Sun*, March 13, 1974.

Tayler, Letta. "Nelson's Still Got It, But Where Is It." *Newsday (Queens Edition)*, August 20, 1998.

Thomas, Barbara. "Willie Nelson's Empire." *Atlanta Constitution*, July 16, 1978.

Tosches, Nick. "Record Review: Waylon & Willie." *Rolling Stone*, May 23, 1978.

Vlerbome, Peggy. "Running with Willie: Nelson Stars in His Own Race through the Hills." *Austin American-Statesman*, June 16, 1980.

Wald, Elijah. "Strong in Music, Stamina, Willie Nelson Never Coasts." *Boston Globe*, March 17, 1998.

Ward, Ed. "Willie Nelson Is Most Unlikely Superstar." Reprinted from *Rolling Stone* in *El Paso Times*, December 28, 1975.

Ward, Ed. "In Nashville They Said My Ideas, My Songs, Were Too Deep." *Rolling Stone*, July 13, 1978.

Weintraub, Boris. "Willie & Waylon at It Again." *Washington Star*, May 29, 1979.

Widner, Ellis. "Willie & Leon: Together Again for the First Time." *Tulsa Tribune*, June 1, 1978.

Willson, Morris. "Bexar Facts: Willie Nelson & Johnny Bush Play Fredericksberg." *The San Antonio Light*, May 5, 1972.

Wilson, John W. "Willie's New Tune: 'My Freaks Don't Scare My Kickers Anymore.'" *Houston Chronicle*, September 2, 1973.

Wolff, Dick. "Willie Nelson's Final July 4th Texas Picnic Like Firecrackers." *Nashville Banner*, July 10, 1980.

Yancy, Matt. "Willie 'Hot' in Texas after Nashville Sours." *Cincinnati Enquirer*, December 14, 1975.

Yarborough, Chuck. "Country Legend Delivers with Voice and Guitar." *Cleveland Plain Dealer*, March 23, 1998.

Yardley, Jonathan. "On The Road With Willie & Kinky." *Washington Post*, October 1, 1997.

Other Media

Anonymous. "CBS Records Bio: Willie Nelson." 1982.

Anonymous. *Farm Aid 2000 In Review* " www.farmaid.com

Anonymous. "Rastaman Vibration On My Mind." *Rolling Stone.com.*

Anonymous. "Record Review: Spirit." jellyroll.com.

Anonymous. "Interview with Willie Nelson." digitalinterviews.com.

Anonymous. "Quotes from many of Willie's friends." sonymusic.com.

Anonymous. "On the road again and again and again. Interview with Willie Nelson." countrymusiclive.com.

Anonymous. "AgProfile interview: Willie Nelson." agjournal.com.

Braun, Liz. "No winners in this alien power struggle." *Toronto Sun* film review of *Starlight* posted canoe.com/JamMovies.

Cash, John R. "Willie and Me." americanrecordings.com

Davis, John T. Liner Notes From "*Willie Nelson, Revolutions of the Journey, 1975–1993*. Boxed Set 1995.

Doyle, Paul. "Brush With Enlightenment: Innerview: Willie Nelson." tripod.com.

Fox, Aaron, Matthew Matlack. "Interview with Willie Nelson on April 13, 2000." " txcountry.com.

Kienzle, Rick. *Liner Notes: Willie Nelson, The Classic Unreleased Collection.* Rhino Records Boxed Set, 1993.

Maltin, Leonard. "Summary for Barbarosa." Internet Movie Data Base.

Nelson Fowler, Lana. Daily road diary of Willie Nelson Family Band 1999 and 2000: "Pedernales Poo Poo." willienelson.com.

Nelson, Willie. "A Letter To America, August 25, 2000." farmaid.com

Nelson, Willie. "Willie Nelson Asks Presidential Hopefuls To Meet With Family Farmers." farmaid.com

Nelson, Willie. "Nelson To Glickman On Organic Standards." farmaid.com

Nelson, Willie. "Actor filmography." Internet Movie Data Base.

Patoski, Joe Nick. "Liner notes to TWISTED WILLIE." justicerecords.com.

Schutt, Roger (aka Captain Midnite). "Liner notes for HONKY TONK HEROES." RCA Records. Produced by Waylon Jennings and many others.

Skanse, Richard. "Willie Nelson Gets The Blues." *Rolling Stone*.com.

Thompson, Matt. "Big Willie Style: A Conversation with Willie Nelson." *Flagpole Magazine Online*.

Willie Nelson: My Life: The Authorized Video Biography. Hallway Productions, 1993.

ACKNOWLEDGEMENTS & CREDITS

Song Lyrics

No Place For Me. By Willie Nelson. Starrite Music/Glad Music, BMI, copyright renewed 1991.

Family Bible. By Willie Nelson, Walt Breeland, Paul Buskirk. Glad Music, BMI, copyright renewed 1988.

The Party's Over. By Willie Nelson. Glad Music, BMI, copyright renewed 1988.

What A Way To Live. By Willie Nelson. Glad Music, BMI, copyright renewed 1988.

Write Your Own Song. By Willie Nelson. Full Nelson Music, BMI, copyright 1982.

Night Life. By Willie Nelson, Walt Breeland, Paul Buskirk. Glad Music, BMI, copyright renewed 1992.

Country Willie. By Willie Nelson. Sony/ATV Songs LLC, BMI, copyright renewed 1992.

Crazy. By Willie Nelson. Sony/ATV Songs LLC, BMI, copyright 1961 (renewed).

Funny How Time Slips Away. By Willie Nelson. Sony/ATV Songs LLC, BMI, copyright 1961 (renewed).

Healing Hands Of Time. By Willie Nelson. Sony/ATV Songs, BMI, copyright 1961 (renewed).

Hello Walls. By Willie Nelson. Sony/ATV Songs, BMI, copyright 1961 (renewed).

I Never Cared For You. By Willie Nelson. Sony/ATV Songs, BMI, copyright 1964 (renewed).

Ridgetop. By Willie Nelson. Sony/ATV Songs, BMI, copyright 1964 (renewed).

In God's Eyes. By Willie Nelson. Sony/ATV Songs, BMI, copyright 1961 (renewed).

Mr. Record Man. By Willie Nelson. Sony/ATV Songs, BMI, copyright 1961 (renewed).

What Can You Do To Me Now. By Willie Nelson & Hank Cochran. Sony/ATV Songs, BMI, copyright 1970.

Do You Know Why You're Here. By Willie Nelson.

Where's the Show /Let Me Be A Man. By Willie Nelson.

Shotgun Willie. By Willie Nelson. Full Nelson Music, copyright 1973.

Phases Stages Circles Cycles And Scenes. By Willie Nelson. Full Nelson Music.

Angel Flying Too Close To The Ground. By Willie Nelson. Full Nelson Music, BMI, copyright 1979.

Island In The Sea. By Willie Nelson. Full Nelson Music, copyright 1987.

Me and Paul. By Willie Nelson. Full Nelson Music, copyright 1971.

Rainy Day Blues. By Willie Nelson. Glad Music, BMI, copyright renewed 1992.

On The Road Again. By Willie Nelson. Full Nelson Music, copyright 1980.

Red Headed Stranger. By Carl Stutz and Edith Lindeman.

Heartland. By Willie Nelson, Bob Dylan. Act V Music, Special Rider Music, 1992.

Nothing I Can Do About It Now and *Ain't Necessarily So*. By Beth Nielsen Chapman. Warner Refuge Music Inc.

The Trouble Maker. By Bruce Belland and David Somerville. Landville Music Ltd./Wilber Publishing Co. ASCAP.

Seven Spanish Angels. By T. Seals and E. Setser. Warner Tamerlane Pub. Corp. BMI. WB Music Corp. ASCAP.

Graceland. By Paul Simon. Copyright, Paul Simon.

Willie the Wandering Gypsy And Me and *We Are The Cowboys*. By Billie Joe Shaver. ATV Music. House of Cash Inc. BMI.

Photographs

Cover	Lisa Rose/Globe Photos
p. 2	Fitzroy Barret/Globe Photos
p. 6	Ralph Dominguez/Globe Photos
p. 97	Andrea Renault/Globe Photos
p. 98	Corbis Images
p. 99	Corbis Images
p. 100	Henry McGee/Globe Photos
p. 101	Sonia Moskowitz/Globe Photos
p. 102	Andrea Renault/Globe Photos
p. 103	Rubin Lombardo/Globe Photos
p. 104	Corbis Images